-Booklist

lagazine

Wiley Publishing, Inc.

Published by:

WILEY PUBLISHING, INC.

111 River St.
Hoboken, NJ 07030-5774

ISBN: 978-0-470-16547-8

Editor: Christine Ryan
Production Editor: Jonathan Scott
Cartographer: Roberta Stockwell
Photo Editor: Richard Fox
Anniversary Logo Design: Richard Pacifico
Production by Wiley Indianapolis Composition Services

For information on our other products and services or to obtain technical support, please contact our Customer Care Department within the U.S. at 800/762-2974, outside the U.S. at 317/572-3993 or fax 317/572-4002.

Wiley also publishes its books in a variety of electronic formats. Some content that appears in print may not be available in electronic formats.

Manufactured in the United States of America

5   4   3   2   1

Contents

List of Maps

ABOUT THE AUTHOR

A resident of the Big Island, **Jeanette Foster** has skied the slopes of Mauna Kea—during a Fourth of July ski meet, no less—and gone scuba diving with manta rays off the Kona Coast. A prolific writer widely published in travel, sports, and adventure magazines, she's also a contributing editor to *Hawaii* magazine and the editor of *Zagat's Survey to Hawaii's Top Restaurants*. In addition to this guide, Jeanette is the author of *Frommer's Hawaii, Frommer's Maui, Frommer's Honolulu, Waikiki & Oahu, Frommer's Hawaii with Kids, Frommer's Maui Day by Day* and *Frommer's Honolulu & Oahu Day by Day.*

AN INVITATION TO THE READER

In researching this book, we discovered many wonderful places—hotels, restaurants, shops, and more. We're sure you'll find others. Please tell us about them, so we can share the information with your fellow travelers in upcoming editions. If you were disappointed with a recommendation, we'd love to know that, too. Please write to:

Frommer's Portable Big Island of Hawaii, 5th Edition
Wiley Publishing, Inc. • 111 River St. • Hoboken, NJ 07030-5774

AN ADDITIONAL NOTE

Please be advised that travel information is subject to change at any time—and this is especially true of prices. We therefore suggest that you write or call ahead for confirmation when making your travel plans. The authors, editors, and publisher cannot be held responsible for the experiences of readers while traveling. Your safety is important to us, however, so we encourage you to stay alert and be aware of your surroundings. Keep a close eye on cameras, purses, and wallets, all favorite targets of thieves and pickpockets.

Frommer's Star Ratings, Icons & Abbreviations

Every hotel, restaurant, and attraction listing in this guide has been ranked for quality, value, service, amenities, and special features using a **star-rating system.** In country, state, and regional guides, we also rate towns and regions to help you narrow down your choices and budget your time accordingly. Hotels and restaurants are rated on a scale of zero (recommended) to three stars (exceptional). Attractions, shopping, nightlife, towns, and regions are rated according to the following scale: zero stars (recommended), one star (highly recommended), two stars (very highly recommended), and three stars (must-see).

In addition to the star-rating system, we also use **seven feature icons** that point you to the great deals, in-the-know advice, and unique experiences that separate travelers from tourists. Throughout the book, look for:

Finds	Special finds—those places only insiders know about
Fun Fact	Fun facts—details that make travelers more informed and their trips more fun
Kids	Best bets for kids and advice for the whole family
Moments	Special moments—those experiences that memories are made of
Overrated	Places or experiences not worth your time or money
Tips	Insider tips—great ways to save time and money
Value	Great values—where to get the best deals

The following **abbreviations** are used for credit cards:

AE	American Express	DISC	Discover	V	Visa
DC	Diners Club	MC	MasterCard		

Frommers.com

Now that you have this guidebook to help you plan a great trip, visit our website at **www.frommers.com** for additional travel information on more than 3,600 destinations. We update features regularly to give you instant access to the most current trip-planning information available. At Frommers.com, you'll find scoops on the best airfares, lodging rates, and car rental bargains. You can even book your travel online through our reliable travel booking partners. Other popular features include:

- Online updates of our most popular guidebooks
- Vacation sweepstakes and contest giveaways
- Newsletters highlighting the hottest travel trends
- Online travel message boards with featured travel discussions

Hawaii, the Big Island

The Big Island of Hawaii—the island that lends its name to the entire 1,500-mile-long Hawaiian archipelago—is where Mother Nature pulled out all the stops. Simply put, it's spectacular.

The Big Island has it all: fiery volcanoes and sparkling waterfalls, black-lava deserts and snowcapped mountain peaks, tropical rainforests and alpine meadows, a glacial lake and miles of golden, black, and even green-sand beaches. The Big Island has an unmatched diversity of terrain and climate. A 50-mile drive will take you from snowy winter to sultry summer, passing through spring or fall along the way. The island looks like the inside of a barbecue pit on one side and a lush jungle on the other.

The Big Island is the largest island in the Hawaiian chain (4,038 sq. miles—about the size of Connecticut), the youngest (800,000 years), and the least populated (with 30 people per sq. mile). It has the highest peaks in the Pacific, the most volcanoes of any Hawaiian island, and the newest land on earth.

Five volcanoes—one still erupting—have created this continental island, which is growing bigger daily. At its heart is snowcapped Mauna Kea, the world's tallest sea mountain (measured from the ocean floor), complete with its own glacial lake. Mauna Kea's nearest neighbor is Mauna Loa (or "Long Mountain"), creator of one-sixth of the island; it's the largest volcano on earth, rising 30,000 feet out of the ocean floor (of course, you can see only the 13,796 ft. that are above sea level). Kilauea's eruptions make the Big Island bigger every day—and, if you're lucky, you can stand just a few feet away and watch it do its work.

Steeped in tradition and shrouded in the primal mist of creation, the Big Island radiates what the Hawaiians call *mana,* a sense of spirituality that's still apparent in the acres of petroglyphs etched in the black lava, the numerous *heiau* (temples), burial caves scattered in the cliffs, sacred shrines both on land and in the sea, and even the sound the wind makes as it blows across the desolate lava fields.

The Big Island is not for everyone, however. It refuses to fit the stereotype of a tropical island. Some tourists are taken aback at

The Big Island

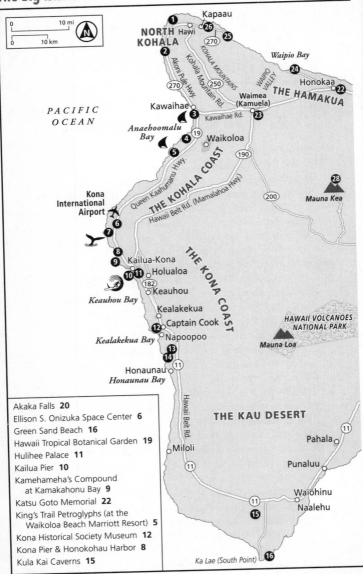

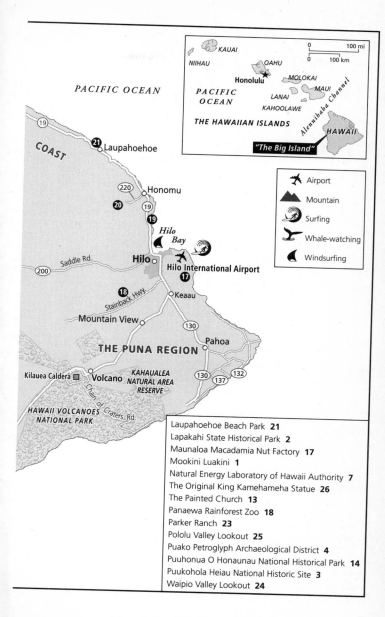

PACIFIC OCEAN

KAUAI

NIIHAU

OAHU

Honolulu

MOLOKAI

MAUI

PACIFIC OCEAN

LANAI

KAHOOLAWE

Alenuihaha Channel

THE HAWAIIAN ISLANDS

HAWAII

"The Big Island"

0 ___ 100 mi
0 ___ 100 km

PACIFIC OCEAN

COAST

(19)

21 Laupahoehoe

(220)

Honomu

20

(19)

19 *Hilo Bay*

Saddle Rd.

(200)

Hilo

Hilo International Airport

17

18

Keaau

Stainback Hwy.

Mountain View

(130)

Pahoa

THE PUNA REGION

Kilauea Caldera

Volcano

KAHAUALEA NATURAL AREA RESERVE

(130) (137) (132)

Chain of Craters Rd.

HAWAII VOLCANOES NATIONAL PARK

Airport

Mountain

Surfing

Whale-watching

Windsurfing

Laupahoehoe Beach Park **21**
Lapakahi State Historical Park **2**
Maunaloa Macadamia Nut Factory **17**
Mookini Luakini **1**
Natural Energy Laboratory of Hawaii Authority **7**
The Original King Kamehameha Statue **26**
The Painted Church **13**
Panaewa Rainforest Zoo **18**
Parker Ranch **23**
Pololu Valley Lookout **25**
Puako Petroglyph Archaeological District **4**
Puuhonua O Honaunau National Historical Park **14**
Puukohola Heiau National Historic Site **3**
Waipio Valley Lookout **24**

the sight of stark fields of lava or black-sand beaches. You must remember that it's *big* (expect to do lots of driving). And you may have to go out of your way if you're looking for traditional tropical beauty, such as a quintessential white-sand beach.

On the other hand, if you're into watersports, this is paradise. The two tall volcanoes mean the water on the leeward side is calm 350 days a year. The underwater landscape of caves, cliffs, and tunnels attracts a stunning array of colorful marine life. The island's west coast is one of the best destinations in the world for big-game fishing. And its miles of remote coastline are a kayaker's dream of caves, secluded coves, and crescent-shaped beaches reachable only by sea.

On land, hikers, bikers, and horseback riders can head up and down a volcano, across beaches, into remote valleys, and through rainforests without seeing another soul. Bird-watchers are rewarded with sightings of the rare, rapidly dwindling native birds of Hawaii. Golfers can find nirvana on a wide variety of courses.

This is the least-explored island in the Hawaiian chain, but if you're looking to get away from it all and back to nature in its most primal state, that might be the best thing about it. Where else can you witness fiery creation and swim with dolphins, ponder the stars from the world's tallest mountain and catch a blue marlin, downhill-ski, and surf the waves in a single day? You can do all this and more on only one island in the world: the Big Island of Hawaii.

1 The Island in Brief

Most people arrive on the Big Island at Kona International Airport, on the island's west coast. From the airport, Kilauea volcano is to the right (counterclockwise), and the ritzy Kohala Coast is to the left (clockwise). (If you land in Hilo, of course, the volcano is clockwise and Kohala is counterclockwise.)

THE KONA COAST ⟨⟨

Kona is synonymous with great coffee and big fish—both of which are found in abundance along this 70-mile-long stretch of black-lava-covered coast.

A collection of tiny communities devoted to farming and fishing along the sun-baked leeward side of the island, the Kona Coast has an amazingly diverse geography and climate for such a compact area. The oceanfront town of **Kailua-Kona,** a quaint fishing village that now caters more to tourists than boat captains, is its commercial center. The lands of Kona range from stark, black, dry coastal desert to cool, cloudy upcountry where glossy green coffee, macadamia nuts, tropical fruit, and a riotous profusion of flowers cover the steep, jagged slopes. Among the coffee fields, you'll find the funky, artsy village of **Holualoa.** Higher yet in elevation are native forests of giant trees filled with tiny, colorful birds, some perilously close to extinction. About 7 miles south of Kailua-Kona, bordering the ocean, is the resort area of **Keauhou,** a suburban-like series of upscale condominiums, a shopping center, and million-dollar homes.

Kona means "leeward side" in Hawaiian—and that means full-on sun every day of the year. This is an affordable vacation spot; an ample selection of midpriced condo units, peppered with a few older hotels and B&Bs, lines the shore, which is mostly rocky lava reef, interrupted by an occasional pocket beach. Here, too, stand two world-class resorts: Kona Village, the site of one of the best luau in the islands, and one of Hawaii's luxury retreats, the Four Seasons at Hualalai.

Away from the bright lights of the town of Kailua lies the rural **South Kona Coast,** home to coffee farmers, macadamia-nut growers, and people escaping to the country. The serrated South Kona Coast is indented with numerous bays, from **Kealakekua,** a marine-life preserve that's the island's best diving spot, down to **Honaunau,** where a national historic park recalls the days of old Hawaii. Accommodations in this area are mainly B&Bs. This coast is a great place to stay if you want to get away from crowds and experience peaceful country living. You'll be within driving distance of beaches and the sites of Kailua.

THE KOHALA COAST 𝕳𝕳

Fringes of palms and flowers, brilliant blankets of emerald green, and an occasional flash of white buildings are your only clues from the road that this black-lava coast north of Kona is more than bleak and barren. But, oh, is it! Down by the sea, pleasure domes rise like palaces no Hawaiian king ever imagined. This is where the Lear jet–set escapes to play in world-class beachfront hotels set like jewels in the golden sand. But you don't have to be a billionaire to visit the Waikoloa, Mauna Lani, and Mauna Kea resorts: The fabulous beaches and abundant historic sites are open to the public, with parking and other facilities, including restaurants, golf courses, and shopping, provided by the resorts.

NORTH KOHALA 𝒜𝒜

Seven sugar mills once shipped enough sugar from three harbors on this knob of land to sweeten all the coffee in San Francisco. **Hawi,** the region's hub and home to the Kohala Sugar Co., was a flourishing town. Today Hawi's quaint, 3-block-long strip of sun-faded, false-fronted buildings and 1920s vintage shops lives on as a minor tourist stop in one of Hawaii's most scenic rural regions, located at the northernmost reaches of the island. North Kohala is most famous as the birthplace of King Kamehameha the Great; a statue commemorates the royal site. It's also home to the islands' most sacred site, the 1,500-year-old **Mo'okini Heiau.**

WAIMEA (KAMUELA) 𝒜𝒜

This old upcountry cow town on the northern road between the coasts is set in lovely country: rolling green pastures, wide-open spaces dotted by *puu* (hills), and real cowpokes who ride mammoth **Parker Ranch,** Hawaii's largest working ranch. The town is also headquarters for the **Keck Telescope,** the largest and most powerful in the world. Waimea is home to several affordable B&Bs, and Merriman's restaurant is a popular foodie outpost at Opelo Plaza.

THE HAMAKUA COAST 𝒜𝒜

This emerald coast, a 52-mile stretch from Honokaa to Hilo on the island's windward northeast side, was once planted with sugar cane; it now blooms with flowers, macadamia nuts, papayas, and marijuana, also known as *pakalolo* (still Hawaii's number-one cash crop). Resort-free and virtually without beaches, the Hamakua Coast still has a few major destinations. Picture-perfect **Waipio Valley** has impossibly steep sides, taro patches, a green riot of wild plants, and a winding stream leading to a broad, black-sand beach; and the historic plantation town of **Honokaa** is making a comeback as the B&B capital on the coastal trail. **Akaka Falls** and **Laupahoehoe Beach Park** are also worth seeking out.

HILO 𝒜𝒜

When the sun shines in Hilo, it's one of the most beautiful tropical cities in the Pacific. Being here is an entirely different kind of island experience: Hawaii's largest metropolis after Honolulu is a quaint, misty, flower-filled city of Victorian houses overlooking a half-moon bay, with a restored historic downtown and a clear view of Mauna Loa's often snowcapped peak. Hilo catches everyone's eye until it rains—it rains a lot in Hilo, and when it rains, it pours.

Hilo is one of America's wettest towns, with 128 inches of rain annually. It's ideal for growing ferns, orchids, and anthuriums, but not for catching a few rays. But there's a lot to see and do in Hilo, so grab your umbrella. The rain is warm (the temperature seldom dips below 70°F/21°C), and there's usually a rainbow afterward.

Hilo's oversize airport and hotels are remnants of a dream: The city wanted to be Hawaii's major port of entry. That didn't happen, but the facilities here are excellent. Hilo is also Hawaii's best bargain for budget travelers. It has plenty of hotel rooms—most of the year, that is. Hilo's magic moment comes in spring, the week after Easter, when hula *halau* (schools) arrive for the annual Merrie Monarch Hula Festival hula competition (see "Big Island Calendar of Events," later in this chapter). This is a full-on Hawaiian spectacle and a wonderful cultural event. Plan ahead if you want to go: Tickets are sold out by the first week in January, and the hotels within 30 miles are usually booked solid.

Hilo is also the gateway to Hawaii Volcanoes National Park; it's just an hour's drive up-slope.

HAWAII VOLCANOES NATIONAL PARK ๛๛๛

This is America's most exciting national park, where a live volcano called Kilauea erupts daily. If you're lucky, it will be a spectacular sight. At other times, you may not be able to see the molten lava at all, but there's always a lot to see and learn. Ideally, you should plan to spend 3 days at the park exploring the trails, watching the volcano, visiting the rainforest, and just enjoying this spectacular place. But even if you have only a day, get here—it's worth the trip. Bring your sweats or jacket (honest!); it's cool up here, especially at night.

If you plan to dally in the park, plan to stay in the sleepy hamlet of Volcano Village, just outside the National Park entrance. Several terrifically cozy B&Bs, some with fireplaces, hide under tree ferns in this cool mountain hideaway. The tiny highland community (elev. 4,000 ft.), first settled by Japanese immigrants, is now inhabited by artists, soul-searchers, and others who like the crisp air of Hawaii's high country. It has just enough civilization to sustain a good life: a few stores, a handful of eateries, a gas station, and a golf course.

KA LAE: SOUTH POINT ๛๛

This is the Plymouth Rock of Hawaii, where the first Polynesians arrived in seagoing canoes, probably from the Marquesas Islands or Tahiti, around A.D. 500. You'll feel like you're at the end of the world on this lonely, windswept place, the southernmost point of the United States (a geographic claim that belonged to Key West, Florida, before Hawaii became a state). Hawaii ends in a sharp, black-lava point. Bold 500-foot cliffs stand against the blue sea to the west and shelter the old fishing village of Waiahukini, which was populated from A.D. 750 until the 1860s. Ancient canoe moorings, shelter caves, and *heiau* (temples) poke through windblown pili grass. The east coast curves inland to reveal a green-sand beach, a world-famous anomaly that's accessible only by foot or four-wheel-drive. For most, the only reason to venture down to the southern tip is to experience the empty vista of land's end.

Everything in **Naalehu** and **Waiohinu,** the two wide spots in the road that pass for towns at South Point, claims to be the southernmost this or that. Except for a monkeypod tree planted by Mark Twain in 1866, there's not much else to crow about. There is, thankfully, a gas station, along with a couple of places to eat, a fruit stand, and a few B&Bs. These end-of-the-world towns are just about as far removed from the real world as you can get.

2 Visitor Information

The **Big Island Visitors Bureau** has two offices on the Big Island: one at 250 Keawe St., Hilo, HI 96720 (© **808/961-5797;** fax 808/961-2126), and on the other side of the island at 250 Waikoloa Beach Dr., Waikoloa, HI 96738 (© **808/886-1652**). Its website is www.bigisland.org.

On the west side of the island, there are two additional sources to contact for information: the **Kona-Kohala Resort Association,** 68–1310 Mauna Lani Dr., suite 101, Kahala Coast, HI 96743 (© **800/318-3637** or 808/885-6414; fax 808/885-6145; www. kohalacoastresorts.com); and **Destination Kona,** P.O. Box 2850, Kailua-Kona, HI 96745 (© **808/322-6809;** fax 808/322-8899). On the east side, you can contact **Destination Hilo,** P.O. Box 1391, Hilo, HI 96721 (© **808/935-5294;** fax 808/969-1984). And in the middle, contact the **Waimea Visitor Center,** P.O. Box 6570, Kamuela, HI 96743 (© **808/885-6707;** fax 808/885-0885).

The Big Island's best free tourist publications are *This Week,* the *Beach and Activity Guide,* and *101 Things to Do on Hawaii the Big Island.* All three offer lots of useful information, as well as discount coupons on a variety of island adventures. Copies are easy to find all around the island.

The *Beach and Activity Guide* is affiliated with the **Activity Connection,** Bougainvillea Plaza, Suite 102, 75–5656 Kuakini Hwy.,

Kailua-Kona (*©* **800/459-7156** or 808/329-1038; fax 808/327-9411; www.beachactivityguide.com), a discount activities desk offering real savings (no fees, no timeshares) of up to 15% on activities including island tours, snorkel and dive trips, submarine and horseback rides, luau, and more. The office is open daily from 7:30am to 5:30pm.

3 Entry Requirements

PASSPORTS

For information on how to get a passport, go to **"Passports"** in the **"Fast Facts"** section of this chapter—the websites listed provide downloadable passport applications as well as the current fees for processing passport applications. For an up-to-date, country-by-country listing of passport requirements around the world, go to the "Foreign Entry Requirement" Web page of the U.S. State Department at **http://travel.state.gov**. International visitors can obtain a visa application at the same website. *Note:* Children are required to present a passport when entering the United States at airports. More information on obtaining a passport for a minor can be found at http://travel.state.gov.

VISAS

For specifics on how to get a visa, go to **"Visas"** in the **"Fast Facts"** section of this chapter.

The U.S. State Department has a **Visa Waiver Program (VWP)** allowing citizens of the following countries (at press time) to enter the United States without a visa for stays of up to 90 days: Andorra, Australia, Austria, Belgium, Brunei, Denmark, Finland, France, Germany, Iceland, Ireland, Italy, Japan, Liechtenstein, Luxembourg,

---

U.S. Entry: Passport Required

New regulations issued by the Homeland Security Department now require virtually every air traveler entering the U.S. to show a passport—and future regulations will cover land and sea entry as well. As of January 23, 2007, all persons, including U.S. citizens, traveling by air between the United States and Canada, Mexico, Central and South America, the Caribbean, and Bermuda are required to present a valid passport. Similar regulations for those traveling by land or sea (including ferries) are expected as early as January 1, 2008.

Monaco, the Netherlands, New Zealand, Norway, Portugal, San Marino, Singapore, Slovenia, Spain, Sweden, Switzerland, and the United Kingdom. Canadian citizens may enter the United States without visas; they will need to show passports and proof of residence, however. *Note:* Any passport issued on or after October 26, 2006, by a VWP country must be an **e-Passport** for VWP travelers to be eligible to enter the U.S. without a visa. Citizens of these nations also need to present a round-trip air or cruise ticket upon arrival. E-Passports contain computer chips capable of storing biometric information, such as the required digital photograph of the holder. (You can identify an e-Passport by the symbol on the bottom center cover of your passport.) If your passport doesn't have this feature, you can still travel without a visa if it is a valid passport issued before October 26, 2005, and includes a machine-readable zone, or between October 26, 2005, and October 25, 2006, and includes a digital photograph. For more information, go to **www.travel.state.gov/visa**.

Citizens of all other countries must have (1) a valid passport that expires at least 6 months later than the scheduled end of their visit to the United States and (2) a tourist visa, which may be obtained without charge from any U.S. consulate.

As of January 2004, many international visitors traveling on visas to the United States will be photographed and fingerprinted on arrival at Customs in airports and on cruise ships in a program created by the Department of Homeland Security called **US-VISIT.** Exempt from the extra scrutiny are visitors entering by land or those that don't require a visa for short-term visits. For more information, go to the Homeland Security website at **www.dhs. gov/dhspublic**.

MEDICAL REQUIREMENTS

Unless you're arriving from an area known to be suffering from an epidemic (particularly cholera or yellow fever), inoculations or vaccinations are not required for entry into the United States. If you have a medical condition that requires **syringe-administered medications,** carry a valid signed prescription from your physician; syringes in carry-on baggage will be inspected. Insulin in any form should have the proper pharmaceutical documentation. If you have a disease that requires treatment with **narcotics,** you should also carry documented proof with you—smuggling narcotics aboard a plane carries severe penalties in the U.S.

For **HIV-positive visitors,** requirements for entering the United States are somewhat vague and change frequently. For up-to-the-minute information, contact **AIDSinfo** (© 800/448-0440 or 301/519-6616 outside the U.S.; www.aidsinfo.nih.gov) or the **Gay Men's Health Crisis** (© 212/367-1000; www.gmhc.org).

CUSTOMS

For information on what you can bring into and take out of Hawaii, go to **"Customs"** in the **"Fast Facts"** section of this chapter.

4 When to Go

Most visitors don't come to Hawaii when the weather's best in the islands; rather, they come when it's at its worst everywhere else. Thus, the **high season**—when prices are up and resorts are often booked to capacity—is generally from mid-December through March or mid-April. The last 2 weeks of December, in particular, are the prime time for travel to Hawaii. If you're planning a holiday trip, make your reservations as early as possible, expect crowds, and prepare to pay top dollar for accommodations, car rentals, and airfare.

The **off season,** when the best rates are available and the islands are less crowded, is spring (mid-Apr to mid-June) and fall (Sept to mid-Dec)—a paradox because these are the best seasons to be in Hawaii, in terms of reliably great weather. If you're looking to save money, or if you just want to avoid the crowds, this is the time to visit. Hotel rates and airfares tend to be significantly lower, and good packages are often available.

Note: If you plan to come to Hawaii between the last week in April and early May, be sure you book your accommodations, inter-island air reservations, and car rentals in advance. In Japan, the last week of April is called **Golden Week** because three Japanese holidays take place one after the other. Waikiki is especially busy with Japanese tourists during this time, but the neighboring islands also see dramatic increases.

Due to the large number of families traveling in **summer** (June–Aug), you won't get the fantastic bargains of spring and fall. However, you'll still do much better on packages, airfare, and accommodations than you will in the winter months.

CLIMATE

Because Hawaii lies at the edge of the tropical zone, it technically has only two seasons, both of them warm. There's a dry season that corresponds to **summer** (Apr–Oct) and a rainy season in **winter** (Nov–Mar). It rains every day somewhere in the islands any time of the year, but the rainy season sometimes brings enough gray weather to spoil your tanning opportunities. Fortunately, it seldom rains in one spot for more than 3 days straight.

The **year-round temperature** doesn't vary much. At the beach, the average daytime high in summer is 85°F (29°C), while the average daytime high in winter is 78°F (26°C); nighttime lows are usually about 10°F cooler. But how warm it is on any given day really depends on *where* you are on the island.

Each island has a leeward side (the side sheltered from the wind) and a windward side (the side that gets the wind's full force). The **leeward** sides (the west and south) are usually hot and dry, while the **windward** sides (east and north) are generally cooler and moist. When you want arid, sunbaked, desertlike weather, go leeward. When you want lush, wet, junglelike weather, go windward.

Hawaii is also full of **microclimates,** thanks to its interior valleys, coastal plains, and mountain peaks. Kauai's Mount Waialeale is the wettest spot on earth, yet Waimea Canyon, just a few miles away, is almost a desert. On the Big Island, Hilo is one of the wettest cities in the nation, with 180 inches of rainfall a year, but at Puako, only 60 miles away, it rains less than 6 inches a year. If you travel into the mountains, the climate can change from summer to winter in a matter of hours because it's cooler the higher you go. So if the weather doesn't suit you, just go to the other side of the island—or head into the hills.

On rare occasions, the weather can be disastrous, as when Hurricane Iniki crushed Kauai in September 1992 with 225-mph winds. Tsunamis have swept Hilo and the south shore of Oahu. But those are extreme exceptions. Mostly, one day follows another here in glorious, sunny procession, each quite like the other.

HOLIDAYS

When Hawaii observes holidays (especially those over a long weekend), travel between the islands increases, interisland airline seats are fully booked, rental cars are at a premium, and hotels and restaurants are busier.

Federal, state, and county government offices are closed on all federal holidays: January 1 (New Year's Day), the third Monday in January (Martin Luther King, Jr., Day), the third Monday in February (Presidents' Day, Washington's Birthday), the last Monday in May (Memorial Day), July 4 (Independence Day), the first Monday in September (Labor Day), the second Monday in October (Columbus Day), November 11 (Veterans Day), the fourth Thursday in November (Thanksgiving Day), and December 25 (Christmas).

State and county offices are also closed on local holidays, including Prince Kuhio Day (Mar 26), honoring the birthday of Hawaii's first delegate to the U.S. Congress; King Kamehameha Day (June 11), a statewide holiday commemorating Kamehameha the Great, who united the islands and ruled from 1795 to 1819; and Admissions Day (third Fri in Aug), which honors the admittance of Hawaii as the 50th state on August 21, 1959.

Other special days celebrated in Hawaii by many people but which involve no closing of federal, state, and county offices are the Chinese New Year (which can fall in Jan or Feb; in 2008, it's Feb 7), Girls' Day (Mar 3), Buddha's Birthday (Apr 8), Father Damien's Day (Apr 15), Boys' Day (May 5), Samoan Flag Day (in Aug), Aloha Festivals (in Sept and Oct), and Pearl Harbor Day (Dec 7).

BIG ISLAND CALENDAR OF EVENTS

Please note that, as with any schedule of upcoming events, the following information is subject to change; always confirm the details before you plan your trip around an event.

For an exhaustive list of events beyond those mentioned here, check www.calendar.gohawaii.com for a list of events throughout the islands, or http://events.frommers.com, where you'll find a searchable, up-to-the-minute roster of what's happening in cities all over the world.

March

Daylight saving time begins. Since 1966, most of the United States has observed daylight saving time from 2am on the first Sunday of April to 2am on the last Sunday of October. In 2007, these dates changed, and now daylight saving time lasts from 2am on the second Sunday in March to 2am on the first Sunday in November. Hawaii does *not* observe daylight saving time. So beginning on March 9, 2008, Hawaii is 3 hours behind the West Coast and 6 hours behind the East Coast.

Kona Brewer's Festival, King Kamehameha's Kona Beach Hotel Luau Grounds, Kailua-Kona. This annual event features microbreweries from around the world, with beer tastings, food, and entertainment. Call © **808/334-1133.** Second Saturday in March.

Annual Kona Chocolate Festival, Kona. A 3-day celebration of the chocolate (cacao) that is grown and produced in Hawaii. Days 1 and 2 are filled with symposiums and seminars on chocolate and its uses. Day 3 features a Gala party with samples of chocolate creations by Big Island chefs, caterers, and ice cream and candy makers. A chocoholic's dream! For information and tickets, call ℂ 808/324-4606 or visit www.konachocolatefestival.com. Mid- to late March.

Prince Kuhio Day Celebrations, various locations. State holiday. Various festivals throughout the state celebrate the birth of Jonah Kuhio Kalanianaole, who was born on March 26, 1871, and elected to Congress in 1902. Kauai, his birthplace, stages a huge celebration in Lihue; call ℂ 808/240-6369 for details. Molokai also hosts a 2-day-long celebration; call ℂ 808/553-3876 to learn more. March 26.

April

Merrie Monarch Hula Festival, Hilo. Hawaii's biggest hula festival features 3 nights of modern *(auana)* and ancient *(kahiko)* dance competition in honor of King David Kalakaua, the "Merrie Monarch" who revived the dance. Tickets sell out by January 30, so reserve early. Call ℂ 808/935-9168; www.merriemonarch festival.org. The week after Easter (Mar 23–30, 2008).

May

Outrigger Canoe Season, various locations. From May to September, canoe paddlers across the state participate in outrigger canoe races nearly every weekend. Call ℂ 808/383-7798, or go to www.y2kanu.com for this year's schedule of events.

Annual Lei Day Celebrations, various locations. May Day is Lei Day in Hawaii, celebrated with lei-making contests, pageantry, arts and crafts, and the real highlight, a Brothers Cazimero concert at the Waikiki Shell. Call ℂ 808/692-5118 or visit www.honolulu.gov/parks/programs/leiday for Oahu events (ℂ 808/597-1888, ext. 232, for the Brothers Cazimero show; ℂ 808/886-1655 for Big Island events; ℂ 808/224-6042 for Maui events; or ℂ 808/245-6931 for Kauai events). May 1.

June

King Kamehameha Celebration. This state holiday features a massive floral parade, *hoolaulea* (party), and much more. Call ℂ 808/586-0333 for Big Island events, or visit www.state.hi.us/dags/kkcc.

Great Waikoloa Food, Wine & Music Festival, Hilton Waikoloa Village. One of the Big Island's best food and wine festivals features Hawaii's top chefs (and a few mainland chefs) showing off their culinary talents, wines from around the world, and an excellent jazz concert with fireworks. Not to be missed.

Call ✆ **808/886-1234** or visit www.hiltonwaikoloavillage.com or www.dolphindays.com. Mid-June.

August

Puukohola Heiau National Historic Site Anniversary Celebration, Kawaihae. This is a weekend of Hawaiian crafts, workshops, and games. Call ✆ **808/882-7218.** Mid-August (Aug 16–17, 2008).

Admissions Day. Hawaii became the 50th state on August 21, 1959. The state takes a holiday (all state-related facilities are closed) on the third Friday in August (Aug 15, 2008).

September

Queen Liliuokalani Canoe Race, Kailua-Kona to Honaunau. The world's largest long-distance canoe race takes places over Labor Day weekend, with hundreds participating. Call ✆ **808/331-8849** or visit www.kaiopua.org.

Parker Ranch Rodeo, Waimea. This is a hot rodeo competition in the heart of cowboy country. Call ✆ **808/885-7311** or go to www.parkerranch.com. Labor Day Weekend (Aug 30–Sept 1, 2008).

Hawaiian Slack-Key Guitar Festival, Sheraton Keauhou Bay Resort & Spa, Kona. The best of Hawaii's folk music (slack-key guitar) performed by the best musicians in Hawaii. It's 5 hours long and absolutely free. Call ✆ **808/239-4336** or e-mail kahoku productions@yahoo.com. September 7, 2008.

Aloha Festivals, various locations. Parades and other events celebrate Hawaiian culture and friendliness throughout the state. Call ✆ **808/589-1771** or visit www.alohafestivals.com for a schedule of events.

Aloha Festivals Poke Recipe Contest, Hapuna Beach Prince Hotel, Mauna Kea Beach Resort, Kohala Coast. Top chefs from across Hawaii and the U.S. mainland, as well as local amateurs, compete in making this Hawaiian delicacy, poke (pronounced po-*kay*): chopped raw fish mixed with seaweed and spices. Here's your chance to sample poke at its best. Call ✆ **808/880-3424** or visit www.pokecontest.com.

October

Hamakua Music Festival, Hamakua. This event features a surprisingly eclectic mix of well-known musicians, ranging from blues and jazz to rock 'n' roll, Hawaiian, and even classical. At press time, the festival was in the midst of reorganization, so first call ✆ **808/775-3378** or check at www.hamakuamusicfestival.org.

Ironman Triathlon World Championship, Kailua-Kona. Some 1,500-plus world-class athletes run a full marathon, swim 2½ miles, and bike 112 miles on the Kona-Kohala coast of the Big Island. Spectators can watch the action along the route for free. The best place to see the 7am start is along the seawall on Alii Drive, facing Kailua Bay; arrive before 5:30am to get a seat. The best place to see the bike-and-run portion is along Alii Drive (which will be closed to traffic; park on a side street and walk down). To watch the finishers come in, line up along Alii Drive from Holualoa Street to the finish at Palani Road/Alii Drive; the first finisher can come as early as 2:30pm, and the course closes at midnight. Call ℂ **808/329-0063** or visit www.ironman.com. October. (As we went to press, they did not have a confirmed date, so check the website.)

November

Daylight saving time ends. Beginning in 2007, most of the U.S. will revert to standard time on the first Sunday in November. Since Hawaii does not observe daylight saving time, starting on November 4, 2008, Hawaii will be 2 hours behind the West Coast and 5 hours behind the East Coast.

Annual Kona Coffee Cultural Festival, Kailua-Kona. Celebrate the coffee harvest with a bean-picking contest, lei contests, song and dance, and the Miss Kona Coffee pageant. Call ℂ **808/326-7820** or go to www.konacoffeefest.com for this year's schedule.

Hawaii International Film Festival, various locations. This cinema festival with a cross-cultural spin features filmmakers from Asia, the Pacific Islands, and the United States. Call ℂ **808/550-8457** or visit www.hiff.org. First 2 weeks in November.

Annual Invitational Wreath Exhibit, Volcano Art Center, Volcano National Park. Thirty-two artists, including painters, sculptors, glass artists, fiber artists, and potters, produce wreaths in a wide variety of styles for this exhibit. Park entrance fees apply. Call ℂ **866/967-7565** or 808/967-7565; www.volcanoartcenter.org. Mid-November through the first of January.

5 Getting There

BY PLANE

Most major U.S. and many international carriers fly to Honolulu International Airport. Some also offer direct flights to Kailua-Kona, on the Big Island.

United Airlines (ℂ **800/225-5825;** www.ual.com) offers the most frequent service from the U.S. mainland, flying not only to

Honolulu, but also offering nonstop flights from Los Angeles and San Francisco to the Big Island, Maui, and Kauai. **Aloha Airlines** (© **800/367-5250** or 808/484-1111; www.alohaairlines.com) has direct flights from Oakland to Maui, Kona, and Honolulu, and from Orange County, California, to Honolulu, Kona, and Maui. Aloha also offers connecting flights from Las Vegas to Oakland and Orange County. **American Airlines** (© **800/433-7300;** www.americanair.com) offers flights from Dallas, Chicago, San Francisco, San Jose, Los Angeles, and St. Louis to Honolulu, plus several direct flights to Maui and Kona. **ATA**/code sharing with **Southwest Airlines** (© **800/I-FLY-ATA** or 800/435-9282; www.ata.com) has direct flights to Honolulu from Oakland, Los Angeles, Orange County, Las Vegas, and Phoenix; direct flights to Maui from Oakland, Orange County, and Phoenix; and direct flights from Oakland to Kona, Hilo, and Lihue. **Continental Airlines** (© **800/231-0856;** www.continental.com) offers the only daily nonstop from the New York area (Newark) to Honolulu. **Delta Air Lines** (© **800/221-1212;** www.delta.com) flies nonstop from the West Coast and from Houston and Cincinnati. **Hawaiian Airlines** (© **800/367-5320;** www.hawaiianair.com) offers nonstop flights to Honolulu from several West Coast cities (including new service from San Diego), plus nonstop flights from Los Angeles to Maui. **Northwest Airlines** (© **800/225-2525;** www.nwa.com) has a daily nonstop from Detroit to Honolulu.

Airlines serving Hawaii from places other than the U.S. mainland include **Air Canada** (© 800/776-3000; www.aircanada.ca); **Air New Zealand** (© 0800/737-000 in Auckland, 643/379-5200 in Christchurch, 800/926-7255 in the U.S.; www.airnewzealand. com); **Qantas** (© 008/177-767 in Australia, 800/227-4500 in the U.S.; www.qantas.com.au); **Japan Air Lines** (© 03/5489-1111 in Tokyo, 800/525-3663 in the U.S.; www.japanair.com); **All Nippon Airways** (**ANA;** © 03/5489-1212 in Tokyo, 800/235-9262 in the U.S.; www.fly-ana.com); **China Airlines** (© 02/715-1212 in Taipei, 800/227-5118 in the U.S.; www.china-airlines.com); **Air Pacific,** serving Fiji, Australia, New Zealand, and the South Pacific (© 800/227-4446; www.airpacific.com); **Korean Air** (© 02/656-2000 in Seoul, 800/223-1155 on the East Coast, 800/421-8200 on the West Coast, 800/438-5000 from Hawaii; www.koreanair.com); and **Philippine Airlines** (© 631/816-6691 in Manila, 800/435-9725 in the U.S.; www.philippineairlines.com).

Operated by the European Travel Network, **www.discounttickets.com** is a great online source for regular and discounted airfares to destinations around the world. You can also use this site to compare rates and book accommodations, car rentals, and tours.

If you're traveling in the United States beyond Hawaii, some large American airlines—such as **American, Delta, Northwest,** and **United**—offer travelers on transatlantic or transpacific flights special discount tickets under the name **Visit USA,** allowing travel between any U.S. destinations at reduced rates. These tickets must be purchased before you leave your foreign point of departure. This system is the best, easiest, and fastest way to see the United States at low cost. You should obtain information well in advance from your travel agent or the office of the airline concerned, since the conditions attached to these discount tickets can change without advance notice.

Locally, **Hawaiian Airlines** (© 800/367-5320; www.hawaiian air.com) flies nonstop to Sydney, Tahiti, and American Samoa.

Visitors arriving by air should cultivate patience and resignation before setting foot on U.S. soil. Getting through immigration control may take as long as 2 hours on some days, especially summer weekends. Add the time it takes to clear Customs, and you'll see that you should make a very generous allowance for delay in planning connections between international and domestic flights—an average of 2 to 3 hours at least.

AGRICULTURAL SCREENING AT THE AIRPORTS   At Honolulu International and the neighbor-island airports, baggage and passengers bound for the mainland must be screened by agricultural officials. Officials will confiscate local produce like fresh avocados, bananas, and mangoes, in the name of fruit-fly control. Pineapples, coconuts, and papayas inspected and certified for export; boxed flowers; leis without seeds; and processed foods (macadamia nuts, coffee, jams, dried fruit, and the like) will pass.

ARRIVING AT THE AIRPORT
The Big Island has two major airports for jet traffic between the islands: **Kona International Airport** and **Hilo International Airport.**

The **Kona Airport** receives direct overseas flights from Japan on **Japan Airlines** (© 800/525-3663; www.jal.co.jp/en) and Vancouver on **Air Canada** (© 888/247-2262; www.aircanada.com). Carriers from the mainland include **Aloha Airlines** (© 800/367-5250; www.alohaairlines.com), with nonstop flights to Oakland and Orange County, both in California; **American Airlines** (© 800/433-7300; www.aa.com), with flights to Los Angeles; **Delta**

Airlines (© 800/221-1212; www.delta.com), with nonstop flights from Salt Lake City (originating in Atlanta); **Northwest Airlines** (© 800/225-2525; www.nwa.com), with flights from Seattle; **U.S. Airways/American West** (© 800/428-4322; www.usairways.com), with flights from Phoenix; and **United Airlines** (© 800/241-6522; www.united.com), with nonstop flights from Denver, Los Angeles and San Francisco, and a direct flight to Chicago.

Hilo Airport has a direct flight from Oakland via **ATA** (© 800/435-9282; www.ata.com), which code-shares with **Southwest Airlines.**

If you cannot get a direct flight to the Big Island, you'll have to pick up an interisland flight in Honolulu: **Aloha Airlines** (see above), **Hawaiian Airlines** (© 800/367-5320; www.hawaiianair.com), and **go!** (© 888/IFLYGO2; www.iflygo.com) offer jet service to both Big Island airports. All major rental companies have cars available at both airports. See "Getting Around," later in this chapter, for more details on interisland travel and car rentals.

IMMIGRATION & CUSTOMS CLEARANCE   Foreign visitors arriving by air, no matter what the port of entry, should cultivate patience and resignation before setting foot on U.S. soil. U.S. airports have considerably beefed up security clearances in the years since the terrorist attacks of 9/11, and clearing Customs and Immigration can take as long as 2 hours.

People traveling by air from Canada, Bermuda, and certain Caribbean countries can sometimes clear Customs and Immigration at the point of departure, which is much faster.

6 Money

It's always advisable to bring money in a variety of forms on a vacation: a mix of cash, credit cards, and traveler's checks. You should also exchange enough petty cash to cover airport incidentals, tipping, and transportation to your hotel before you leave home, or withdraw money upon arrival at an airport ATM.

ATMS

Nationwide, the easiest and best way to get cash away from home is from an ATM (automated teller machine), sometimes referred to as a "cash machine" or "cashpoint." ATMs are everywhere in Hawaii—at banks, supermarkets, Long's Drugs, and Honolulu International Airport, and in some resorts and shopping centers. The **Cirrus** (© 800/424-7787; www.mastercard.com) and **PLUS** (© 800/843-7587;

www.visa.com) networks span the country; you can find them even in remote regions. Go to your bank card's website to find ATM locations at your destination. Be sure you know your daily withdrawal limit before you depart.

Note: Many banks impose a fee every time you use a card at another bank's ATM, and that fee is often higher for international transactions (up to $5 or more) than for domestic ones (where they're rarely more than $2). In addition, the bank from which you withdraw cash may charge its own fee. To compare banks' ATM fees within the U.S., use **www.bankrate.com**. Visitors from outside the U.S. should also find out whether their bank assesses a 1% to 3% fee on charges incurred abroad.

CREDIT CARDS & DEBIT CARDS

Credit cards are the most widely used form of payment in the United States: **Visa** (Barclaycard in Britain), **MasterCard** (Euro-Card in Europe, Access in Britain, Chargex in Canada), **American Express, Diners Club,** and **Discover.** They also provide a convenient record of all your expenses and offer relatively good exchange rates. You can withdraw cash advances from your credit cards at banks or ATMs, but high fees make credit card cash advances a pricey way to get cash.

It's highly recommended that you travel with at least one major credit card. You must have a credit card to rent a car, and hotels and airlines usually require a credit card imprint as a deposit against expenses.

ATM cards with major credit card backing, known as **"debit cards,"** are now a commonly acceptable form of payment in most stores and restaurants. Debit cards draw money directly from your checking account. Some stores enable you to receive cash back on your debit card purchases as well. The same is true at most U.S. post offices.

TRAVELER'S CHECKS

Though credit cards and debit cards are more often used, traveler's checks are still widely accepted in the U.S. Foreign visitors should make sure that traveler's checks are denominated in U.S. dollars; foreign-currency checks are often difficult to exchange.

You can buy traveler's checks at most banks. Most are offered in denominations of $20, $50, $100, $500, and sometimes $1,000. Generally, you'll pay a service charge ranging from 1% to 4%.

The most popular traveler's checks are offered by **American Express** (© 800/807-6233; © 800/221-7282 for card holders—this number accepts collect calls, offers service in several foreign languages, and exempts Amex gold and platinum cardholders from the 1% fee.); **Visa** (© 800/732-1322—AAA members can obtain Visa checks for a $9.95 fee for checks up to $1,500 at most AAA offices or by calling © 866/339-3378); and **MasterCard** (© 800/223-9920).

Be sure to keep a copy of the traveler's checks serial numbers separate from your checks in case they are stolen or lost. You'll get a refund faster if you know the numbers.

Another option is the new **prepaid traveler's check cards,** reloadable cards that work much like debit cards but aren't linked to your checking account. The **American Express Travelers Cheque Card,** for example, requires a minimum deposit ($300), sets a maximum balance ($2,750), and has a one-time issuance fee of $14.95. You can withdraw money from an ATM ($2.50 per transaction, not including bank fees), and the funds can be purchased in dollars, euros, or pounds. If you lose the card, your available funds will be refunded within 24 hours.

7 Travel Insurance

The cost of travel insurance varies widely, depending on the cost and length of your trip, your age and health, and the type of trip you're taking, but expect to pay between 5% and 8% of the vacation itself. You can get estimates from various providers through **InsureMyTrip.com.** Enter your trip cost and dates, your age, and other information, for prices from more than a dozen companies.

For **U.K. citizens,** insurance is always advisable when traveling in the States. Travelers or families who make more than one trip abroad per year may find an annual travel insurance policy works out cheaper. Check **www.moneysupermarket.com**, which compares prices across a wide range of providers for single- and multitrip policies.

Most big travel agents offer their own insurance and will probably try to sell you their package when you book a holiday. Think before you sign. **Britain's Consumers' Association** recommends that you insist on seeing the policy and reading the fine print before buying travel insurance. **The Association of British Insurers** (© 020/7600-3333; www.abi.org.uk) gives advice by phone and publishes *Holiday Insurance,* a free guide to policy provisions and prices. You might also shop around for better deals: Try **Columbus Direct** (✆ **0870/033-9988;** www.columbusdirect.net).

TRIP-CANCELLATION INSURANCE

Trip-cancellation insurance will help retrieve your money if you have to back out of a trip or depart early, or if your travel supplier goes bankrupt. Trip cancellation traditionally covers such events as sickness, natural disasters, and State Department advisories. The latest news in trip-cancellation insurance is the availability of **expanded hurricane coverage** and the **"any-reason"** cancellation coverage—which costs more but covers cancellations made for any reason. You won't get back 100% of your prepaid trip cost, but you'll be refunded a substantial portion. **TravelSafe** (✆ **888/885-7233;** www.travel safe.com) offers both types of coverage. Expedia also offers any-reason cancellation coverage for its air-hotel packages.

For details, contact one of the following recommended insurers: **Access America** (✆ 866/807-3982; www.accessamerica.com), **Travel Guard International** (✆ 800/826-4919; www.travelguard. com), **Travel Insured International** (✆ 800/243-3174; www. travelinsured.com), and **Travelex Insurance Services** (✆ 888/457-4602; www.travelex-insurance.com).

MEDICAL INSURANCE

Although it's not required of travelers, health insurance is highly recommended. Most health insurance policies cover you if you get sick away from home—but check your coverage before you leave.

International visitors should note that, unlike many European countries, the United States does not usually offer free or low-cost medical care to its citizens or visitors. Doctors and hospitals are expensive and, in most cases, will require advance payment or proof of coverage before they render their services. Good policies will cover the costs of an accident, repatriation, or death. Packages such as **Europ Assistance's "Worldwide Healthcare Plan"** are sold by European automobile clubs and travel agencies at attractive rates. **Worldwide Assistance Services, Inc.** (✆ **800/777-8710;** www. worldwideassistance.com) is the agent for Europ Assistance in the United States.

Though lack of health insurance may prevent you from being admitted to a hospital in nonemergencies, don't worry about being left on a street corner to die: The American way is to fix you now and bill the living daylights out of you later.

If you're ever hospitalized more than 150 miles from home, **MedjetAssist** (✆ 800/527-7478; www.medjetassistance.com) will pick you up and fly you to the hospital of your choice in a medically equipped and staffed aircraft 24 hours day, 7 days a week. Annual memberships are $225 individual, $350 family; you can also purchase short-term memberships.

Canadians should check with their provincial health plan offices or call **Health Canada** (✆ 866/225-0709; www.hc-sc.gc.ca) to find out the extent of their coverage and what documentation and receipts they must take home in case they are treated in the United States.

LOST-LUGGAGE INSURANCE

On flights within the U.S., checked baggage is covered up to $2,500 per ticketed passenger. On flights outside the U.S. (and on U.S. portions of international trips), baggage coverage is limited to approximately $9.07 per pound, up to approximately $635 per checked bag. If you plan to check items more valuable than what's covered by the standard liability, see if your homeowner's policy covers your valuables, get baggage insurance as part of your comprehensive travel-insurance package, or buy Travel Guard's "BagTrak" product.

If your luggage is lost, immediately file a lost-luggage claim at the airport, detailing the luggage contents. Most airlines require that you report delayed, damaged, or lost baggage within 4 hours of arrival. The airlines are required to deliver luggage, once found, directly to your house or destination free of charge.

8 Specialized Travel Resources

TRAVELERS WITH DISABILITIES

Most disabilities shouldn't stop anyone from traveling in the U.S. There are more options and resources out there than ever before.

Travelers with disabilities are made to feel very welcome in Hawaii. There are more than 2,000 ramped curbs in Oahu alone, hotels are usually equipped with wheelchair-accessible rooms, and tour companies provide many special services. The **Hawaii Center for Independent Living,** 414 Kauwili St., Suite 102, Honolulu, HI 96817 (✆ 808/522-5400; fax 808/586-8129), can provide information.

The only travel agency in Hawaii specializing in needs for travelers with disabilities is **Access Aloha Travel** (✆ 800/480-1143; www.accessalohatravel.com), which can book anything, including rental vans (available on Maui and Oahu only), accommodations, tours, cruises, airfare, and anything else you can think of.

The **America the Beautiful—National Park and Federal Recreational Lands Pass—Access Pass** (formerly the **Golden Access Passport**) gives the visually impaired persons or those with permanent disabilities (regardless of age) free lifetime entrance to federal recreation sites administered by the National Park Service, including the Fish and Wildlife Service, the Forest Service, the Bureau of Land Management, and the Bureau of Reclamation. This may include national parks, monuments, historic sites, recreation areas, and national wildlife refuges.

The America the Beautiful Access Pass can be obtained only in person at any NPS facility that charges an entrance fee. You need to show proof of medically determined disability. Besides free entry, the pass offers a 50% discount on some federal-use fees charged for such facilities as camping, swimming, parking, boat launching, and tours. For more information, go to www.nps.gov/fees_passes.htm or call ✆ **888/467-2757.**

Organizations that offer a vast range of resources and assistance to travelers with disabilities include **MossRehab** (✆ **800/CALL-MOSS;** www.mossresourcenet.org), the **American Foundation for the Blind** (AFB; ✆ **800/232-5463;** www.afb.org), and **SATH (Society for Accessible Travel & Hospitality;** ✆ **212/447-7284;** www.sath.org). **AirAmbulanceCard.com** is now partnered with SATH and allows you to preselect top-notch hospitals in case of an emergency.

Access-Able Travel Source (✆ **303/232-2979;** www.access-able.com) offers a comprehensive database on travel agents from around the world with experience in accessible travel, destination-specific access information, and links to such resources as service animals, equipment rentals, and access guides.

Many travel agencies offer customized tours and itineraries for travelers with disabilities. Among them are **Flying Wheels Travel** (✆ **507/451-5005;** www.flyingwheelstravel.com) and **Accessible Journeys** (✆ **800/846-4537** or 610/521-0339; www.disability travel.com).

Flying with Disability (www.flying-with-disability.org) is a comprehensive information source on airplane travel. **Avis Rent a Car** (✆ **888/879-4273**) has an "Avis Access" program that offers services for customers with special travel needs. These include specially outfitted vehicles with swivel seats, spinner knobs, and hand controls; mobility scooter rentals; and accessible bus service. Be sure to reserve well in advance.

Also check out the quarterly magazine *Emerging Horizons* (www.emerginghorizons.com), available by subscription ($16.95 year U.S.; $21.95 outside U.S.).

The "Accessible Travel" link at **Mobility-Advisor.com** (www.mobility-advisor.com) offers a variety of travel resources to persons with disabilities.

British travelers should contact **Holiday Care** (℃ **0845-124-9971** in U.K. only; www.holidaycare.org.uk) to access a wide range of travel information and resources for elderly people and those with disabilities.

GAY & LESBIAN TRAVELERS

Hawaii is known for its acceptance of all groups. The number of gay- or lesbian-specific accommodations on the islands is limited, but most properties welcome gays and lesbians like any other travelers.

The Center, mailing address P.O. Box 22718, Honolulu, 96823, or 2424 S. Beretania St., between Isenberg and University, Honolulu (℃ **808/951-7000;** fax 808/951-7001; www.thecenter hawaii.org), open Monday through Friday from 10am to 6pm and on Saturday from noon to 4pm, is a referral center for nearly every kind of gay-related service you can think of, including the latest happenings on Oahu. Check out their community newspaper, *Outlook* (published quarterly), for information on local issues in the gay community in the islands.

For information on Kauai's gay community and related events, contact the **Gay/Lesbian/Bisexual/Transgender Audio Bulletin Board** (℃ 808/823-6248).

For the Big Island, Oahu, Maui, and Kauai, check out the website for **Out in Hawaii,** www.outinhawaii.com, for vacation ideas and a calendar of events.

The International Gay and Lesbian Travel Association (**IGLTA;** ℃ **800/448-8550** or 954/776-2626; www.iglta.org) is the trade association for the gay and lesbian travel industry, and offers an online directory of gay- and lesbian-friendly travel businesses and tour operators.

Many agencies offer tours and travel itineraries specifically for gay and lesbian travelers. **Above and Beyond Tours** (℃ **800/397-2681;** www.abovebeyondtours.com) are gay Australia tour specialists. San Francisco–based **Now, Voyager** (℃ **800/255-6951;** www.now voyager.com) offers worldwide trips and cruises, and **Olivia** (℃ **800/631-6277;** www.olivia.com) offers lesbian cruises and resort vacations.

Pacific Ocean Holidays (© **800/735-6600** or 808/944-4700; www.gayhawaiivacations.com) offers vacation packages that feature gay-owned and gay-friendly lodgings. Also on their website is *A Guide for Gay Visitors & Kamaaina.*

Gay.com Travel (© **800/929-2268** or 415/644-8044; www.gay. com/travel or www.outandabout.com) is an excellent online successor to the popular *Out & About* print magazine. It provides regularly updated information about gay-owned, gay-oriented, and gay-friendly lodging, dining, sightseeing, nightlife, and shopping establishments in every important destination worldwide. British travelers should click on the "Travel" link at **www.uk.gay.com** for advice and gay-friendly trip ideas.

The Canadian website **GayTraveler** (**gaytraveler.ca**) offers ideas and advice for gay travel all over the world.

The following travel guides are available at many bookstores, or you can order them from any online bookseller: *Spartacus International Gay Guide, 35th Edition* (Bruno Gmünder Verlag; www.spartacusworld.com/gayguide/) and *Odysseus: The International Gay Travel Planner, 17th Edition* (www.odyusa.com); and the *Damron* guides (www.damron.com), with separate annual books for gay men and lesbians.

SENIOR TRAVEL

Discounts for seniors are available at almost all of Hawaii's major attractions and occasionally at hotels and restaurants. The Outrigger hotel chain, for instance, offers travelers ages 50 and older a 20% discount off regular published rates—and an additional 5% off for members of AARP. Always ask when making hotel reservations or buying tickets. And always carry identification with proof of your age—it can really pay off.

Members of **AARP,** 601 E St. NW, Washington, DC 20049 (© **888/687-2277;** www.aarp.org), get discounts on hotels, airfares, and car rentals. AARP offers members a wide range of benefits, including *AARP: The Magazine* and a monthly newsletter. Anyone over 50 can join.

The U.S. National Park Service offers an **America the Beautiful— National Park and Federal Recreational Lands Pass—Senior Pass** (formerly the **Golden Age Passport**), which gives seniors 62 years or older lifetime entrance to all properties administered by the National Park Service—national parks, monuments, historic sites, recreation areas, and national wildlife refuges—for a one-time processing fee of $10. The pass must be purchased in person at any NPS facility that charges an entrance fee. Besides free entry, the America the Beautiful Senior Pass offers a 50% discount on some federal-use fees charged for such facilities as camping, swimming, parking, boat launching, and tours. For more information, go to www.nps.gov/fees_passes.htm or call © **888/467-2757.**

Many reliable agencies and organizations target the 50-plus market. **Elderhostel** (© **800/454-5768;** www.elderhostel.org) arranges worldwide study programs for those aged 55 and over. **ElderTreks** (© **800/741-7956** or 416/558-5000 outside North America; www. eldertreks.com) offers small-group tours to off-the-beaten-path or adventure-travel locations, restricted to travelers 50 and older.

Recommended publications offering travel resources and discounts for seniors include the quarterly magazine *Travel 50 & Beyond* (www.travel50andbeyond.com) and the bestselling paperback *Unbelievably Good Deals and Great Adventures That You Absolutely Can't Get Unless You're Over 50 2005–2006, 16th Edition* (McGraw-Hill), by Joann Rattner Heilman.

FAMILY TRAVEL

Hawaii is paradise for children: beaches to run on, water to splash in, and unusual sights to see. Be sure to look for the "kids" icon in each chapter for kid-friendly places to stay and family activities.

The larger hotels and resorts offer supervised programs for children and can refer you to qualified babysitters. By state law, hotels can accept only children ages 5 to 12 in supervised activities programs, but they often accommodate younger children by simply hiring babysitters to watch over them. You can also contact **People Attentive to Children (PATCH),** which can refer you to babysitters who have taken a training course on child care. On Oahu call © 808/839-1988; on the Big Island call © 808/325-3864 in Kona or © 808/961-3169 in Hilo; on Maui call © 808/242-9232; on Kauai call © 808/246-0622; on Molokai and Lanai call © 800/ 498-4145; or visit www.patchhawaii.org.

Baby's Away (www.babysaway.com) rents cribs, strollers, highchairs, playpens, infant seats, and the like on Maui (© 800/942-9030 or 808/875-9030), the Big Island (© 800/996-9030 or 808/987-9236), and Oahu (© 800/496-6386 or 808/222-6041). The staff will deliver whatever you need to wherever you're staying and pick it up when you're done.

To locate accommodations, restaurants, and attractions that are particularly kid-friendly, refer to the "Kids" icon throughout this guide.

Recommended family travel websites include **Family Travel Forum** (www.familytravelforum.com), a comprehensive site that offers customized trip planning; **Family Travel Network** (www.familytravelnetwork.com), an online magazine providing travel tips; and **TravelWithYourKids.com** (www.travelwithyourkids.com), a comprehensive site written by parents for parents offering sound advice for long-distance and international travel with children.

Also look for *Frommer's Hawaii with Kids* (Wiley Publishing, Inc.).

9 Getting Around

INTERISLAND FLIGHTS

Since September 11, 2001, the major interisland carriers have cut way, way, way back on the number of interisland flights. The airlines warn you to show up at least 90 minutes before your flight, and believe me, with all the security inspections, you will need all 90 minutes to catch your flight.

In 2006, a new airline entered the Hawaiian market: **go!** (© 888/IFLYGO2; www.iflygo.com), owned by Mesa Air Group (which has more than 1,000 flights to 166 cities across the U.S., Canada, and Mexico). The new airline began service with 50-passenger Bombardier CRJ 200 jets with service from Honolulu to Maui, Kauai, and both Hilo and Kona on the Big Island. go! offers the cheapest interisland fares in Hawaii.

Aloha Airlines (© 800/367-5250 or 808/484-1111; www.alohaairlines.com) is the state's largest provider of interisland air transport service. It offers daily flights throughout Hawaii, using an all-jet fleet of Boeing 737 aircraft. **Hawaiian Airlines** (© 800/367-5320 or 808/835-3700; www.hawaiianair.com), Hawaii's first interisland airline, has carried more than 100 million passengers to and around the state.

In 2007, visitors to Molokai and Lanai got not one, but two new commuter airlines, which began flying from Honolulu to Molokai and Lanai. go! started a new commuter service from Honolulu to Molokai and Lanai, under the name **go!Express,** on their new fleet of Cessna Grand Caravan 208B planes. Another commuter airline, **Pacific Wings,** started operating a discount airline, **PW Express** (© 888/866-5022 or 808/873-0877; www.flypwx.com), with daily nonstop flights between Honolulu and Molokai and Lanai, plus flights from Kahului, Maui, and Molokai.

Island Air (© **800/323-3345** or 808/484-2222) serves Hawaii's small interisland airports on Maui, Molokai, and Lanai. However, I have to tell you that I have not had stellar service from Island Air and recommend that you book on go!Express or PW Express if you are headed to Molokai or Lanai.

Overseas visitors can take advantage of the APEX (Advance Purchase Excursion) reductions offered by all major U.S. and European carriers. In addition, some large airlines offer transatlantic or transpacific passengers special discount tickets under the name **Visit USA,** which allows mostly one-way travel from one U.S. destination to another at very low prices. Unavailable in the U.S., these discount tickets must be purchased abroad in conjunction with your international fare. This system is the easiest, fastest, cheapest way to see the country.

BY CAR

You'll need a rental car on the Big Island; not having one will really limit you. To rent a car in Hawaii, you must be at least 25 years of age and have a valid driver's license and credit card. ***Note:*** Foreign driver's licenses are usually recognized in the U.S., but you should get an international one if your home license is not in English.

At Honolulu International Airport and most neighbor-island airports, you'll find most major car-rental agencies, including **Alamo** (© 800/327-9633; www.goalamo.com), **Avis** (© 800/321-3712; www.avis.com), **Budget** (© 800/572-0700; www.budget.com), **Dollar** (© 800/800-4000; www.dollarcar.com), **Enterprise** (© 800/325-8007; www.enterprise.com), **Hertz** (© 800/654-3011; www.hertz.com), **National** (© 800/227-7368; www.nationalcar.com), and **Thrifty** (© 800/367-2277; www.thrifty.com). It's almost always cheaper to rent a car at the airport than in Waikiki or through your hotel (unless there's one already included in your package deal).

INSURANCE   Hawaii is a no-fault state, which means that if you don't have collision-damage insurance, you are required to pay for all damages before you leave the state, whether or not the accident was your fault. Your personal car insurance may provide rental-car coverage; check before you leave home. Bring your insurance identification card if you decline the optional insurance, which usually costs from $12 to $20 a day. Obtain the name of your company's local claim representative before you go. Some credit card companies also provide collision-damage insurance for their customers; check with yours before you rent.

DRIVING RULES   Hawaiian state law mandates that all car passengers must wear a **seat belt** and all infants must be strapped into car seats. You'll pay a $50 fine if you don't buckle up. **Pedestrians** always have the right of way, even if they're not in the crosswalk. You can turn **right on red** after a full and complete stop, unless otherwise posted.

ROAD MAPS   There are more than 480 miles of paved road on the Big Island. The highway that circles the island is called the **Hawaii Belt Road.** On the Kona side of the island, you have two choices: the scenic "upper" road, **Mamalahoa Highway** (Hwy. 190), or the speedier "lower" road, **Queen Kaahumanu Highway** (Hwy. 19). The road that links east to west is called the **Saddle Road** (Hwy. 200). Saddle Road looks like a shortcut from Kona to Hilo, but it usually doesn't make for a shorter trip. It's rough, narrow, and plagued by bad weather; as a result, most rental-car agencies forbid you from taking their cars on it.

The best and most detailed maps for activities are published by **Franko Maps** (www.frankosmaps.com); they feature a host of island maps, plus a terrific "Hawaiian Reef Creatures Guide" for snorkelers curious about those fish they spot under water. Free road maps are published by *This Week Magazine,* a free visitor publication available on Oahu, the Big Island, Maui, and Kauai. For even greater road map detail, check out Odyssey Publishing (© 888/729-1074; www.hawaiimapsource.com). They have very detailed maps of East and West Hawaii, Maui, and Kauai. Another source of good maps is the University of Hawaii Press maps, which include a detailed network of island roads, large-scale insets of towns, historical and contemporary points of interest, parks, beaches, and hiking trails. If you can't find them in a bookstore near you, contact **University of Hawaii Press,** 2840 Kolowalu St., Honolulu, HI 96822 (© 888/847-7737; www.uhpress.hawaii.edu). For topographic and other maps of the islands, go to the **Hawaii Geographic Society,** 49 S. Hotel St., Honolulu, or contact P.O. Box 1698, Honolulu, HI 96806 (© 800/538-3950 or 808/538-3952).

BY TAXI

Taxis are readily available at both Kona and Hilo airports. In Hilo call **Ace-1** (© 808/935-8303). In Kailua-Kona call **Kona Airport Taxi** (© 808/329-7779). Taxis will take you wherever you want to go on the Big Island, but it's prohibitively expensive to use them for long distances.

BY BUS & SHUTTLE

For transportation from the Kona Airport, there are three options: two shuttle services that will come when you call them, and a discount shuttle that leaves the airport every hour on the hour and drops you at your hotel. Door-to-door service is provided by **Speedi-Shuttle** (© 808/329-5433; www.speedishuttle.com). Some sample rates: From the airport to Kailua-Kona, the fare is $21 per person; to the Four Seasons, it's $21; and to Mauna Lani Resort, it's $46.

The islandwide bus system is the **Hele-On Bus** (© 808/961-8744; www.co.hawaii.hi.us/mass_transit/heleonbus.html); as we went to press, the Hele-On Bus had the best deal on the island: ride free. The recently created Kokua Zone allows riders in West Hawaii to travel from as far south as Ocean View to as far north as Kawaihae for free; in East Hawaii, riders can ride free from Pahoa to Hilo. Visitors to Hawaii can pick up the free, air-conditioned bus from the Kohala hotels or from the Kona International Airport and ride the bus south to shopping centers like Costco, Lanihau Center, Kmart, Wal-Mart, and Keauhou Shopping Center. The Hele-On Bus also stops at the Kona Community Hospital and provides wheelchair access.

In the Keauhou Resort area, there's a free, open-air, 44-seat **Keauhou Resort Trolley,** with stops at the Keauhou Bay, Sheraton Keauhou Bay Resort & Spa, Kona Country Club, Keauhou Shopping Center, Outrigger Keauhou Beach Resort, and Kahaluu Beach Park. In addition, three times a day the Trolley travels round-trip, via Alii Drive to Kailua Village, stopping at White Sands Beach on the way. For information, contact concierges at either the Sheraton Keauhou Bay Resort & Spa (© 808/930-4900) or the Outrigger Keauhou Beach Hotel (© 808/322-3411).

FAST FACTS: The Big Island

American Express There's an office on the Kohala Coast at the **Hilton Waikoloa Village** (© 808/886-7958) and **The Fairmont Orchid** in Mauna Lani Resort (© 808/885-2000). To report lost or stolen traveler's checks, call © 800/221-7282.

Area Code All the Hawaiian Islands are in the **808** area code. Note that if you're calling one island from another, you'll have to dial 1-808 first.

ATM Networks See "Money," p. 19.

Automobile Organizations Auto clubs will supply maps, suggested routes, guidebooks, accident and bail-bond insurance, and emergency road service. The **American Automobile Association (AAA)** is the major auto club in the United States. If you belong to an auto club in your home country, inquire about AAA reciprocity before you leave. You may be able to join AAA even if you're not a member of a reciprocal club; to inquire, call AAA (*©* **800/222-4357**). AAA is actually an organization of regional auto clubs, so look under "AAA Automobile Club" in the White Pages of the telephone directory. AAA has a nationwide emergency road service telephone number (*©* 800/AAA-HELP).

Business Hours Most offices are open Monday through Friday from 8am to 5pm. Bank hours are Monday through Thursday from 8:30am to 3pm and Friday from 8:30am to 6pm; some banks are open on Saturday as well. Shopping centers are open Monday through Friday from 10am to 9pm, Saturday 10am to 5:30pm, and Sunday from noon to 5 or 6pm.

Car Rentals See "Getting Around," p. 28.

Currency The most common bills are the $1 (a "buck"), $5, $10, and $20 denominations. There are also $2 bills (seldom encountered), $50 bills, and $100 bills (the last two are usually not welcome as payment for small purchases).

Coins come in seven denominations: 1¢ (1 cent, or a penny); 5¢ (5 cents, or a nickel); 10¢ (10 cents, or a dime); 25¢ (25 cents, or a quarter); 50¢ (50 cents, or a half-dollar); the gold-colored Sacagawea coin, worth $1; and the rare silver dollar.

For additional information, see "Money," p. 19.

Customs **What You Can Bring into Hawaii** Every visitor more than 21 years of age may bring in, free of duty, the following: (1) 1 liter of wine or hard liquor; (2) 200 cigarettes, 100 cigars (but not from Cuba), or 3 pounds of smoking tobacco; and (3) $100 worth of gifts. These exemptions are offered to travelers who spend at least 72 hours in the United States and who have not claimed them within the preceding 6 months. It is altogether forbidden to bring into the country foodstuffs (particularly fruit, cooked meats, and canned goods) and plants (vegetables, seeds, tropical plants, and the like). Foreign tourists may carry in or out up to $10,000 in U.S. or foreign currency with no formalities; larger sums must be declared to U.S. Customs on entering or leaving, which includes filing form CM 4790. For details regarding U.S. Customs and Border Protection, consult your nearest U.S. embassy or consulate, or **U.S. Customs** (☏ **202/927-1770**; www. customs.ustreas.gov).

What You Can Take Home from Hawaii:

Canadian Citizens: For a clear summary of Canadian rules, write for the booklet *I Declare*, issued by the **Canada Border Services Agency** (☏ **800/461-9999** in Canada, or 204/983-3500; **www.cbsa-asfc.gc.ca**).

U.K. Citizens: For information, contact **HM Customs & Excise** at ☏ **0845/010-9000** (from outside the U.K., 020/8929-0152), or consult their website at **www.hmce.gov.uk**.

Australian Citizens: A helpful brochure available from Australian consulates or Customs offices is *Know Before You Go*. For more information, call the **Australian Customs Service** at ☏ **1300/363-263**, or log on to **www.customs.gov.au**.

New Zealand Citizens: Most questions are answered in a free pamphlet available at New Zealand consulates and Customs offices: *New Zealand Customs Guide for Travellers, Notice no. 4*. For more information, contact **New Zealand Customs,** The Customhouse, 17–21 Whitmore St., Box 2218, Wellington (☏ **04/473-6099** or 0800/428-786; **www.customs. govt.nz**).

Dentists In an emergency, contact **Dr. Craig C. Kimura** at Kamuela Office Center (☏ **808/885-5947**); in Kona, call **Dr. Frank Sayre,** Frame 10 Center, behind Lanihau Shopping Center on Palani Road (☏ **808/329-8067**); in Hilo, call **Hawaii Smile Center,** Hilo Lagoon Center, 101 Aupuni St. (☏ **808/961-9181**).

Doctors In Hilo, the **Hilo Medical Center** is at 1190 Waianuenue Ave. (☏ **808/974-4700**); on the Kona side, call **Hualalai Urgent Care,** 75–1028 Henry St., across the street from Safeway (☏ **808/327-HELP**).

Drinking Laws The legal drinking age in Hawaii is 21. Bars are allowed to stay open daily until 2am; places with cabaret licenses are able to keep the booze flowing until 4am. Grocery and convenience stores are allowed to sell beer, wine, and liquor 7 days a week. Proof of age is required and often requested at bars, nightclubs, and restaurants, so it's always a good idea to bring ID when you go out.

Do not carry open containers of alcohol in your car or any public area that isn't zoned for alcohol consumption. The police can fine you on the spot. And nothing will ruin your trip faster than getting a citation for DUI ("driving under the influence"), so don't even think about driving while intoxicated.

Driving Rules See "Getting Around," p. 28.

Electricity Like Canada, the United States uses 110 to 120 volts AC (60 cycles), compared to 220 to 240 volts AC (50 cycles) in most of Europe, Australia, and New Zealand. Downward converters that change 220–240 volts to 110–120 volts are difficult to find in the United States, so bring one with you.

Embassies & Consulates All embassies are located in the nation's capital, Washington, D.C. Some consulates are located in major U.S. cities, and most nations have a mission to the United Nations in New York City. If your country isn't listed below, call for directory information in Washington, D.C. (© 202/555-1212), or log on to **www.embassy.org/embassies**.

The embassy of **Australia** is at 1601 Massachusetts Ave. NW, Washington, DC 20036 (© 202/797-3000; www.austemb.org). There are consulates in New York, Honolulu, Houston, Los Angeles, and San Francisco.

The embassy of **Canada** is at 501 Pennsylvania Ave. NW, Washington, DC 20001 (© 202/682-1740; www.canadian embassy.org). Other Canadian consulates are in Buffalo (New York), Detroit, Los Angeles, New York, and Seattle.

The embassy of **Ireland** is at 2234 Massachusetts Ave. NW, Washington, DC 20008 (© 202/462-3939; www.irelandemb. org). Irish consulates are in Boston, Chicago, New York, San Francisco, and other cities. See the website for complete listing.

The embassy of **New Zealand** is at 37 Observatory Circle NW, Washington, DC 20008 (© 202/328-4800; www.nzemb. org). New Zealand consulates are in Los Angeles, Salt Lake City, San Francisco, and Seattle.

The embassy of the **United Kingdom** is at 3100 Massachusetts Ave. NW, Washington, DC 20008 (© 202/588-7800; www. britainusa.com). Other British consulates are in Atlanta, Boston, Chicago, Cleveland, Houston, Los Angeles, New York, San Francisco, and Seattle.

Emergencies For ambulance, fire, and rescue services, dial © 911 or call © 808/961-6022. The **Poison Control Center** hotline is © 800/362-3585.

Gasoline (Petrol) At press time, in the U.S., the cost of gasoline (also known as gas, but never petrol) is abnormally high. Taxes are already included in the printed price. One U.S. gallon equals 3.8 liters or .85 imperial gallons. Fill-up locations are known as gas or service stations.

Holidays Banks, government offices, post offices, and many stores, restaurants, and museums are closed on the following legal national holidays: January 1 (New Year's Day), the third Monday in January (Martin Luther King, Jr., Day), the third Monday in February (Presidents' Day), the last Monday in May (Memorial Day), July 4 (Independence Day), the first Monday in September (Labor Day), the second Monday in October (Columbus Day), November 11 (Veterans Day/ Armistice Day), the fourth Thursday in November (Thanksgiving Day), and December 25 (Christmas). The Tuesday after the first Monday in November is Election Day, a federal government holiday in presidential-election years (held every 4 years, and next in 2008).

For more information on holidays, see "When to Go," earlier in this chapter.

Hospitals Hospitals offering 24-hour urgent-care facilities include the **Hilo Medical Center,** 1190 Waianuenue Ave., Hilo (© 808/974-4700); **North Hawaii Community Hospital,** Waimea (© 808/885-4444); and **Kona Community Hospital,** on the Kona Coast in Kealakekua (© 808/322-9311).

Legal Aid If you are "pulled over" for a minor infraction (such as speeding), never attempt to pay the fine directly to a police officer; this could be construed as attempted bribery, a much more serious crime. Pay fines by mail or directly into the hands of the clerk of the court. If accused of a more serious offense, say and do nothing before consulting a lawyer. Here the burden is on the state to prove a person's guilt beyond a reasonable doubt, and everyone has the right to remain silent, whether he or she is suspected of a crime or actually arrested. Once arrested, a person can make one telephone call to a party of his or her choice. International visitors should call their embassy or consulate.

Lost & Found Be sure to tell all of your credit card companies the minute you discover your wallet has been lost or stolen, and file a report at the nearest police precinct. Your credit card company or insurer may require a police report number or record of the loss. Most credit card companies have an emergency toll-free number to call if your card is lost or stolen; they may be able to wire you a cash advance immediately or deliver an emergency credit card in a day or two. Visa's U.S. emergency number is © **800/847-2911** or 410/581-9994. American Express cardholders and traveler's check holders should call © **800/221-7282.** MasterCard holders should call © **800/307-7309** or 636/722-7111. For other credit cards, call the toll-free number directory at © **800/555-1212.**

If you need emergency cash over the weekend when all banks and American Express offices are closed, you can have money wired to you via **Western Union** (© **800/325-6000;** www.westernunion.com).

Mail At press time, domestic postage rates were 26¢ for a postcard and 41¢ for a letter. For international mail, a postcard or first-class letter of up to 1 ounce costs 90¢ (69¢ to Canada and Mexico). For more information, go to **www. usps.com** and click on "Calculate Postage."

If you aren't sure what your address will be in the United States, mail can be sent to you, in your name, c/o General Delivery at the main post office of the city or region where you expect to be. (Call © **800/275-8777** for information on the nearest post office.) The addressee must pick up mail in person and must produce proof of identity (driver's license, passport, and the like). Most post offices will hold your mail for up to 1 month and are open Monday to Friday from 8am to 6pm and Saturday from 9am to 3pm.

Always include zip codes when mailing items in the U.S. If you don't know your zip code, visit www.usps.com/zip4.

Maps See "Getting Around," p. 28.

Measurements See the chart on the inside front cover of this book for details on converting metric measurements to U.S. equivalents.

Passports **For Residents of Australia:** You can pick up an application from your local post office or any branch of Passports Australia, but you must schedule an interview at the passport office to present your application materials. Call the **Australian Passport Information Service** at © **131-232,** or visit the government website at www.passports.gov.au.

For Residents of Canada: Passport applications are available at travel agencies throughout Canada or from the central **Passport Office,** Department of Foreign Affairs and International Trade, Ottawa, ON K1A 0G3 (© 800/567-6868; www.ppt.gc.ca). *Note:* Canadian children who travel must have their own passport. However, if you hold a valid Canadian passport issued before December 11, 2001, that bears the name of your child, the passport remains valid for you and your child until it expires.

For Residents of Ireland: You can apply for a 10-year passport at the **Passport Office,** Setanta Centre, Molesworth Street, Dublin 2 (© 01/671-1633; www.irlgov.ie/iveagh). Those under age 18 and over 65 must apply for a 3-year passport. You can also apply at 1A South Mall, Cork (© 021/272-525), or at most main post offices.

For Residents of New Zealand: You can pick up a passport application at any New Zealand Passports Office or download it from their website. Contact the **Passports Office** at © 0800/225-050 in New Zealand or 04/474-8100, or log on to www.passports.govt.nz.

For Residents of the United Kingdom: To pick up an application for a standard 10-year passport (5-yr. passport for children under 16), visit your nearest passport office, major post office, or travel agency, or contact the **United Kingdom Passport Service** at © 0870/521-0410 or search its website at www.ukpa.gov.uk.

Police Dial © 911 in case of emergency; otherwise, call the **Hawaii Police Department** at © 808/326-4646 in Kona, © 808/961-2213 in Hilo.

Post Office All calls to the U.S. Post Office can be directed to © 800/275-8777. There are local branches in Hilo at 1299 Kekuanaoa Ave., in Kailua-Kona at 74–5577 Palani Rd., and in Waimea on Lindsey Road.

Smoking It's against the law to smoke in public buildings, including airports, shopping malls, grocery stores, retail shops, buses, movie theaters, banks, convention facilities, and all government buildings and facilities. There is no smoking in restaurants, bars, and nightclubs. Most bed-and-breakfasts prohibit smoking indoors, and more and more hotels and resorts are becoming nonsmoking even in public area. Also, there is no smoking within 20 feet of a doorway, window, or ventilation intake (no hanging around outside a bar to smoke—you must go 20 feet away).

Taxes The United States has no value-added tax (VAT) or other indirect tax at the national level. Every state, county, and city may levy its own local tax on all purchases, including hotel and restaurant checks and airline tickets. These taxes will not appear on price tags.

Telegraph, Telex, & Fax **Telegraph and telex services** are provided primarily by Western Union. You can telegraph money, or have it telegraphed to you, very quickly over the Western Union system, but this service can cost as much as 15% to 20% of the amount sent.

Most hotels have **fax machines** available for guest use (be sure to ask about the charge to use it). Many hotel rooms are even wired for guests' fax machines. A less expensive way to send and receive faxes may be at stores such as **The UPS Store** (formerly Mail Boxes Etc.).

Time The continental United States is divided into **four time zones:** Eastern Standard Time (EST), Central Standard Time (CST), Mountain Standard Time (MST), and Pacific Standard Time (PST). Alaska and Hawaii have their own zones. For example, when it's 9am in Los Angeles (PST), it's 7am in Honolulu (HST),10am in Denver (MST), 11am in Chicago (CST), noon in New York City (EST), 5pm in London (GMT), and 2am the next day in Sydney.

Daylight saving time is in effect from 1am on the second Sunday in March to 1am on the first Sunday in November, except in Arizona, Hawaii, the U.S. Virgin Islands, and Puerto Rico. Daylight saving time moves the clock 1 hour ahead of standard time.

Tipping Tips are a very important part of certain workers' income, and gratuities are the standard way of showing appreciation for services provided. (Tipping is certainly not compulsory if the service is poor!) In hotels, tip **bellhops** at least $1 per bag ($2–$3 if you have a lot of luggage) and tip the **chamber staff** $1 to $2 per day (more if you've left a disaster area for him or her to clean up). Tip the **doorman** or **concierge** only if he or she has provided you with some specific service (for example, calling a cab for you or obtaining difficult-to-get theater tickets). Tip the **valet-parking attendant** $1 every time you get your car.

In restaurants, bars, and nightclubs, tip **service staff** 15% to 20% of the check, tip **bartenders** 10% to 15%, tip **checkroom attendants** $1 per garment, and tip **valet-parking attendants** $1 per vehicle.

As for other service personnel, tip **cab drivers** 15% of the fare; tip **skycaps** at airports at least $1 per bag ($2–$3 if you have a lot of luggage); and tip **hairdressers** and **barbers** 15% to 20%.

Toilets You won't find public toilets or "restrooms" on the streets in most U.S. cities, but they can be found in hotel lobbies, bars, restaurants, museums, department stores, railway and bus stations, and service stations. Large hotels and fast-food restaurants are often the best bet for clean facilities. If possible, avoid the toilets at parks and beaches, which tend to be dirty; some may be unsafe. Restaurants and bars in resorts or heavily visited areas may reserve their restrooms for patrons.

Useful Phone Numbers

U.S. Dept. of State Travel Advisory: ℭ **202/647-5225** (manned 24 hr.)

U.S. Passport Agency: ℭ **202/647-0518**

U.S. Centers for Disease Control International Traveler's Hotline: ℭ **404/332-4559**

Visas For information about U.S. visas, go to **http://travel.state.gov** and click on "Visas." Or go to one of the following websites:

Australian citizens can obtain up-to-date visa information from the **U.S. Embassy Canberra,** Moonah Place, Yarralumla, ACT 2600 (ℭ **02/6214-5600**), or by checking the U.S. Diplomatic Mission's website at **http://usembassy-australia.state.gov/consular**.

British subjects can obtain up-to-date visa information by calling the **U.S. Embassy Visa Information Line** (ℭ **0891/200-290**) or by visiting the "Visas to the U.S." section of the American Embassy London's website at **www.usembassy.org.uk**.

Irish citizens can obtain up-to-date visa information through the **Embassy of the USA Dublin,** 42 Elgin Rd., Dublin 4, Ireland (ℭ **353/1-668-8777**) or by checking the "Consular Services" section of the website at **http://dublin.usembassy.gov**.

Citizens of **New Zealand** can obtain up-to-date visa information by contacting the **U.S. Embassy New Zealand,** 29 Fitzherbert Terrace, Thorndon, Wellington (© **644/472-2068**), or get the information directly from the website at **http://wellington.usembassy.gov**.

Weather For conditions in and around Hilo, call © **808/935-8555**; for the rest of the Big Island, call © **808/961-5582**. For marine forecasts, call © **808/935-9883**.

2

Where to Stay

Before you reach for the phone to book your accommodations, refer to "The Island in Brief," in chapter 1, to decide where to base yourself.

If you're interested in additional information on bed-and-breakfasts, contact the **Hawaii Island B&B Association,** P.O. Box 1890, Honokaa, HI 96727 (no phone; **www.stayhawaii.com**).

In the listings below, all rooms come with a full private bathroom (with tub or shower) and free parking unless otherwise noted. Remember to add Hawaii's 11.42% in taxes to your final bill.

1 The Kona Coast
IN & AROUND KAILUA-KONA
For a detailed map of central Kailua-Kona, see p. 43.

VERY EXPENSIVE
Four Seasons Resort Hualalai at Historic Kaupulehu 𝒦𝒦𝒦
Kids This is a great place to relax in the lap of luxury. Low-rise clusters of oceanview villas nestle between the sea and the greens of a new golf course. The Four Seasons looks like a two-story townhouse project, clustered around three seaside swimming pools and a snorkeling pond. The rooms are furnished in Pacific tropical style: light gold walls, hand-knotted rugs over clay-colored slate, and rattan-and-bamboo settees. The ground-level rooms have bathrooms with private outdoor gardens, so you can shower under the tropical sun or nighttime stars. All rooms have new flatscreen plasma TVs.

If you can afford it, this is the place to go to be pampered—sit back and relax as the pool attendants bring you ice-cold water, chilled towels, and fresh fruit kabobs. Other pluses include a Hawaiian history and cultural interpretive center, complimentary scuba lessons, a complimentary valet, twice-daily maid service, and a multilingual concierge. The spa has been selected by *Condé Nast Traveller* magazine as the world's best resort spa. One of the five pools is a saltwater pond carved out of black-lava rock with reef fish swimming about. The new Lava Lounge offers entertainment and the best view for watching the sun sink into the Pacific.

The complimentary Kids for All Seasons program features plenty of activities to keep the little ones busy. The resort also offers children's menus in all restaurants, a game room, videos, complimentary infant gear (cribs, highchairs, and so on), and more.

72-100 Ka'upulehu Dr., Kailua-Kona, HI 96745. ⓒ 888/340-5662 or 808/325-8000. Fax 808/325-8053. www.fourseasons.com/hualalai. 243 units. $695–$995 double; from $1,300 suite. Extra person $170. Children under 18 stay free in parent's room (maximum occupancy is 3 people; couples with more than one child must get 2 rooms). AE, DC, DISC, MC, V. **Amenities:** 3 restaurants (including Pahu i'a, p. 68, and Beach Tree Bar & Grill, p. 70); 3 bars (nightly entertainment ranging from contemporary Hawaiian to pianist); 5 exquisite outdoor pools (including a giant infinity pool and a lap pool); 18-hole Jack Nicklaus signature golf course exclusively for guests and residents; 8 tennis courts (4 lit for night play); complete fitness center; award-winning spa; 6 whirlpools; watersports equipment rentals; complimentary year-round children's program; game room; concierge; activities and car rental through the concierge; business center; salon; room service; both in-room and spa massage; babysitting; complimentary washer/dryers; same-day laundry service and dry cleaning; Wi-Fi Internet access in lobby, guest rooms, pools, and other places on property. *In room:* A/C, plasma TV, dataport, fridge, coffeemaker, hair dryer, iron, safe.

EXPENSIVE

Outrigger Royal Sea Cliff Resort *Kids*   Families will love these luxuriously appointed apartments and their affordable rates. The architecturally striking, five-story white buildings that make up this resort/condo complex, 2 miles from Kailua-Kona, are stepped back from the ocean for maximum views and privacy. (The downside is that there's no ocean swimming here, but the waves are near enough to lull you to sleep, and there's a decent swimming beach about a mile away.) Atrium gardens and hanging bougainvillea soften the look. Spacious units are furnished in tropical rattan with a large, sunny lanai, a full kitchen, and a washer/dryer, and there are barbecue and picnic facilities for oceanfront dining.

75–6040 Alii Dr., Kailua-Kona, HI 96740. ⓒ 800/688-7444 or 808/329-8021. Fax 808/326-1887. www.outrigger.com. 148 units. $215–$255 studio double; $249–$415 1-bedroom apt for 4; $289–$459 2-bedroom apt for 6. AE, DC, DISC, MC, V. **Amenities:** 2 outdoor pools; complimentary tennis courts; Jacuzzi; activities desk. *In room:* A/C, TV, wireless Internet access, kitchen, fridge, coffeemaker, hair dryer, iron, safe, washer/dryer.

MODERATE

King Kamehameha's Kona Beach Hotel   The location is terrific, downtown Kailua Kona, right on the ocean. The problem here

Where to Stay on the Kona Coast

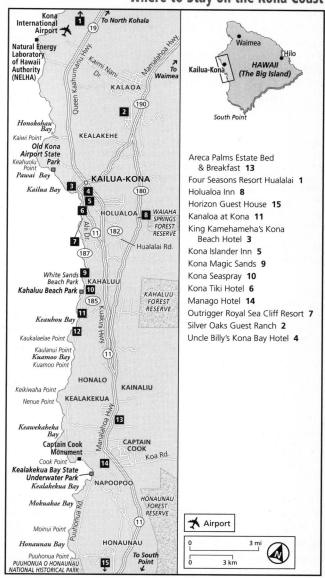

Areca Palms Estate Bed & Breakfast **13**
Four Seasons Resort Hualalai **1**
Holualoa Inn **8**
Horizon Guest House **15**
Kanaloa at Kona **11**
King Kamehameha's Kona Beach Hotel **3**
Kona Islander Inn **5**
Kona Magic Sands **9**
Kona Seaspray **10**
Kona Tiki Hotel **6**
Manago Hotel **14**
Outrigger Royal Sea Cliff Resort **7**
Silver Oaks Guest Ranch **2**
Uncle Billy's Kona Bay Hotel **4**

is this is a 30-plus-years-old hotel that looks tired. Rooms are showing their age, but they are clean and can have views of an ancient banyan tree, the Kailua Pier, or sparkling Kailua Bay. The hotel's own small, gold-sand beach is right out the front door. The hotel's restaurant is forgettable, but you're within walking distance of dozens of other options. The best deal here is the Paradise on Wheels, which comes with a double room, a compact car, and breakfast for two starting at just $170—a price that makes the "King Kam" (as locals call it) attractive to travelers on a budget.

75–5660 Palani Rd., Kailua-Kona, HI 96740. ✆ **800/367-6060** or 808/329-2911. Fax 808/922-8061. www.konabeachhotel.com. 460 units. $170–$250 double. Room, car, and breakfast packages from $170 (subject to availability). Extra person $30. AE, DC, DISC, MC, V. Parking $7. **Amenities:** Restaurant; outdoor bar w/Hawaiian entertainment; outdoor pool; 4 tennis courts; Jacuzzi; watersports equipment rentals; activities desk; shopping arcade; salon; room service; coin-op washer/dryers; laundry service; dry cleaning. *In room:* A/C, TV, dataport, fridge, coffeemaker, hair dryer, iron, safe.

Silver Oaks Guest Ranch 🏆🏆 *Finds*   Book this place! This is a true "guest ranch," consisting of two cottages spread over a 10-acre working ranch complete with friendly horses (no riding, just petting), the cutest Nigerian dwarf goats, chickens, and wild turkeys. The ranch sits at 1,300 feet, where the temperatures are in the 70s (low to middle 20s Celsius) year-round. The views are spectacular, some 40 miles of coastline from the ocean to Mauna Loa, yet it's just 5 miles from the airport and 5 miles from downtown Kailua-Kona. Hosts Amy and Rick Decker have impeccable taste, and each unit is uniquely decorated. You'll get breakfast items (cereals, milk, yogurt, coffee, fruit, and bread) for your first day. They have a closet full of beach gear for guests, not to mention books, videos, binoculars, even a couple of backpacks.

Reservations: 75–1027 Henry St., Suite 310, Kailua-Kona, HI 96740. ✆ **877/325-2300** or 808/325-2000. Fax 808/325-2200. www.silveroaksranch.com. 2 units, plus additional space available for large groups. $175 double. Extra person $15. 5-night minimum. MC, V. **Amenities:** Outdoor pool; Jacuzzi; washer/dryers. *In room:* TV/VCR, high-speed Internet access, kitchen, fridge, coffeemaker.

INEXPENSIVE

Kona Islander Inn *Value*   This is the most affordable place to stay in Kailua-Kona. These plantation-style, three-story buildings are surrounded by lush, palm-tree-lined gardens with torch-lit pathways that make it hard to believe you're smack-dab in the middle of downtown. The central location—across the street from the historic

Kona Inn Shops—is convenient but can be noisy. Built in 1962, the complex is showing some signs of age, but the units were recently outfitted with new appliances, new bedspreads and curtains, and a fresh coat of paint. The studios are small, but extras like lanais and kitchenettes outfitted with microwaves, minifridges, and coffeemakers make up for the lack of space.

75–5776 Kuakini Hwy. (south of Hualalai Rd.), Kailua-Kona. c/o Hawaii Resort Management, P.O. Box 39, Kailua-Kona, HI 96745. © **800/622-5348** or 808/329-3333. Fax 808/329-4137. www.konahawaii.com. 80 units. $70–$100 double. DC, DISC, MC, V. **Amenities:** Outdoor pool; hot tub; activities desk; coin-op washer/dryers. *In room:* A/C, TV, kitchenette, fridge, coffeemaker.

Kona Magic Sands ★ *Value*

If you want to stay right on the ocean without spending a fortune, this is the place to do it—it's one of the best oceanfront deals you'll find on a Kona condo, and the only one with a beach for swimming and snorkeling right next door. Every unit in this older complex has a lanai that steps out over the ocean and sunset views that you'll dream about long after you return home. These studio units aren't luxurious; they're small (two people max) and cozy, great for people who want to be lulled to sleep by the sound of the waves crashing on the shore. Each consists of one long, narrow room with a small kitchen at one end and the lanai at the other, with a living room/dining room/bedroom combo in between.

77–6452 Alii Dr. (next to Magic Sands Beach Park). c/o Hawaii Resort Management, P.O. Box 39, Kailua-Kona, HI 96745. © **800/622-5348** or 808/329-3333. Fax 808/326-4137. www.konahawaii.com. 37 units, shower only. High season $135 double; low season $105 double; plus $60 cleaning fee. 3-night minimum. DC, DISC, MC, V. **Amenities:** Excellent restaurant; bar; oceanfront outdoor pool. *In room:* TV, kitchen, fridge, coffeemaker.

Kona Tiki Hotel ★★ *Finds*

It's hard to believe that places like this still exist. The Kona Tiki, located right on the ocean, away from the hustle and bustle of downtown Kailua-Kona, is one of the best budget deals in Hawaii. All of the rooms are tastefully decorated and feature queen-size beds, ceiling fans, minifridges, and private lanais overlooking the ocean. Although it's called a hotel, this small, family-run operation is more like a large B&B, with lots of aloha and plenty of friendly conversation at the morning breakfast buffet around the pool. The staff is helpful in planning activities. There are no TVs or phones in the rooms, but there's a pay phone in the lobby. If a double with a kitchenette is available, grab it—the extra few bucks will save you a bundle in food costs. Book way in advance.

75–5968 Alii Dr. (about a mile from downtown Kailua-Kona), Kailua-Kona, HI 96740. ℂ **808/329-1425.** Fax 808/327-9402. www.konatiki.com. 15 units. $66–$79 double; $88 double with kitchenette. Rates include continental breakfast. Extra person $8; children 2–12 $6. 3-night minimum. No credit cards. **Amenities:** Outdoor pool. *In room:* Kitchenette (in some rooms), fridge, no phone.

Uncle Billy's Kona Bay Hotel   An institution in Kona, Uncle Billy's is where visitors from the other islands stay. A thatched roof hangs over the lobby area, and a Polynesian longhouse restaurant is next door. The rooms are old but comfortable and come with large lanais; most also have minifridges (request one at booking), and 16 are condo-style units with kitchenettes. This budget hotel is a good place to sleep, but don't expect new furniture or carpets, or fancy soap in the bathroom. It can be noisy at night when big groups book in; avoid Labor Day weekend, when all the canoe paddlers in the state want to stay here and rehash the race into the wee morning hours.

75–5739 Alii Dr., Kailua-Kona, HI 96740. ℂ **800/367-5102** or 808/961-5818. Fax 808/935-7903. www.unclebilly.com. 139 units. $119–$129 double; Check the website for specials starting at $99 and car/room deals for just $30 more a night. Extra person $14. Children 18 and under stay free in parent's room. AE, DC, DISC, MC, V. **Amenities:** Restaurant; bar (w/Hawaiian entertainment); 2 outdoor pools (1 just for children); watersports equipment rentals; activities desk; coin-op washer/dryers. *In room:* A/C, TV, dataport, kitchenette (in some rooms), fridge, hair dryers (in some rooms).

UPCOUNTRY KONA: HOLUALOA

Holualoa Inn ⭐⭐ *(Finds*   The quiet, secluded setting of this B&B—40 pastoral acres just off the main drag of the artsy village of Holualoa, 1,350 feet above Kailua-Kona—provides stunning panoramic views of the entire coast. Recently sold to Sandy Hazen, a local Kona coffee farmer, this contemporary 7,000-square-foot Hawaiian home has six private suites and window-walls that roll back to embrace the gardens and views. Sandy resorted the guest rooms with new furnishings and upgraded bathrooms, and put lahala matting on the ceilings. Plus, the Inn now has a renowned chef cooking your gourmet breakfast. Cows graze on the bucolic pastures below the garden Jacuzzi and pool, and the 30-acre estate includes 3,000 coffee trees, which are the source of the morning brew. The inn offers a gas grill for a romantic dinner beside the pool, a telescope for stargazing, and a billiard table. It's a 15-minute drive down the hill to busy Kailua-Kona and about 20 minutes to the beach, but the pool has a stunning view of Kailua-Kona and the sparkling Pacific below.

P.O. Box 222 (76–5932 Mamalahoa Hwy.), Holualoa, HI 96725. © **800/392-1812** or 808/324-1121. Fax 808/322-2472. www.holualoainn.com. 6 units, 1 with shower only. $225–$475 double. Rates include full breakfast. 2-night minimum. If you mention Frommer's when you book, they promise a discount. 15% discount for 7 nights or more. AE, DC, DISC, MC, V. On Mamalahoa Hwy., just after the Holualoa Post Office, look for Paul's Place General Store; the next driveway is the inn. Children must be 13 or older. **Amenities:** Huge outdoor pool; Jacuzzi. *In room:* Hair dryer, no phone.

KEAUHOU

Sheraton Keauhou Bay Resort and Spa ⭐ *(Kids)*   In 2005, nearly 6 years after the old Kona Surf Resort closed, and after $70 million in renovations, the Sheraton Keauhou Bay Resort had a formal opening. The complete overhaul of this 1970s resort is remarkable: Walls were torn out in the lobby and the main dining room to allow access to the incredible view of Keauhou Bay, and the 420-square-foot rooms were completely redone to bring them into the 21st century. The best addition to the rooms is Sheraton's "Sweet Sleeper" bed, with a cushy mattress top, a feather-weight duvet, and five pillows to choose from. The next biggest change to the resort is the mammoth pool: Tucked in around the tropical gardens and splashing waterfalls, this enormous freshwater pool includes its own small man-made beach, the island's largest water slide, bubbling whirlpool spas, and a children's play area. Speaking of kids, there's a children's center and program on property and plenty of activities to keep the little ones occupied (water activities, cultural games and arts and crafts, video games, and so on). Plus, the Sheraton has a golf course next door, tennis courts on-property, and a shopping center (with restaurants) close by.

78–128 Ehukai St., Kailua-Kona, HI 96740. © **888/488-3535** or 808/930-4900. Fax 808/930-4800. www.sheratonkeauhou.com. 522 units. $350–$460 double. Children 18 and younger stay free in parent's room with existing bedding. $60 extra person. AE, DC, DISC, MC, V. Self-parking $5, valet parking $10. **Amenities:** 2 restaurants (luau twice a week); bar; multilevel pool w/200-ft. water slide; 36-hole golf course nearby w/preferred guest rate; 2 tennis courts; fitness center; spa; whirlpool; year-round children's program; concierge; activities desk; business center; room service; babysitting; coin-op washer/dryers; laundry service; dry cleaning; sand volleyball court; basketball court. *In room:* A/C, TV, dataport, high-speed Internet (additional fee), fridge, coffeemaker, hair dryer, iron, safe.

EXPENSIVE

Kanaloa at Kona ⭐⭐ *(Kids)*   These big, comfortable, well-managed, and spacious vacation condos, on 16 landscaped acres, border the

rocky coast beside Keauhou Bay, 6 miles south of Kailua-Kona. They're exceptional units, ideal for families, with comforts such as huge bathrooms with whirlpool bathtubs, dressing rooms, and bidets. In addition, the spacious lanais, tropical decor, and many appliances make for free and easy living. It's easy to stock up on supplies at the supermarket at the new mall just up the hill, but the oceanfront restaurant offers an alternative to your own cooking. Guests receive discounted golf rates at a nearby country club.

78–261 Manukai St., Kailua-Kona, HI 96740. ℂ 800/688-7444 or 808/322-9625. Fax 800/622-4852. www.outrigger.com. Managed by Outrigger Resorts. 76 units. $239–$349 1-bedroom apt (sleeps up to 4); $259–$429 2-bedroom apt (up to 6); $395–$479 2-bedroom apt with loft (up to 8). AE, DC, DISC, MC, V. **Amenities:** Restaurant; ocean-side bar; 3 outdoor pools (1 for adults only); 2 tennis courts (lit); 3 Jacuzzis; concierge; activities desk; babysitting; coin-op washer/dryers. *In room:* TV, kitchen, fridge, coffeemaker, hair dryer, iron, safe.

MODERATE

Kona Seaspray ✿ *Value*   The Kona Seaspray has a couple of great things going for it: location and price. It's just across from the Kahaluu Beach Park, possibly the best snorkeling area in Kona. The rates are a great deal when you consider that the one-bedroom apartments easily sleep four and the two-bedroom unit can sleep six. It's under new ownership, and all the units are undergoing renovations that include upgraded furniture and new carpets. All apartments have a full kitchen, and there's also a barbecue area. Every unit has a lanai and fabulous ocean view. Golf and tennis are nearby. This is the place to book if you are going to spend a lot of time lounging around, or if you need the extra space.

78–6671 Alii Dr. (reservations c/o Johnson Resort Properties, 78–6665 Alii Dr.), Kailua-Kona, HI 96740. ℂ 808/322-2403. Fax 808/322-0105. www.konaseaspray. com. 12 units. $115–$140 1-bedroom double; $125–$155 1-bedroom/2-bathroom double; $140–$180 2-bedroom/2-bathroom; plus $55–$75 cleaning fee. 3-night minimum. Extra person $20. AE, DISC, MC, V. **Amenities:** Gorgeous outdoor pool w/waterfall; whirlpool hot tub; washer/dryers. *In room:* TV/VCR, kitchen, full-size fridge, coffeemaker, hair dryer, iron.

SOUTH KONA
EXPENSIVE

Horizon Guest House ✿✿ *Finds*   If you're planning to stay in South Kona, get on the phone right now and book this place—this is the Hawaiian hideaway of your dreams. Host Clem Classen spent 2 years researching the elements of a perfect B&B, and the Horizon Guest House is the result. Its 40 acres of pastureland are located at an altitude of 1,100 feet. You can see 25 miles of coastline, from

Kealakekua to just about South Point, yet you cannot see another structure or hear any sounds of civilization. The carefully thought-out individual units (all under one roof but positioned at an angle to one another so you don't see any other units) are filled with incredible Hawaiian furnishings, including hand-quilted Hawaiian bedspreads. Units also include private lanais with coastline views. The property features barbecue facilities, gardens everywhere, an outdoor shower, and plenty of beach toys. Clem whips up a gourmet breakfast in the main house, which also features a media room with library, video collection, TV (which you can take to your room if you use headphones so you won't disturb other guests), DVD, VCR, and cordless phone. At first glance, the rate may seem high, but once you're ensconced on the unique property, I think you'll agree it's worth every penny.

P.O. Box 268, Honaunau, HI 96726. © **888/328-8301** or 808/328-2540. Fax 808/328-8707. www.horizonguesthouse.com. 4 units. $250 double. Rates include full gourmet breakfast. 2-night minimum. MC, V. 21 miles south of Kailua-Kona on Hwy. 11, just before mile marker 100. Children must be 14 or older. **Amenities:** Large outdoor pool worthy of a big resort; Jacuzzi perfectly placed to watch the sunset behind Kealakekua Bay; complimentary washer/dryers; dataport; wireless Internet access. *In room:* Fridge, coffeemaker, hair dryer, no phone.

INEXPENSIVE

Areca Palms Estate Bed & Breakfast ⟨ *Finds* Everything about this upcountry B&B is impeccable: the landscaping, the furnishings, the fresh flowers in every room—even breakfast is served with attention to every detail. This charming cedar home, surrounded by immaculate parklike landscaping, sits above the Captain Cook–Kealakekua area, close to beaches, shopping, and restaurants. Guests enjoy watching the sun sink into the ocean from the large lanai or gazing at the starry sky as they soak in the hot tub. Hosts Janice and Steve Glass serve memorable breakfasts (orange-oatmeal quiche, tropical stuffed French toast, tree-ripened banana cakes), offer daily maid service, provide guests with beach equipment, and gladly help with reservations for activities and dinner.

P.O. Box 489, Captain Cook, HI 96704. © **800/545-4390** or 808/323-2276. Fax 808/323-3749. www.konabedandbreakfast.com. 4 units. $110–$145 double. Rates include full breakfast. Extra person $25. 2-night minimum. MC, V. From Hwy. 11, make a left at the Pacific Island Tire dealer (after mile marker 111) and follow the signs. **Amenities:** Outdoor Jacuzzi. *In room:* TV, hair dryer, no phone.

Manago Hotel *Value* If you want to experience the history and culture of the 50th state, the Manago Hotel may be the place for you. This living relic is still operated by the third generation of the

same Japanese family that opened it in 1917. It offers clean accommodations, tasty home cooking, and generous helpings of aloha, all
at budget prices. The older rooms (with community bathrooms) are
ultraspartan—strictly for desperate budget travelers. The rooms
with private bathrooms in the new wing are still pretty sparse
(freshly painted walls with no decoration and no TV), but they're
spotlessly clean and surrounded by Japanese gardens with a koi
pond. The room prices increase as you go up; the third-floor units
have the most spectacular views of the Kona coastline. Adventure-
some travelers might want to try the Japanese rooms with tatami
mats to sleep on and *furo* (deep hot tubs) in each room to soak in.
By the end of your stay, you may leave with new friends (the Manago family is very friendly).

P.O. Box 145, Captain Cook, HI 96704. ℂ **808/323-2642.** Fax 808/323-3451.
www.managohotel.com. 63 units, some with shared bathroom. $33 double with
shared bathroom; $54–$59 double with private bathroom; $73 double Japanese
room with small *furo* tub and private bathroom. Extra person $3. DISC, MC, V.
Amenities: Restaurant (Manago Hotel Restaurant, p. 76); bar. *In room:* No phone.

2 The Kohala Coast

VERY EXPENSIVE
Hapuna Beach Prince Hotel ✴✴   This hotel enjoys one of the
best locations on the Kohala Coast, adjacent to the magnificent
white sands of Hapuna Beach. The Hapuna Beach Prince is more
formal than other hotels on the Kohala Coast; guests, many from
Japan, dress up here, some in the latest Tokyo fashions. You won't
feel comfortable parading around in your T-shirt and flip-flops.

The rooms are comfortable, all attuned to the fabulous ocean
view and the sea breezes. Although the rooms are small for a luxury
hotel, the sprawling grounds make up for it (some guests, however,
complain about the long walk from the lobby to their rooms). Service is friendly and caring.

There is also a wealth of activities on the property, from the 18-
hole championship golf course (designed by Arnold Palmer and Ed
Seay, and reserved for guests and residents) to the state-of-the-art fitness center and world-class Paul Brown Salon and Spa, one of the
state's top salons.

At Mauna Kea Resort, 62–100 Kaunaoa Dr., Kohala Coast, HI 96743. ℂ **800/
882-6060** or 808/880-1111. Fax 808/880-3112. www.princeresortshawaii.com.
350 units. $395–$690 double; from $1,300 suite. Extra person $60. Children 17 and
under stay free in parent's room using existing bedding. AE, DC, MC, V. **Amenities:**
5 restaurants (including the Coast Grille, p. 79); 2 bars (1 is an open-air beachfront

Where to Stay & Dine in North Kohala & Waimea

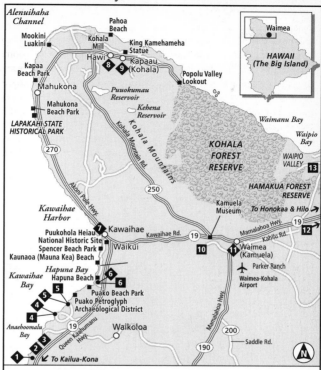

ACCOMMODATIONS ■

Aaah, the Views B&B **10**
Belle Vue **12**
The Cliff House **13**
The Fairmont Orchid, Hawaii **5**
Hapuna Beach Prince Hotel **6**
Hilton Waikoloa Village **3**
Luana Ola B&B Cottages **12**
Mauna Lani Bay Hotel
  & Bungalows **4**
Waianuhea **12**
Waikoloa Beach Marriott & Spa **1**
Waimea Garden Cottages **12**
Waipio Wayside B&B Inn **13**

DINING ◆

Bamboo **8**
Brown's Beach House **5**
Café Pesto **7**
CanoeHouse **4**
Coast Grille **6**
Daniel Thiebaut Restaurant **11**
Kohala Rainbow Café **9**
Merriman's **11**
Merriman's Market Café **2**
Norio's Sushi Bar
  & Restaurant **5**
Roy's Waikoloa Bar & Grill **2**
Tako Taco Takeria **11**

bar w/live evening entertainment); huge outdoor pool; golf course; 13 tennis courts; fitness center; salon and spa; Jacuzzi; watersports equipment rentals; year-round Keiki Kamp children's program; concierge; activities desk; car-rental desk; business center; shopping arcade; room service; massage; babysitting; same-day laundry service and dry cleaning. *In room:* A/C, TV, high-speed Internet access, fridge, coffeemaker, hair dryer, iron, safe.

Mauna Lani Bay Hotel & Bungalows ★★ Kids

Burned out? In need of tranquillity and gorgeous surroundings? Look no further. Sandy beaches and lava tide pools are the focus of this serene seaside resort, where gracious hospitality is dispensed in a historic setting. From the lounge chairs on the pristine beach to the turndown service at night, everything here is done impeccably.

Louvered doors open onto the plush guest rooms, which are outfitted in natural tones with teak accents, each with a lanai. They're arranged to capture maximum ocean views, and they surround interior atrium gardens and pools in which endangered baby sea turtles are raised. A shoreline trail leads across the whole 3,200-acre resort, giving you an intimate glimpse into the ancient past, when people lived in lava caves and tended the large complex of fish ponds.

The hotel offers a very complete children's program, plus "kid-friendly" restaurants, but in addition to that, this is just a great place for kids to explore. The saltwater stream that meanders through the hotel and out onto the property outside is filled with reef fish and even a shark. The fish ponds on the property are a great educational experience for *keiki*, and the beach has plenty of room for the youngsters to run and play. Next door to the resort are ancient Hawaiian petroglyph fields, where older kids can learn about Hawaii's past.

The Sports and Fitness Club (one of the best on the island) was just renovated, and The Shops at Mauna Lani recently opened with great retail-therapy opportunities and several food options.

68–1400 Mauna Lani Dr., Kohala Coast, HI 96743. ℂ **800/367-2323** or 808/885-6622. Fax 808/885-1484. www.maunalani.com. 342 units. $430–$920 double; from $980 suite; $620–$1,860 villa (3-day minimum); $5,500–$6,225 bungalow (sleeps up to 4). AE, DC, DISC, MC, V. **Amenities:** 5 excellent restaurants (including CanoeHouse, p. 79); bar (live music nightly); large outdoor pool; 2 celebrated 18-hole championship golf courses; 10 Plexipave tennis courts; full-service fitness facility; range of massage treatments at the spa; Jacuzzi; watersports equipment rentals; bike rentals; year-round children's program; concierge; activities desk; business center; shopping arcade; salon; room service; massage; babysitting; laundry service; dry cleaning. *In room:* A/C, TV, dataport, fridge, coffeemaker, hair dryer, iron, safe.

Waikoloa Beach Marriott Resort & Spa ★

There have been big, big changes here. First they gutted all the guest rooms (back down to the bare concrete) and redesigned them, added 27-inch flatscreen TVs, put in glass lanai railings (which actually glow at sunset), and topped everything off with a very comfy Marriott "Revive" bed. This resort has always had one outstanding attribute: an excellent location on Anaehoomalu Bay (or A-Bay, as the locals call it), one of the best ocean-sports bays on the Kohala Coast. The gentle sloping beach has everything: swimming, snorkeling, diving, kayaking, windsurfing, and even old royal fish ponds. The property still isn't as posh as other luxury hotels along the Kohala Coast, but it also isn't nearly as expensive. The size and layout of the guest rooms remain the same—perfectly nice, but not luxurious. Families might want to book the deluxe rooms, which are oversized. A new adults-only infinity swimming pool was added in 2006, and the Mandara Spa was expanded to 5,000 sq. ft on two levels. The main dining room, Hawaii Calls, also was expanded with a new patio area outside and has a new menu. Guests may use the two championship golf courses at the adjacent Hilton Waikoloa Village.

69–275 Waikoloa Beach Dr., Waikoloa, HI 96738. © **877/359-3696** or 808/886-6789. Fax 808/886-3601. www.marriotthawaii.com. 555 units. $425–$565 double; cabana from $600 suite. Extra person $40. Children 17 and under stay free in parent's room. Resort fee $16 for overnight self-parking, daily mai tais for 2, 1 child meal (11 years and under) with purchase of adult entree (dinner), half-day snorkel rental for 2, 1-hr. daily tennis court time, free local calls (Big Island), and high-speed wireless Internet access. AE, DC, DISC, MC, V. Valet parking $15. **Amenities:** 2 restaurants; 1 bar w/nightly live entertainment; outdoor swimming pools (a huge pool w/water slide and separate children's pool); 2 tennis courts; fitness center; full-service Mandara Spa; Jacuzzi; watersports equipment rentals; year-round children's program; concierge; activities desk; business center; salon; room service; babysitting; coin-op washer/dryers; laundry service; dry cleaning; Hawaiian cultural activities, including petroglyphs tour and evening luau. *In room:* A/C, flatscreen TV, dataport, fridge, coffeemaker, hair dryer, iron, safe.

EXPENSIVE

The Fairmont Orchid, Hawaii ★★★ *Kids*   Located on 32 acres of oceanfront property, the Orchid is the place for watersports nuts, cultural explorers, families with children, or someone who just wants to lie back and soak up the sun. This elegant beach resort takes full advantage of the spectacular ocean views and historical sites on its grounds. The sports facilities here are extensive, and there's an excellent Hawaiiana program: The "beach boys" demonstrate how to do everything from creating drums from the trunks of coconut trees to paddling a Hawaiian canoe or strumming a ukulele.

I recommend spending a few dollars more to book a room on The Fairmont's Gold Floor, which offers personalized service, a lounge (serving complimentary continental breakfast, finger sandwiches in the afternoon, and appetizers in the evening), and exquisite ocean views. All 540 guest rooms in this luxury hotel underwent complete renovation in 2006 (to the tune of $9.3 million) and sport new carpets, paint, artwork, lani furniture, and amenities. All guest rooms feature big lanais, sitting areas, and marble bathrooms, each with a double vanity and separate shower. The Spa Without Walls allows you to book a massage just about anywhere on the property—overlooking the ocean, nestled deep in the lush vegetation, or in your room. The Orchid's four restaurants are all wonderful, with a casual, relaxed atmosphere.

The Keiki Aloha program, for kids 5 to 12, features supervised activities like watersports and Hawaiian cultural activities. Some special money-saving family packages are also available.

The award-winning Norio's Sushi Bar & Restaurant has expanded, with three sushi chefs chopping, rolling, and performing magic at the sushi bar. The recently opened Polynesian revue ("The Gathering of Kings") and luau is making a big splash with everything from fire-knife dancing performances to culinary creations from Samoa, Tahiti, and New Zealand.

I applaud The Fairmont Orchid for dropping the obnoxious "resort fee" and allowing guests to pay for the extra services they want.

1 N. Kaniku Dr., Kohala Coast, HI 96743. (C) **800/845-9905** or 808/885-2000. Fax 808/885-1064. www.fairmont.com/orchid. 540 units. $359–$799 double; $799–$1,499 double Gold Floor; from $999 suite. Extra person $75. Children 17 and under stay free in parent's room. AE, DC, DISC, MC, V. Valet parking $15; self-parking $8. **Amenities:** 4 restaurants (including Norio's Sushi Bar & Restaurant, p. 79, and Brown's Beach House, p. 78); 5 bars (w/evening entertainment in the Paniolo Lounge); large outdoor pool; 2 championship golf courses; 10 award-winning Plexipave tennis courts (7 lit for night play); well-equipped fitness center; outstanding spa; 2 lava rock whirlpools; watersports equipment rentals; bike rentals; year-round children's program; concierge; activities desk; car-rental desk; business center; shopping arcade; salon; room service; babysitting; same-day laundry service and dry cleaning. *In room:* A/C, TV, high-speed Internet access $15/day, minibar, hair dryer, iron, safe.

Hilton Waikoloa Village 🐟

This hotel is a fantasy world all its own, perfect for those who love Vegas and Disneyland. Its high-rise towers are connected by silver-bullet trams, boats, and museum-like walkways lined with $7 million in Asian/Pacific reproductions. The kids will love it, but Mom and Dad may get a little weary waiting for the tram or boat to take them to breakfast (sometimes a 20-min. ordeal or a mile-long walk). The 62 acres feature tropical gardens, cascading waterfalls, exotic wildlife, exaggerated architecture, a 175-foot water slide twisting into a 1-acre pool, hidden grottoes, and man-made lagoons, including a dolphin lagoon (you can swim with the dolphins for a fee).

The contemporary guest rooms are spacious and luxurious, with built-in platform beds, lanais, and loads of amenities, from spacious dressing areas to a second phone line in all units. All rooms and bathrooms have recently undergone renovations from top to bottom, including new drapes, new beds and bedding, bigger televisions, and new furniture, carpet, and tile. With nine restaurants to choose from, you'll never lack for culinary choices, and golfers can choose from one of the two championship golf courses, one designed by Robert Trent Jones, Jr., and the other by Tom Weiskopf.

Even if you aren't staying here, drop by for the Kohala Spa, one of the best spas on the Kohala Coast, with 25,000 square feet of treatment rooms, saunas, whirlpools, and a host of treatments, including acupuncture and Eastern medicine practices—there's even an astrologer on staff!

69-425 Waikoloa Beach Dr., Waikoloa, HI 96738. ℂ **800/HILTONS** or 808/886-1234. Fax 808/886-2900. www.hiltonwaikoloavillage.com. 1,240 units, including 57 suites. $249–$599 double; from $1,095 suite. Daily resort fee $15 for seaside putting course, access to Kohala spa, 1 hr. of tennis court time, and $25 beach toy credit. Extra person $40. Children 18 and under stay free in parent's room. AE, DC, DISC, MC, V. Valet parking $15; self-parking $7. **Amenities:** 9 restaurants; 9 bars (many w/entertainment); 3 huge outdoor pools (w/waterfalls, slides, whirlpools, and an adults-only pool); 2 18-hole golf courses; 8 tennis courts; excellent spa w/cardio machines, weights, and a multitude of services; Jacuzzi; watersports equipment rentals; bike rentals; fabulous children's program; game room; concierge; activities desk; car-rental desk; business center; shopping arcade; salon; room service; in-room massage; babysitting; coin-op washer/dryers; same-day laundry service and dry cleaning; concierge-level rooms; art gallery. *In room:* A/C, TV, dataport, high-speed Internet ($14/day), minibar/fridge, coffeemaker, hair dryer, iron, safe.

3 Waimea

MODERATE

Waimea Garden Cottages ★★ (Finds)   Imagine rolling hills on pastoral ranch land. Then add a babbling stream and two cozy Hawaiian cottages. Complete the picture with mountain views, and you have Waimea Garden Cottages. One unit has the feel of an old English country cottage, with oak floors, a fireplace, and French doors opening onto a spacious brick patio. The other is a remodeled century-old Hawaiian wash house, filled with antiques, eucalyptus-wood floors, and a full kitchen. Extra touches keep guests returning again and again: plush English robes, sandalwood soaps in the bathroom, mints next to the bed, and fresh flower arrangements throughout. Hosts Barbara and Charlie Campbell live on the spacious property.

Off Mamalahoa Hwy., 2 miles west of Waimea town center. Reservations c/o Hawaii's Best Bed & Breakfasts, P.O. Box 758, Volcano, HI 96785. © 800/262-9912 or 808/263-3100. Fax 808/962-6360. www.bestbnb.com. 2 units. $150–$160 double. Rates include continental breakfast. Extra person $20. 3-night minimum. No credit cards. *In room:* TV/VCR, kitchen, fridge, coffeemaker, hair dryer, iron, whirlpool bathtub (in 1 unit), fireplace (in 1 unit).

INEXPENSIVE

Aaah, the Views Bed & Breakfast ⋒ *Value*   This quiet B&B, just 15 minutes from the fabulous beaches of the Kohala Coast and 5 minutes from the cowboy town of Waimea, lives up to its name— each of the four units has huge picture windows from which you can watch the sun rise or set, or gaze out over green pastureland to the slopes of Mauna Kea. New owners Erika and Derek Stuart recently took over this B&B and have added a new deck to the stream-side property. One unit is a studio apartment, complete with kitchen. Two rooms share one bathroom, and the fourth unit has its own private bathroom down the hall.

P.O. Box 6593, Kamuela, HI 96743. © 808/885-3455. Fax 808/885-4031. www. aaahtheviews.com. 4 units. $85–$165 double. Rates include continental breakfast. Extra person $20. 2-night minimum. MC, V. *In room:* TV/VCR, high-speed Internet access, kitchenette, fridge, coffeemaker, hair dryer, iron.

Belle Vue ⋒   This two-story vacation rental has a truly beautiful view. Sitting in the hills overlooking Waimea and surrounded by manicured gardens, the charming home is just 15 minutes from the Kohala Coast beaches. The penthouse unit is a large, cathedral-ceilinged studio apartment with a small kitchen, huge bedroom, luxurious bathroom, and view of Mauna Loa and Mauna Kea mountains down to the Pacific Ocean. The one-bedroom apartment has a full kitchen and sofa bed. Each unit has a separate entrance. The rates include breakfast fixings (toast, juice, fruit, cereal, coffee) inside the kitchenettes.

1351 Konokohau Rd., off Opelo Rd. (P.O. Box 1295), Kamuela, HI 96743. © 800/ 772-5044 or ©/fax 808/885-7732. www.hawaii-bellevue.com. 3 units. $95–$185 double. Extra person $25. 2-night minimum. AE, MC, V. *In room:* TV, dataport, kitchenette, fridge, coffeemaker, hair dryer, iron.

4 The Hamakua Coast

Note: You'll find the following hotels on the "Where to Stay & Dine in North Kohala & Waimea" map on p. 51.

EXPENSIVE

Waianuhea ★★ *Finds*   Located in the rural rolling hills above Honokaa, totally off the grid, and nestled in seven beautifully landscaped acres (with a lily pond, fruit trees, a vegetable garden, and a bucolic horse pasture) lies this oasis of luxury and relaxation. Just off a narrow country road, this two-story inn features five posh rooms with soaking tubs, gas or wood stoves, phones, and flatscreen LCD satellite TV, all on photovoltaic solar power. The sumptuous main room has highly polished wood floors, a rock fireplace, and custom Italian sofas. The "Great Room" has wraparound glass windows with multicolored glass balloons hanging from the ceiling. There are five guest rooms, but splurge a little and ask for the Malamalama suite with a cherrywood sleigh bed, extra-large soaking tub, glass-enclosed shower, and separate living room. Other amenities are nightly wine tasting (featuring different wines every month) with gourmet hors d'oeuvres, an outdoor hot tub, a guest minikitchen stocked with a range of goodies (enough to make a meal), and beverages at surprisingly reasonable prices. Complete multicourse gourmet breakfasts are served every morning.

45-3503 Kahana Dr. (P.O. Box 185), Honokaa, Hi 96727. © **888/775-2577** or 808/77-1118, fax 888/296-6302. www.waianuhea.com. 5 units. $195–$400. Includes full breakfast. AE, MC, V. **Amenities:** Hot tub, minikitchen. *In room:* TV/DVD, hair dryer, iron.

MODERATE

The Cliff House ★★ *Finds*   Perched on the cliffs above the ocean is this romantic two-bedroom getaway, surrounded by horse pastures and million-dollar views. A large deck takes in the ocean vista, where whales frolic offshore in winter. Impeccably decorated (the owner also owns Waipio Valley Artworks), the unit features a very well equipped kitchen, two large bedrooms, and a full bathroom. Lots of little touches make this property stand out from the others: an answering machine for the phone, a pair of binoculars, a chess set, and even an umbrella for the rain squalls. Four people could comfortably share this unit.

P.O. Box 5070, Kukuihaele, HI 96727. © **800/492-4746** or 808/775-0005. Fax 808/775-0058. www.cliffhousehawaii.com. 1 unit. $195 double. Extra person $35. 2-night minimum. MC, V. *In room:* TV, dataport, kitchen, fridge, coffeemaker, hair dryer, iron.

INEXPENSIVE

Waipio Wayside B&B Inn ★★ *(Finds)*   Jackie Horne's restored Hamakua Sugar supervisor's home, built in 1938, sits nestled among fruit trees, surrounded by sweet-smelling ginger, fragile orchids, and blooming birds-of-paradise. The comfortable house, done in old Hawaii style, abounds with thoughtful touches, such as the help-yourself tea-and-cookies bar with 26 different kinds of tea. A sunny lanai with hammocks overlooks a yard lush with banana, lemon, lime, tangerine, and avocado trees; the cliff-side gazebo has views of the ocean 600 feet below. There are five vintage rooms to choose from: My favorite is the master bedroom suite (dubbed the "bird's-eye" room), with double doors that open onto the deck; I also love the Library Room, which has an ocean view, hundreds of books, and a skylight in the shower. There's a shared living room with a TV (including VCR and DVD). Jackie's friendly hospitality and excellent continental breakfasts round out the experience.

P.O. Box 840, Honokaa, HI 96727. ℂ **800/833-8849** or 808/775-0275. www.waipiowayside.com. 5 units. $99–$190 double. Rates include full organic tropical continental breakfast with coffee, fruit (sunrise papayas, mangoes, fresh tangerines), granola, yogurts, and muffins. Extra person $25. MC, V. On Hwy. 240, 2 miles from the Honokaa Post Office; look on the right for a long, white picket fence and sign on the ocean side of the road; the 2nd driveway is the parking lot. **Amenities:** Concierge. *In room:* TV/VCR/DVD in living room.

5 Hilo

EXPENSIVE

The Palms Cliff House Inn ★★ *(Finds)*   This inn is a 15-minute drive north of Hilo town, at Honomu (where Akaka Falls is located). Perched on the side of a cliff, this grand old Victorian-style inn is surrounded by manicured lawns and macadamia-nut, lemon, banana, lime, orange, avocado, papaya, star fruit, breadfruit, grapefruit, and mango trees. Eight oversize suites, filled with antiques and equipped with DVD players, fireplaces, and private lanais, all overlook the ocean. Four rooms have private Jacuzzis; other extras include custom-made Italian-lace sheets, cooking classes, yoga classes, and private massage and other spa treatments. A gourmet hot breakfast (entrees range from banana–mac nut pancakes to asparagus–sweet potato quiche) is served on the wrap-around lanai overlooking the rolling surf. Lots of activities on-site,

Hilo

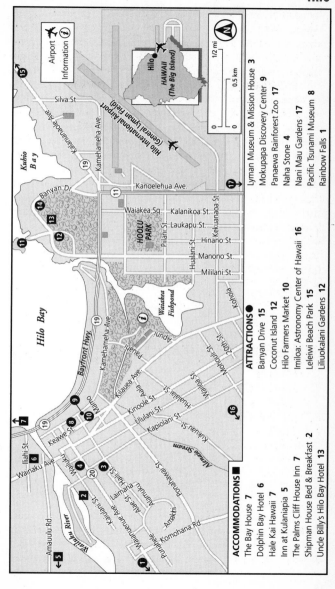

Airport ✈
Information ⓘ

HAWAII
(The Big Island)
Hilo

Silva St.
Kaumana Ave.
Kamehameha Ave.
Hilo International Airport
(General Lyman Field)

Kuhio Bay

Banyan Dr.
Kanoelehua Ave.

Waiakea Sq.   Kalanikoa St.

HOOLU PARK

Pilani St.   Laukapu St.   Kekuanaoa St.

Hinano St.

Manono St.

Mililani St.

Kohola

Waiakea Fishpond

Hilo Bay

Kamehameha Ave.

Bayfront Hwy.

Manono

Keawe St.
Kilauea Ave.
Aala St.
Kinoole St.
Ululani St.
Kapiolani St.
Hualalai St.
Waianuenue Ave.
Kinoole St.
Mohouli St.
20th St.

Akau St.

Alenaio Stream

Wailuku River

Amauulu Rd.

Wainaku Ave.
Akolea Rd.
Alae St.
Hall St.
Waianuenue Ave.
Kaiulani St.
Komohana Rd.
Ponahawai St.

ACCOMMODATIONS ■

The Bay House **7**
Dolphin Bay Hotel **6**
Hale Kai Hawaii **7**
Inn at Kulaniapia **5**
The Palms Cliff House Inn **7**
Shipman House Bed & Breakfast **2**
Uncle Billy's Hilo Bay Hotel **13**

ATTRACTIONS ●

Banyan Drive **15**
Coconut Island **12**
Hilo Farmers Market **10**
Imiloa: Astronomy Center of Hawaii **16**
Leleiwi Beach Park **15**
Liliuokalani Gardens **12**

Lyman Museum & Mission House **3**
Mokupapa Discovery Center **9**
Panaewa Rainforest Zoo **17**
Naha Stone **4**
Nani Mau Gardens **17**
Pacific Tsunami Museum **8**
Rainbow Falls **1**

1/2 mi
0.5 km

from gourmet cooking classes to hula lessons to high tea. A magnificent getaway.

P.O. Box 189, Honomu, 96728. (C) **866/963-6076** or 808/963-6076. Fax 808/963-6316. www.palmscliffhouse.com. 8 units. $250–$395 double. Rates include full gourmet breakfast. AE, DC, DISC, MC, V. **Amenities:** Hot tub. *In room:* A/C (only upper units), TV/DVD, dataport, fridge, hair dryer, iron, Jacuzzi (some units).

MODERATE

Shipman House Bed & Breakfast ★★ *Finds*   Built in 1900, the Shipman House is on both the national and state registers of historic places. This Victorian mansion has been totally restored by Barbara Andersen, the great-granddaughter of the original owner, and her husband, Gary. Despite the home's historic appearance, Barbara has made sure that its conveniences are strictly 21st century, including full bathrooms with all the amenities. All five guest bedrooms are large, with 10- to 12-foot ceilings and touches like heirloom furnishings and hand-woven lauhala mats. Wake up to a large continental homemade (with fresh fruit from the garden) breakfast buffet. On Wednesdays, guests can join in with the hula class practicing on the lanai. Recently they've added lei making and other cultural activities.

131 Kaiulani St., Hilo, HI 96720. (C) **800/627-8447** or 808/934-8002. Fax 808/934-8002. www.hilo-hawaii.com. 5 units. $205–$225 double. Rates include continental breakfast. Extra person $25. AE, MC, V. From Hwy. 19, take Waianuenue Ave.; turn right on Kaiulani St. and go 1 block over the wooden bridge; look for the large house on the left. *In room:* No phone.

INEXPENSIVE

The Bay House ★ *Finds*   Overlooking Hilo Bay, this B&B offers immaculate rooms (each with oak floors, king-size bed, sofa, private bathroom, and oceanview lanai) at reasonable prices. A continental breakfast (tropical fruit, pastries, Kona coffee) is set out in a common area every morning (which also has a refrigerator, coffeemaker, toaster, and microwave for common use); you can take all you want to eat back to your lanai and watch the sun rise over Hilo Bay. In the evening, relax in the cliff-side Jacuzzi as the stars come out.

42 Pukihae St., Hilo, HI 96720. (C) **888/235-8195** or (C)/fax 808/961-6311. www.bayhousehawaii.com. 3 units. $125 double. Rates include continental breakfast. Extra person $15. AE, MC, V. **Amenities:** Hot tub. *In room:* TV, hair dryer.

Dolphin Bay Hotel ★ *Value*   This two-story, motel-like building, 4 blocks from downtown, is a clean, family-run property that offers good value in a quiet garden setting. Ripe star fruit hang from the trees, flowers abound, and there's a junglelike trail by a stream. The tidy concrete-block apartments are small and often breezeless, but they're equipped with ceiling fans and jalousie windows. Rooms are brightly painted and outfitted with rattan furniture and Hawaiian prints. There are no phones in the rooms, but there's one in the lobby. You're welcome to all the papayas and bananas you can eat.

333 Iliahi St., Hilo, HI 96720. © 808/935-1466. Fax 808/935-1523. www.dolphin bayhilo.com. 18 units. $99–$109 studio double; $129 1-bedroom apt double; $149 2-bedroom apt double. Extra person $10. From Hwy. 19, turn mauka (toward the mountains) on Hwy. 200 (Waianuenue St.), and then right on Pueeo St.; go over the bridge and turn left on Iliahi St. MC, V. **Amenities:** Concierge; car-rental desk; coin-op washer/dryer. *In room:* TV, high-speed Internet access, kitchenette, fridge, coffeemaker, hair dryer (on request), iron, no phone.

Hale Kai Hawaii 🏖 *(Value)*

An eye-popping view of the ocean runs the entire length of this house; you can sit on the wide deck and watch the surfers slide down the waves. All rooms have that fabulous ocean view through sliding-glass doors. There's one suite, with a living room, kitchenette, and separate bedroom. Guests have access to a pool, hot tub, and small guest area with fridge, telephone, and library. Breakfast is a treat, with entrees like homemade mac-nut waffles or double cheese soufflé. New owners Maria Macias and Ricardo Zepeda have breathed new life into this B&B: The rooms are now all painted in vibrant tropical colors, Maria has improved the landscaping, and they've installed privacy barriers between each room.

111 Honolii Pali, Hilo, HI 96720. © 808/935-6330. Fax 808/935-8439. www.halekaihawaii.com. 4 units. $125–$139 double; $155 suite. Rates include gourmet breakfast. Extra person $20. 2-night minimum. MC, V. **Amenities:** Oceanfront outdoor pool; Jacuzzi. *In room:* TV, no phone.

The Inn at Kulaniapia 🏖 *(Finds)*

The view from this off-the-beaten-track inn is worth the price alone: the 120-foot Kulaniapia Waterfall in one direction and the entire town of Hilo sprawled out 850 feet below in another direction. This is *the* place for a romantic getaway. In addition to luxury accommodations, you get a royal breakfast with egg dishes, fresh fruit grown on the 22-acre property, and just-baked breads. Wander along the 2-mile pathways that follow the Waiau River (check out the exotic bamboo garden) or swim at the base of the waterfall in the 300-foot pond. The rooms are well appointed, with balconies. It's just 15 minutes from Hilo but feels a zillion miles away from everything in the peaceful surroundings of a 2,000-acre macadamia-nut grove.

P.O. Box 11338, Hilo, HI 96720. © 866/935-6789 or 808/935-6789. Fax 808/935-6789. www.waterfall.net. 4 units. $109 double. Rates include breakfast. Extra person $20. AE, MC, V. **Amenities:** Hot tub; high-speed Internet access. *In room:* TV.

Uncle Billy's Hilo Bay Hotel   Uncle Billy's is one of the least expensive places to stay along Hilo's hotel row, Banyan Drive. This oceanfront budget hotel boasts a dynamite location, and the car/room package offers an extra incentive to stay here. You enter via a tiny lobby, gussied up Polynesian style; it's slightly overdone, with sagging fishnets and tapa (bark cloth) on the walls. The guest rooms are simple: bed, TV, phone, closet, and bathroom—that's about it. The walls seem paper thin, and it can get very noisy at night (you may want to bring ear plugs), but at these rates, you're still getting your money's worth.

87 Banyan Dr. (off Hwy. 19), Hilo, HI 96720. © **800/367-5102** or 808/961-5818. Fax 808/935-7903. www.unclebilly.com. 144 units. $104–$114 double; $119 studio with kitchenette. Car/room packages and special senior rates available. Extra person $14. Internet specials from $89. Children 18 and under stay free in parent's room. AE, DC, DISC, MC, V. **Amenities:** Restaurant; bar w/hula show nightly; oceanfront outdoor pool; activities desk; coin-op washer/dryers. *In room:* A/C, TV, kitchenette (some rooms), fridge, coffeemaker (some rooms), hair dryer (some rooms), iron (some rooms).

6 Hawaii Volcanoes National Park

As a result of Hawaii Volcanoes being officially designated a National Park in 1916, a village has popped up at its front door. Volcano Village isn't so much a town as a wide spot in Old Volcano Road, with two general stores, a handful of restaurants, a post office, a coffee shop, a new firehouse, and a winery.

Except for Volcano House (see below), which is within the national park, all of the accommodations in this section are in Volcano Village. It gets cool here at night—Volcano Village is located at 3,700 feet—so a fireplace might be an attractive amenity. It also rains a lot in Volcano—100 inches a year—which makes everything grow Jack-and-the-Beanstalk style.

I recommend spending at least 3 days to really see and enjoy the park. The best way to do this is to rent a cottage or house, and the best rental agency is **Hawaii Volcano Vacations** ★★ (P.O. Box 913, Volcano, HI 96785; © **800/709-0907** or 808/967-7271; www. hawaiivolcanovacations.com). Manager Aurelia Gutierrez selects only the top cottages, cabins, and houses in Volcano and makes sure that they are perfect for you. Her reasonably priced units range from $99 to $200, and each one is outfitted with a full kitchen, plus an outdoor grill, cooler, flashlight, umbrella, and fresh flower arrangement for your arrival. Many of them are great options for families traveling with kids.

Where to Stay & Dine in the Volcano Area

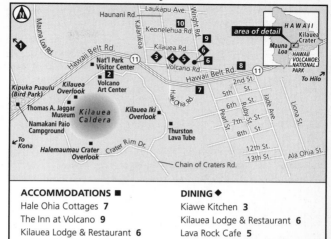

ACCOMMODATIONS ■
Hale Ohia Cottages **7**
The Inn at Volcano **9**
Kilauea Lodge & Restaurant **6**
Volcano Bed & Breakfast **10**
Volcano House **2**
Volcano Inn **8**

DINING ◆
Kiawe Kitchen **3**
Kilauea Lodge & Restaurant **6**
Lava Rock Cafe **5**
Thai Thai Restaurant **4**
Volcano Golf & Country Club **1**

EXPENSIVE

The Inn at Volcano   Formerly called Chalet Kilauea, this is the most expensive B&B in Volcano. It has a storybook, enchanting quality to it. I found some rooms, although exquisitely decorated, were not very practical for things like hanging clothes, storing toiletries, and so on. The least expensive room is decorated in memorabilia from the owners' extensive travels to eastern and southern Africa. Other rooms include an Oriental Jade room with collectibles from the Far East, a Continental Lace suite with Victorian decor, a treetop suite, and a separate cabin located next door to The Inn.

P.O. Box 998, Volcano, HI 96785. ✆ **800/937-7786** or 808/967-7786. Fax 808/ 967-8660. www.volcano-hawaii.com. 5 units. $170–$400 double. Rates include full gourmet breakfast and afternoon tea. AE, DC, DISC, MC, V. **Amenities:** Hot tub; 3 of the rooms share a fridge, microwave, and coffeemaker on the porch. *In room:* TV/VCR, fridge (some rooms), coffeemaker (some rooms), microwave (some rooms).

MODERATE

Kilauea Lodge ★   This popular roadside lodge, built in 1938 as a YMCA camp, sits on 10 wooded and landscaped acres. Its rooms offer heating systems and hot-towel warmers, beautiful art on the walls, fresh flowers, and, in some, fireplaces. There's also a 1929 two-bedroom cottage with a fireplace and a full kitchen, just a couple of blocks down the street. A full gourmet breakfast is served to guests at the restaurant.

P.O. Box 116 (1 block off Hwy. 11 on Old Volcano Rd.), Volcano, HI 96785. ℭ **808/ 967-7366.** Fax 808/967-7367. www.kilauealodge.com. 17 units. $150–$165 double room; $180–$190 cottages. Rates include full breakfast. Extra person $20. AE, MC, V. **Amenities:** Restaurant (p. 92); hot tub. *In room:* Coffeemaker, no phone.

INEXPENSIVE

Hale Ohia Cottages ✿ *(Finds)*   Take a step back in time to the 1930s. Here you'll have a choice of suites, each with private entrance. There are also four guest cottages, ranging from one bedroom to three. The surrounding botanical gardens contribute to the overall tranquil ambience of the estate. They were groomed in the 1930s by a resident Japanese gardener, who worked with the natural volcanic terrain but gently tamed the flora into soothing shapes and designs. The lush grounds are just a mile from Hawaii Volcanoes National Park. The latest addition is a romantic, cozy cottage with fireplace, hot tub, and unusual bedroom made from a 1930s redwood water tank.

P.O. Box 758 (Hale Ohia Rd., off Hwy. 11), Volcano, HI 96785. ℭ **800/455-3803** or 808/967-7986. Fax 808/967-8610. www.haleohia.com. 8 units. $95–$179 double. Rates include continental breakfast. Extra person $20. MC, V. *In room:* Fridge, coffeemaker, hair dryer, no phone.

Volcano Bed & Breakfast *(Value)*   If you're on a tight budget, check into this charming restored 1912 historic home offering comfortable, clean, quiet rooms, all with shared bathrooms. The restored house sits on beautifully landscaped grounds and has new carpeting throughout and new furnishings in the common area. The rooms are tiny but clean and inviting. The common rooms include a living room with TV/VCR, a reading room, and a sunroom.

P.O. Box 998 (on Keonelehua St., off Hwy. 11 on Wright Rd.), Volcano, HI 96785. ℭ **800/937-7786** or 808/967-7779. Fax 808/967-8660. www.volcano-hawaii. com. 6 units, none with private bathroom. $65–$85 double. Rates include continental breakfast. Extra person $15. AE, DC, DISC, MC, V. From Hwy. 11, turn north onto Wright Rd.; go 1 mile to Chalet Kilauea on the right, where you'll check in. *In room:* No phone.

Volcano House   Volcano House has a great location—inside the boundaries of the national park—and that's about all. This mountain lodge, which evolved out of a grass lean-to in 1865, is Hawaii's oldest visitor accommodations. It stands on the edge of Halemaumau's bubbling crater, and although the view of the crater is still an awesome sight, don't expect the Ritz here—rooms are very plain and heated with volcanic steam. *Tip:* Book only if you can get a room facing the volcano; if they are filled, don't bother—you can do better elsewhere.

P.O. Box 53, Hawaii Volcanoes National Park, HI 96718. © 808/967-7321. Fax 808/967-8429. www.volcanohousehotel.com. 42 units. $130–$250 double. Extra person $20. AE, DC, DISC, MC, V. **Amenities:** Restaurant w/great view; bar.

Volcano Inn   Located in the rainforest, this property is a combination of two inns, one with four rooms and one with three, plus a separate cabin with kitchenette, all in the heart of Volcano Village. The rooms at the inn are quite luxurious for the price; each comes with a fireplace and daily maid service. The amenities here include complimentary use of the bicycles, a great video library at one inn and a regular book library at the other, and coffee service daily.

19–3820 Old Volcano Rd., Volcano, HI 96785. © 800/997-2292 or 808/967-7293. Fax 808/985-7349. www.volcanoinn.com. 8 units. $105–$145 double. AE, DC, DISC, MC, V. *In room:* TV/VCR/DVD, fridge, hair dryer, iron, no phone.

7 South Point

Bougainvillea Bed & Breakfast ☆ *Finds*   Don and Martie Jean Nitsche bought this 3-acre property in the Hawaiian Rancho subdivision of Ocean View and had a *Field of Dreams* experience: They decided that if they built a bed-and-breakfast, people would come. Where some people just saw lava, the Nitsches saw the ancient Hawaiian path that went from the mountain to the sea. So they built. And out of the lava came gardens—colorful bougainvillea, a pineapple patch, and a fish pond to add to the pool and hot tub. Word got out. Martie's breakfast—her secret-recipe banana and mac-nut pancakes, sausage, fruit, and coffee—drew people from all over. Things got so good, they had to add more rooms (all with their own private entrances) and expand the living room (complete with TV, VCR, and video library) and dining room. Guests usually take their breakfast plates out to the lanai, which boasts ocean views. Or you can wander over to the pavilion, located next to the pool, which has a big barbecue area (with a minikitchen, including a microwave), a game area (darts, Ping-Pong table, and so on), a satellite TV, some exercise equipment, even a horseshoe pit. You can borrow snorkeling gear, beach mats, coolers, and other beach equipment.

P.O. Box 6045, Ocean View, HI 96737. © 800/688-1763 or 808/929-7089. Fax 808/929-7089. www.hawaii-inn.com. 4 units. $89 double. Rates include full breakfast. Extra person $15. AE, DC, DISC, MC, V. **Amenities:** Big outdoor pool; concierge; car-rental desk; massage in-room or outdoors; hot tub; satellite TV; minikitchen in pavilion; game area; microwave. *In room:* TV/VCR, hair dryer, no phone.

Macadamia Meadows Bed & Breakfast (Kids) Near the southernmost point in the United States and just 45 minutes from Volcanoes National Park lies one of the Big Island's most welcoming B&Bs. It's located on an 8-acre working macadamia-nut farm, in a great place for stargazing, and the warmth and hospitality of host Charlene Cowan is unsurpassed. This is an excellent place for children; because the owner has children herself, the entire property is very kid-friendly. In addition to exploring the groves of mac-nut trees, kids can swim in the pool or play tennis. Charlene also has puzzles, games, and other "rainy day" items to entertain children. Two of the units can be reserved together as a two-bedroom suite. All rooms have private entrances and are immaculately clean. Ask Charlene about the free orchid tours.

94–6263 Kamaoa Rd., Waiohinu. Reservations: P.O. Box 756, Naalehu, HI 96772. © 888/929-8118 or 808/929-8097. Fax 808/929-8097. www.macadamia meadows.com. 5 units. $89–$139 double. Rates include continental breakfast. Extra person $10 children under 18, $15 adults; children under 5 stay free in parent's room. AE, DISC, MC, V. **Amenities:** Resort-size outdoor pool; tennis courts; activities desk. *In room:* TV, fridge, microwave, no phone.

South Point Banyan Tree House (Finds) Couples looking for an exotic place to nest should try this tree house nestled inside a huge Chinese banyan tree. The cottage comes complete with see-through roof that lets the outside in, plus a comfy, just-for-two hot tub on the wraparound deck. Inside there's a queen-size bed and a kitchen with microwave and two-burner stove. The scent of ginger brings you sweet dreams at night, and the twitter of birds greets you in the morning.

At Hwy. 11 and Pinao St., Waiohinu. © 715/302-8180. www.southpointbth.com. 1 unit. $185 double. 2-night minimum. MC, V. **Amenities:** Hot tub; washer/dryer; outside grill. *In room:* TV/VCR, kitchen, fridge, coffeemaker.

3

Where to Dine

So many restaurants, so little time. What's a traveler to do? The Big Island's delicious dilemma is its daunting size and abundant offerings. Its gastronomic environment—the fruitful marriage of creative chefs, good soil, and rich cultural traditions—has made this island as much a culinary destination as a recreational one.

The Big Island's volcanic soil produces fine tomatoes, lettuces, beets, beans, fruit, and basic herbs and vegetables that were once difficult to find locally. Southeast Asian fruit, such as mangosteen and rambutan, are beginning to appear in markets, along with the sweet white pineapple that is by now a well-established Big Island crop. Along with the lamb and beef from Big Island ranches and seafood from local fishermen, this fresh produce forms the backbone of ethnic cookery and Hawaii Regional Cuisine.

Kailua-Kona is teeming with restaurants for all pocketbooks, while the haute cuisine of the island is concentrated in the Kohala Coast resorts. Waimea, also known as Kamuela, is a thriving upcountry community, a haven for yuppies, techies, and retirees who know a good place when they see it. In Hawi, North Kohala, expect bakeries, neighborhood diners, and one tropical-chic restaurant that's worth a special trip. In Hilo in eastern Hawaii, you'll find pockets of trendiness among the precious old Japanese and ethnic restaurants that provide honest, tasty, and affordable meals in unpretentious surroundings.

Warning: Big Island restaurants, especially along the Kona coast, seem to have a chronic shortage of waitstaff. Come prepared for a leisurely meal; sit and enjoy the warm moonlit night, sip a liquid libation, and realize time is relative here.

In the listings below, reservations are not necessary unless otherwise noted.

1 The Kona Coast

IN & AROUND KAILUA-KONA

Note: Hualalai Club Grille, Pahu i'a, and Beach Tree Bar & Grill are located north of Kailua-Kona, 6 miles north of the airport and just south of the Kohala Coast.

VERY EXPENSIVE

Hualalai Grille ✻✻ CONTEMPORARY PACIFIC   This open-air oasis of koa, marble, and island artwork just got better. Chef Alan Wong, who put the CanoeHouse restaurant (p. 79) on the map and was one of the founders of Hawaii Regional Cuisine, has taken the helm at this popular golf club restaurant, which overlooks the course and has an ocean view. Lunch features soups (including Wong's famous chilled red-and-yellow-tomato soup poured in a yin-yang design), sandwiches (like grass-fed Kamuela beef burgers with bacon, cheese, avocado, and salsa), and daily specials (seared peppered ahi over crispy Asian slaw). Dinner entrees include ginger-crusted onaga, steamed moi (raised on property at Hualalai Resort), mac nut–crusted lamb chops, and a host of other mouthwatering offerings. Save room for dessert: chocolate crunch bars, caramel sea salt cheesecake, and other tempting delights. The only thing missing is good service. I have had two kinds of service here—service with an attitude and very bad service.

In the Hualalai Resort, Queen Kaahumanu Hwy., Kaupulehu-Kona. ✆ 808/325-8525. www.hualalairesort.com. Reservations recommended. Main courses $12–$21 lunch, $36–$56 dinner. AE, DC, MC, V. Daily 11:30am–2:30pm and 5:30–9pm; bar menu served 11:30am–9:00pm.

Pahu i'a ✻ CONTEMPORARY PACIFIC CUISINE   You can't find a better oceanfront location on the Big Island (maybe in the entire state)—Pahu i'a sits just feet from the lapping waves. A small bridge of natural logs leads to this enchanting oceanfront dining room, where views on three sides expand on the aquatic theme (*pahu i'a* is Hawaiian for "aquarium," and there's a large one at the entrance). The food features fresh produce and seafood from the island—and even from the resort's own aquaculture ponds, which teem with shrimp and moi (threadfin), a rich Island fish. The day begins with the coast's most elegant breakfast buffet, featuring excellent omelets, meats, fresh fruit, and regional specialties. At dinner, part of the menu changes daily and always includes several fresh seafood preparations; the Pahu i'a bento box, a tasting of the specials of the day; crispy skin opakapaka meunière; mac nut–crusted lamb rack; veal Oscar; dry-aged prime New York steak; and Hawaiian whole lobster thermidor. From ambience to execution to presentation, Pahu i'a is top-drawer.

In the Four Seasons Resort Hualalai, Queen Kaahumanu Hwy., Kaupulehu-Kona. ✆ 808/325-8000. Reservations recommended. Breakfast buffet $28; dinner main courses $30–$60. AE, DC, DISC, MC, V. Daily 6:30–11:30am (buffet 7–11:30am); dinner 5:30–9:30pm.

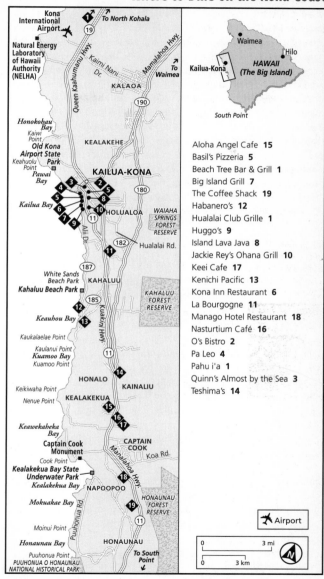

Kona International Airport

Natural Energy Laboratory of Hawaii Authority (NELHA)

Kaimi Nani Dr.

Queen Kaahumanu Hwy.

Mamalahoa Hwy.

To North Kohala

19

To Waimea

KALAOA

190

Waimea

Hilo

Kailua-Kona

HAWAII (The Big Island)

South Point

Honokohau Bay

Kaiwi Point

Old Kona Airport State Park

Keahuolu Point

Pawai Bay

KEALAKEHE

KAILUA-KONA

180

Kailua Bay

HOLUALOA

WAIAHA SPRINGS FOREST RESERVE

Alii Dr.

182

Hualalai Rd.

187

White Sands Beach Park

Kahaluu Beach Park

KAHALUU

185

Keauhou Bay

KAHALUU FOREST RESERVE

Kuakini Hwy.

Kaukalaelae Point

Kaulanui Point

Kuamoo Bay

Kuamoo Point

11

Keikiwaha Point

Nenue Point

HONALO

KEALAKEKUA

KAINALIU

Keawekaheka Bay

Captain Cook Monument

Cook Point

Kealakekua Bay State Underwater Park

Kealakekua Bay

CAPTAIN COOK

Koa Rd.

Mamalahoa Hwy.

NAPOOPOO

Mokuakae Bay

HONAUNAU FOREST RESERVE

Puuhonua Rd.

Moinui Point

11

Honaunau Bay

Puuhonua Point

PUUHONUA O HONAUNAU NATIONAL HISTORICAL PARK

HONAUNAU

To South Point

Aloha Angel Cafe **15**
Basil's Pizzeria **5**
Beach Tree Bar & Grill **1**
Big Island Grill **7**
The Coffee Shack **19**
Habanero's **12**
Hualalai Club Grille **1**
Huggo's **9**
Island Lava Java **8**
Jackie Rey's Ohana Grill **10**
Keei Cafe **17**
Kenichi Pacific **13**
Kona Inn Restaurant **6**
La Bourgogne **11**
Manago Hotel Restaurant **18**
Nasturtium Café **16**
O's Bistro **2**
Pa Leo **4**
Pahu i'a **1**
Quinn's Almost by the Sea **3**
Teshima's **14**

✈ Airport

0   3 mi
0   3 km

EXPENSIVE

Beach Tree Bar & Grill ☆ CASUAL GOURMET   Here's an
example of outstanding cuisine in a perfect setting, without being
fancy, fussy, or prohibitively expensive. The bar on the sand is a sunset paradise, and the sandwiches, seafood, and grilled items at the
casual outdoor restaurant (a few feet from the bar) are in a class of
their own—simple, excellent, and imaginatively prepared. The
menu, which varies, includes items like grilled fresh fish sandwiches,
steaks, alternative healthy cuisine, and vegetarian specialties. On
Saturday the "Surf, Sand and Stars" feast offers an array of buffet-
style items from fresh fish to grilled New York sirloin, and on
Wednesday there's a special "Viva Italia" menu. An added attraction
is entertainment from 5 to 8pm nightly.

In the Four Seasons Resort Hualalai, Queen Kaahumanu Hwy., Kaupulehu-Kona.
ⓒ 808/325-8000. Reservations recommended for Sat-night buffet. Lunch main
courses $17–$22; dinner main courses $42–$47; Sat buffet: "Surf, Sand and Stars"
$78 adults, $37 kids 5–12; Wed "Viva Italia" menu entrees $17–$35. AE, DC, DISC,
MC, V. Daily 11:30am–8:30pm.

Huggo's ☆ PACIFIC RIM/SEAFOOD   The main Huggo's dining room still hums with diners murmuring dreamily about the
view, but it's the thatched-bar fantasy that's *really* on the rocks.
Huggo's on the Rocks ☆, a mound of thatch, rock, and grassy-
sandy ground right next to Huggo's, is a sunset-lover's nirvana. At
sundown it's packed with people sipping mai tais and noshing on
salads, poke, sandwiches, plate lunches, sashimi, and fish and chips.
For lunch the new menu ranges from a spicy grilled mahi taco plate
to a huge burger with barbecue sauce. From 6:30 to 11am, this same
location turns into the **Java on the Rocks** ☆☆ espresso bar, which
is *not* to be missed—sip Kona coffee, enjoy your eggs, and watch the
waves roll onto the shore.

   At the senior Huggo's, fresh seafood remains the signature, as
does the coral-strewn beach with tide pools just beyond the
wooden deck. The tables are so close to the water you can see the
entire curve of Kailua Bay. Feast on sautéed mahimahi, steamed
clams, seared ahi, or imu-style chicken cooked in ti leaves. At
lunch, specialties include *kalua* chicken quesadillas, brick-oven
pizzas, and sandwiches ranging from hot turkey to prime rib and
fresh fish.

75–5828 Kahakai Rd. ⓒ **808/329-1493.** www.huggos.com. Reservations recommended. Main courses $9–$19 lunch; $21–$49 dinner. AE, DC, DISC, MC, V. Daily
6–11am; 11:30am–2:30pm and 5:30–10pm.

Kona Inn Restaurant ☆ AMERICAN/SEAFOOD This is touristy, but it can be a very pleasant experience, especially if the sun is setting. The wide-ranging menu and fresh seafood in the open-air oceanfront setting remind you why you have come to Kailua-Kona. The large, open room and panoramic view of the Kailua shoreline are the most attractive features, especially for sunset cocktails and appetizers. It's a huge menu—everything from nachos and chicken Caesar salad to sandwiches, pasta, stir-fried dishes, and the highlight: the fresh fish served Cajun style or broiled and basted in lemon butter. Watch for the daily specials on the less expensive Cafe Grill menu (coconut shrimp, stuffed mushrooms, fish and chips, and so on).

In Kona Inn Shopping Village, 75–5744 Alii Dr. © 808/329-4455. Reservations recommended at dinner. Main courses $16–$36; Cafe Grill $7–$13. AE, MC, V. Dinner menu daily 5:30–9pm; Cafe Grill daily 11:30am–9:30pm.

La Bourgogne ☆☆ *(Finds* CLASSIC FRENCH An intimate spot with 10 tables, La Bourgogne serves classic French fare with simple, skillful elegance. Baked brie in puff pastry is a taste treat, and the fresh Maine lobster salad, served on a bed of greens with mango slices and a passion-fruit vinaigrette, is a master stroke. Other offerings include classic onion soup, fresh catch of the day, *osso buco,* and New Zealand mussels steamed in apple cider, thyme, shallots, and cognac. The roast duck breast with raspberries and pine nuts is exactly the kind of dish that characterizes La Bourgogne—done to perfection, presented attractively, and with an unbeatable match of flavors and textures. Classically trained chef Ron Gallaher expresses his allegiance to *la cuisine Française* down to the last morsel of flourless chocolate cake and lemon tartlette.

Hwy. 11, 3 miles south of Kailua-Kona. © 808/329-6711. Reservations recommended. Main courses $28–$36. AE, DC, DISC, MC, V. Tues–Sat 6–10pm.

MODERATE

Jackie Rey's Ohana Grill ☆☆ *(Finds* ECLECTIC This off-the-beaten-path eatery is hard to categorize: part sports bar, part family restaurant, part music/dancing (salsa, country western), part neighborhood cafe. No matter what you call it, you'll get great food at wallet-pleasing prices. Locals pile in at lunch for burgers, roasted turkey sandwiches, and seared ahi poke. On weekdays, a happy-hour crowd downs a few brews and pupu (appetizers). Starting at 5pm, families with kids in tow show up for the delicious curry-crusted ahi (over organic greens), pork loin with coconut shrimp stuffing, seafood pasta, and beef short ribs (with a ko-chu-jang glaze). Weekends bring music and dancing starting at 8:30pm.

75–5995 Kuakini Hwy., Kailua-Koha. ℂ **808/327-0209.** Reservations recommended for dinner. Lunch entrees $7–$12; dinner entrees $11–$24; pupu menu $5–$12. MC, V. Mon–Fri 11am–9pm; Sat 5–9pm.

Kenichi Pacific ★★★ *Finds* PACIFIC RIM FUSION/SUSHI BAR Hidden in the Keauhou Shopping Center is this gem of a restaurant, decorated in muted tones and understated furnishings, featuring both Pacific Rim fusion cuisine and a sushi bar. The fantastic food and efficient service will leave you smiling. The appetizer menu is so tempting (ginger-marinated squid, blackened tuna, Dungeness crab cakes, fresh lobster summer rolls), you might just want to graze from one dish to the next. Entrees include pan-seared mahimahi with eggplant mousse, hearts of palm, and asparagus in a miso beurre blanc sauce; macadamia-crusted lamb accompanied by taro risotto; ono tataki; lemon grass ahi; and bamboo salmon. If you love duck, don't miss Kenichi's duck confit, which has Chinese five-spice cured duck leg with celeriac purée, ali'i mushrooms, pea tendrils, red-pepper coulis, and balsamic reduction. Leave room for the warm, flourless molten cake with Kona coffee-chip ice cream.

Keauhou Shopping Center, Keauhou. ℂ **808/322-6400.** Reservations recommended for dinner. Entrees $19–$36. AE, DC, DISC, MC, V. Tues–Fri 11:30am–1:30pm; daily 5–9:30pm.

O's Bistro ★ NOODLES/PASTA   Chef Amy Ferguson-Ota's wildly popular gourmet noodle house Oodles of Noodles has been replaced by O's Bistro but offers nearly the same menu, with a staggering assortment of noodles from far-flung cultures and countries. Diners can tuck into udon, cake noodles, saimin, ramen, spaghetti, orzo, somen, and more. Plus there are entrees like fresh local-style steamed fish, Provençal-style fish, Peking duck in fresh plum sauce, and rib-eye steak with mashed potatoes. Breakfast (which starts at 10am) includes hearty egg and fish dishes, a healthful breakfast taco, and French toast with pecans.

In Crossroads Shopping Center, 75–1027 Henry St. ℂ **808/327-6565.** Main courses $12–$16 lunch, $21–$34 dinner. DC, DISC, MC, V. Daily 10am–9pm.

Pa Leo PACIFIC RIM   Pa Leo dishes up very good fresh fish (crusted with taro and drizzled with lehua honey-lime tarter sauce), chicken (in a pineapple ginger-apple sauce), and meats (rack of lamb served with ginger cream). It overlooks the pier and Ahuena Heiau (King Kamehameha's temple). The new owners have painted the second-story restaurant with bold colors and filled it with orchids. The service is friendly, but when the place is busy, it can be slow, so have another liquid libation and enjoy the view. One very pressing problem is there is virtually no parking. Your options are to park in the pay lot at the King Kamehameha Hotel across the street or hope you luck into a spot on the street.

Alii Dr., Kailua-Kona. © **808/329-5550.** Reservations a must. Entrees $12–$32. AE, MC, V. Daily 11:00am–9pm.

INEXPENSIVE

Basil's Pizzeria PIZZA/ITALIAN   Two dining rooms seat 100 in a garlic-infused atmosphere where pizza is king, sauces sizzle, and pasta is cheap. The oceanview restaurant, in a prime location in Kailua-Kona, is redolent with cheeses, garlic, and fresh organic herbs (a big plus). Shrimp pesto and the original barbecue-chicken pizzas are long-standing favorites, as is the artichoke-olive-caper version, a Greek-Italian hybrid. Recently they have expanded the menu to included sandwiches and burgers. Very popular with the 20-something crowd.

75–5707 Alii Dr. © **808/326-7836.** Individual pizzas $9.95–$12; main courses $9–$15. MC, V. Daily 11am–9:30pm.

Big Island Grill (Finds) AMERICAN   One of the best-kept secrets among local residents is the Big Island Grill, where you get huge servings of home cooking at 1970s prices. The place is always packed, from the first cup of coffee at breakfast to the last bite of dessert at night. Chef Bruce Gould has been cooking in Kona for decades and has a loyal following for his localized American cuisine. This is a place to take the family for dinner (excellent fresh salmon, generous salads, and the world's tastiest mashed potatoes) without having to go into debt. *Warning:* You'll likely have to wait (no reservations), and once you finally land a table, service can sometimes be slow. Relax, it's Hawaii and people are not in much of a hurry.

75–5702 Kuakini Hwy. © **808/326-1153.** Reservations not accepted. Main courses $6.25–$20. AE, MC, V. Mon–Sat 6–10am, 11am–9pm.

Habanero's (Value) MEXICAN   There's no leisurely dining at this small eatery, just great, fast Mexican food at budget prices. You order at one counter and pick up at another. Habanero's starts off with huevos rancheros and other egg dishes, such as a chorizo-egg burrito, for breakfast. Lunch and dinner items include burritos (the fish with black bean is my favorite), soft and hard tacos (the veggie is surprisingly tasty and filling), nachos, tostadas, quesadillas, enchiladas, and daily specials (Fri night is shrimp Vallarta). Bring cash.

Keauhou Shopping Center, Keauhou. ℭ **808/324-HOTT.** All items under $7.75. No credit cards. Mon–Sat 9am–9pm.

Island Lava Java (Value) ☆ AMERICAN   Perched directly across the street from the ocean with an unimpaired view of the water activities in Kailua Bay, this inexpensive outdoor coffee shop started as a small espresso joint with a few pastries a few years ago. Eventually they added lunch and then dinner. Today Lava Java is the "in" place to sip espresso drinks, chow down on good food, and enjoy the ocean view. A handful of tables ring the small shop outside, and a few more tiny tables are located inside at this counter service-only restaurant. The breakfast menu features stacks of pancakes and eggs in various preparations, such as in a massive omelet, wrapped in a tortilla, or on an English muffin or bagel. The lunch menu is big on sandwiches, burgers, and salads. Dinners can be small (sandwiches or salads) or big (New York steak with all the trimmings, veggie lasagna, and fresh fish). Be sure to come with a laid-back attitude; service can be slow or forgetful (I once had to reorder a couple of times because the counter person kept getting my order wrong), but the price and the view more than make up for it.

75-5799 Alii Dr., Kailua-Kona. ℭ **808/327-2161.** Breakfast $3.75–$13; lunch $6.25–$15; dinner $6.95–$17. AE, DISC, MC, V. Daily 6am–10pm.

Quinn's Almost by the Sea ☆ STEAK/SEAFOOD   Late-night noshers, take note: This is one of the few places you can grab a bite to eat in Kona after 9pm. Quinn's, located at the northern gateway to town, has a nautical/sports-bar atmosphere and offers casual alfresco dining on a garden lanai, with an air-conditioned, non-smoking area also available. The menu is surf-and-turf basic: burgers, sandwiches, and a limited dinner menu of dependably good fresh fish, filet mignon, and a few shrimp dishes. There are eight burger selections and, when available, fresh ahi or ono sandwiches.

75–5655A Palani Rd. ℭ **808/329-3822.** Main courses $7.95–$24. MC, V. Daily 11am–11pm.

2 South Kona

MODERATE

Aloha Angel Cafe ISLAND CUISINE   The former Aloha Cafe is under new management, but it kept the trademark large servings, heroic burgers and sandwiches, and a home-style menu for vegetarians and carnivores alike. Breakfast and lunch are served on the veranda that wraps around the old Aloha Theatre, with sweeping views down from the coffee fields to the shoreline. Dinner is in the tiny dining room (which, unfortunately, has no view); space is limited, so phone ahead to ensure that you get a table. The cheaper daytime staples include omelets, burritos, tostadas, quesadillas, and home-baked goods (breakfast is served all day). Most of the produce is organic, and fresh-squeezed orange juice and fresh-fruit smoothies are served daily. Sandwiches, from turkey to tofu-avocado and a wonderful fresh ahi, are heaped with vegetables on tasty whole-wheat buns. The dinner entrees cover the basics, from fresh catch to grilled New York steak and Cajun chicken with tropical salsa.

Hwy. 11, Kainaliu. (C) **808/322-3383**. Reservations recommended for dinner. Breakfast $6.95–$9.95; dinner main courses $13–$22. AE, MC, V. Thurs–Mon 7:30am–8pm, Tues–Wed 7:30am–2:30pm.

Keei Cafe *Overrated*   MEDITERRANEAN/LATINO/ISLAND When this bistro cafe opened in a former fish market in Keei, it was fabulous in every respect—delicious food at frugal prices, friendly service, and quirky decor. The restaurant became so popular it moved a few years ago to a new location with hardwood floors, first-class artwork, and a view of the coast. It got really big really fast and didn't seem to keep up with the rapid growth. The first thing that went was seating people on time. On my last visit, I waited more than an hour for a 7:30pm reservation (the staff was unapologetic). Then the food, once the draw, was no longer dependably good. I'm including the restaurant in this guide because it's so popular, but I can no longer recommend it—not only because of the not-up-to-par food and the slow service, but more because of the cavalier atti-tude: The owners are making money (right now) and don't really care how they treat their clientele.

By the 113 mile marker on Hwy. 11, in Kalakekua. (C) **808/322-9992**. Main courses $9–$12 lunch, $14–$23 dinner. No credit cards. Tues–Sat 10:30am–2:00pm and 5:15–9pm.

INEXPENSIVE

The Coffee Shack 🎋🎋 *Kids*   COFFEEHOUSE/DELI   Great food, crisp air, and a sweeping ocean view make The Coffee Shack one of South Kona's great finds. It's an informal place with counter service, pool chairs, and white trellises on the deck, which is framed by ferns, palms, and banana and avocado trees. The fare is equally inviting: French toast made with homemade poi bread, lemon bars and carrot cake, and eggs Benedict with a delectable hollandaise. At

Kona Coffee Craze!

Coffeehouses are booming on the Big Island—this is, after all, the home of Kona coffee, with dozens of vendors who want to compete for your loyalty and dollars.

Most of the farms are concentrated in the North and South Kona districts, where coffee remains a viable industry. Notable among them is the **Kona Blue Sky Coffee Company,** in Holualoa (© **877/322-1700** or 808/322-1700; www.konabluesky coffee.com), which handles its own beans exclusively. The Christian Twigg-Smith family and staff grow, handpick, sundry, roast, grind, and sell their coffee on a 400-acre estate. You can buy coffee on the farm itself and see the operation from field to final product. You can also find Blue Sky at the Waikoloa Beach Marriott Resort and at KTA in Kailua-Kona and Keauhou, open Wednesday through Sunday.

Also in Holualoa, 10 minutes above Kailua-Kona, **Holualoa Kona Coffee Company** (© **800/334-0348** or 808/ 322-9937; www.konalea.com) purveys organic Kona from its own farm and other growers. Not only can you buy premium, unadulterated Kona coffee here, but you can also witness the hulling, sorting, roasting, and packaging of beans on a farm tour Monday through Friday from 8am to 3pm. Also in this upcountry village, the **Holuakoa Cafe,** Highway 180 (© **808/322-2233**), is famous for high-octane espresso, ground from fresh-roasted Kona Blue Sky beans.

lunch you'll find an assortment of imported beers, excellent sandwiches on home-baked breads, and fresh, hearty salads made with organic lettuces. Let the kids order peanut-butter-and-jelly or grilled-cheese sandwiches while you head for the smoked Alaskan salmon sandwich or the hot, authentic Reuben.

Hwy. 11, 1 mile south of Captain Cook. © **808/328-9555.** Most items less than $8.95; pizzas $9–$13. DISC, MC, V. Daily 7:30am–3pm.

Manago Hotel Restaurant *Value* AMERICAN The dining room of the decades-old Manago Hotel is a local legend, greatly loved for its unpretentious, tasty food at bargain prices. At breakfast, $5 buys you eggs, bacon, papaya, rice, and coffee. At lunch or dinner, you can dine on a 12-ounce T-bone, fried ahi, opelu, or the

Some other coffees to watch for: **Bong Brothers** (© 808/ 328-9289; www.bongbrothers.com) thrives with its coffees, roadside fruit stand, and natural-foods deli that sells smoothies and healthful foods. Aficionados know that **Langenstein Farms** (© 808/328-8356; www.kona-coffee.com/ konastore), a name associated with quality and integrity, distributes excellent Kona coffee and distinctively tasty macadamia nuts in the town of Honaunau. They also have great tours of the farm; just give them a call and they'll set something up. **Rooster Farms,** also in Honaunau (© 808/ 328-9173; www.roosterfarms.com), enjoys an excellent reputation for the quality of its organic coffee beans. The **Bad Ass Coffee Company** (www.badasscoffee.com) has franchises in Kainaliu, Kawaihae, Honokaa, Keauhou, and Kailua-Kona (and even a number of branches on the mainland), all selling its 100% Kona as well as coffees from Molokai, Kauai, and other tropical regions.

A good bet in Hilo is **Bears' Coffee,** 106 Keawe St. (© 808/ 935-0708), the quintessential sidewalk coffeehouse and a Hilo stalwart. Regulars love to start their day here, with coffee and specialties such as souffléed eggs, cooked light and fluffy in the espresso machine and served in a croissant. It's a great lunchtime spot as well, and recently they added a dinner menu.

house specialty, pork chops—the restaurant serves nearly 1,500 pounds monthly. When the akule or opelu are running, count on a rush by the regular customers. This place is nothing fancy, and lots of things are fried, but the local folks would riot if anything were to change after so many years.

In the Manago Hotel, Hwy. 11, Captain Cook. © 808/323-2642. Reservations recommended for dinner. Main courses $8–$14. DISC, MC, V. Tues–Sun 7–9am, 11am–2pm, and 5–7:30pm.

Nasturtium Café 🏵🏵 *(Finds)* HEALTHY GOURMET This once-tiny cafe recently expanded into the space next door and now has plenty of seating. It's a true find for those who love healthy gourmet food with an international flair—and, best of all, it comes at budget prices. Chef Diane Tomac-Campogan cooks up interesting dishes like Moroccan chicken wrap (with range-fed, hormone- and antibiotic-free chicken), a to-die-for fresh fish wrap, a very unusual ostrich burger, and a mean Mexican corn soup. Save room for dessert: ginger macadamia-nut tart (wheat- and dairy-free), fresh ginger spice cake, homemade fruit crisp a la mode, or the very yummy chocolate mousse (which chef Diane claims is cholesterol-free). Takeout is available, so you can take your mouthwatering treats and go to the beach for a picnic.

79–7491-B Mamalahoa Hwy. (Hwy. 11), Kainaliu. ☎ 808/322-5083. Lunch under $15. MC, V. Tues–Fri 11am–4pm; Sat 11am–2:30pm. Live guitar music Wed–Sat.

Teshima's JAPANESE/AMERICAN This is local style all the way. Shizuko Teshima has a strong following among those who have made her miso soup and sukiyaki an integral part of their lives. The early morning crowd starts gathering for omelets or Japanese breakfasts (soup, rice, and fish) while it's still dark outside. As the day progresses, the orders pour in for shrimp tempura and sukiyaki. By dinner, Number 3 teishoku trays—miso soup, sashimi, sukiyaki, shrimp, pickles, and other delights—are streaming out of the kitchen. Other combinations include steak and shrimp tempura, beef teriyaki and shrimp tempura, and the deep-sea trio of shrimp tempura, fried fish, and sashimi.

Hwy. 11, Honalo. ☎ 808/322-9140. Reservations recommended. Complete dinners $19 and under. No credit cards. Daily 6:30am–1:45pm and 5–9pm.

3 The Kohala Coast

Note: You'll find the following restaurants on the "Where to Stay & Dine in North Kohala & Waimea" map on p. 51.

VERY EXPENSIVE

Brown's Beach House 🎊🎊 BIG ISLAND CUISINE The nearby lagoon takes on the pink-orange glow of sunset, while torches flicker between the coconut trees. With white tablecloths, candles, and seating near the lagoon, this is a spectacular setting, complemented by a menu that keeps getting better by the year. The chef de cuisine, David Abrahams, serves up Big Island cuisine with a flare that includes unusual dishes like kiawe-grilled fresh island catch with tomato fondue, quinoa and almond–crusted free-range chicken paillarde, Big Island swordfish poached in seasoned olive oil, sizzling ahi tataki with local exotic mushrooms, and crab-crusted sautéed opakapaka. Next door is **Brown's Deli,** with freshly made breads, pastries, and espresso coffees for breakfast, and pizza, salads, and sandwiches for lunch and dinner.

At The Fairmont Orchid, Hawaii, 1 N. Kaniku Dr., Mauna Lani Resort. © 808/885-2000. www.fairmont.com/orchid. Reservations recommended for dinner. Lunch main courses $15–$22; dinner main courses $29–$59. AE, DC, DISC, MC, V. Daily 11:30am–2:30pm and 5:30–9:30pm.

CanoeHouse ✹✹ HAWAII REGIONAL

The setting is as gorgeous as ever, but it is not the same restaurant as it was when Alan Wong was the chef and the food coming out of the kitchen was nothing short of extraordinary. However, Wong didn't take the ambience with him, and the legendary sunset views remain, along with a koa canoe hanging from the ceiling in the open-air dining room. *Tip:* Ask for a table outside and go at sunset to get the real flavor of this incredible setting. The menu, which changes seasonally, includes great fish items (Shanghai lobster, sautéed moi, steamed opakapaka), meats (honey-roasted rack of lamb, grilled beef tenderloin, and braised short rib of beef), and even vegetarian items (spice-lacquered tofu). Save room for dessert!

At Mauna Lani Bay Hotel and Bungalows, 68–1400 Mauna Lani Dr. © 808/881-7911. Reservations recommended. Main courses $29–$45. AE, DC, DISC, MC, V. Summer daily 6–9pm; winter daily 5:30–9pm.

Coast Grille ✹✹ STEAK/SEAFOOD/HAWAII REGIONAL

It's a 3-minute walk from the main lobby to the open-air Grille, but the view along the way is nothing to complain about and will help you work up an appetite. The split-level dining room has banquettes and wicker furniture, open-air seating, and an oyster bar that is famous. The extensive seafood selection includes poke, clams, and fresh oysters from all over the world, as well as fresh seafood from island waters, served in multicultural preparations.

In the Hapuna Beach Prince Hotel, 62–100 Kaunaoa Dr. © 808/880-1111. www.hapunabeachprincehotel.com. Reservations recommended. Main courses $28–$55. AE, DISC, MC, V. Daily 6–9:30pm.

EXPENSIVE

Norio's Sushi Bar & Restaurant ✹ JAPANESE This new upscale sushi bar and restaurant at The Fairmont Orchid features master sushi chef Norio Yamamoto, who trained in Tokyo and most recently worked at the sushi bar at the Ritz-Carlton Kapalua on Maui. His menu reflects a reverence for traditional Japanese delicacies like sushi and tempura dishes, plus a few signature items like *kushi katsu* (a panko-fried pork loin and onion skewer served with sesame katsu sauces), or *sukiyaki* (thinly sliced beef and vegetables).

Also on the menu are a selection of sakes, Japanese beers, and green teas. Sushi lovers can sit at the newly expanded 15-seat sushi bar to watch the master and his team of three at work.

Fairmont Orchid, Mauna Lani Resort, Kohala Coast, Mauna Lani Resort. ℭ **808/ 885-2000.** www.fairmont.com/orchid. Reservations recommended. Entrees $32–$50. AE, DC, DISC, MC, V. Daily 6–9:30pm.

Roy's Waikoloa Bar & Grill 𝄞𝄞𝄞 PACIFIC RIM/EURO-ASIAN Don't let the strip mall location fool you—Roy's Waikoloa has several distinctive and inviting features, such as a golf-course view, large windows overlooking a 10-acre lake, and the East-West cuisine and upbeat service that are Roy Yamaguchi signatures. This is a clone of his Oahu restaurant, offering favorites like Szechuan baby back ribs, blackened island ahi, hibachi-style salmon, and six other types of fresh fish prepared charred, steamed, or seared, and topped with exotic sauces such as shiitake miso and gingered lime-chile butter. Yamaguchi's tireless exploration of local ingredients and world traditions produces food that keeps him at Hawaii's culinary cutting edge. **Be warned:** Roy's is always packed (make reservations) and always noisy, but the food is always great and the service is excellent.

Kings' Shops, Waikoloa Beach Resort, 250 Waikoloa Beach Dr. ℭ **808/886-4321.** www.roysrestaurant.com. Reservations recommended. Main courses $26–$33 dinner. AE, DC, DISC, MC, V. Daily 5–9:30pm.

MODERATE

Cafe Pesto 𝄞𝄞 MEDITERRANEAN/ITALIAN Fans drive miles for the gourmet pizzas, calzones, and fresh organic greens grown from Kealakekua to Kamuela. The herb-infused Italian pies are adorned with lobster from the aquaculture farms on Keahole Point, shiitake mushrooms from a few miles mauka (inland), and fresh fish, shrimp, and crab. Honey-miso crab cakes, Santa Fe chicken pasta, and sweet roasted peppers are other favorites.

In Kawaihae Shopping Center, at Kawaihae Harbor, Pule Hwy. and Kawaihae Rd. ℭ **808/882-1071.** Main courses $8.95–$20 lunch, $15–$32 dinner. AE, DC, DISC, MC, V. Sun–Thurs 11am–9pm; Fri–Sat 11am–10pm.

Merriman's Market Cafe 𝄞 MEDITERRANEAN/DELI Peter Merriman, who has long reigned as king of Hawaii Regional Cuisine with Merriman's restaurant in Waimea (p. 82), has opened this tiny "market cafe" featuring cuisines of the Mediterranean made with fresh local produce, house-made sausages, artisan-style breads, and great cheese and wines. This is a fun place for lunch or a light dinner. The 3,000-square-foot restaurant and deli features full-service indoor and outdoor dining in a casual atmosphere and a gourmet deli with daily specials. Lunch ranges from salads to sandwiches. Dinner has small plate dishes, pizzas, and entrees from grilled fish to large salads.

Kings' Shops, Waikoloa Beach Resort, 250 Waikoloa Beach Dr., Waikoloa. © **808/ 886-1700.** Main courses $9.95–$16 lunch, $14–$29 dinner. AE, MC, V. Daily 11am–9:30pm.

4 North Kohala

Note: You'll find the following restaurants on the "Where to Stay & Dine in North Kohala & Waimea" map on p. 51.

Bamboo *★★* *Finds* PACIFIC RIM   Serving fresh fish and Asian specialties in a historic building, Hawaii's self-professed "tropical saloon" is a major attraction on the island's northern coastline. The exotic interior is a nod to nostalgia, with high wicker chairs from Waikiki's historic Moana Hotel, works by local artists, and old Matson liner menus accenting the bamboo-lined walls. The fare, island favorites in sophisticated presentations, is a match for all this style: imu-smoked pork quesadillas, fish prepared several ways, sesame nori-crusted or tequila-lime shrimp, and selections of pork, beef, and chicken. There are even some local faves, such as teriyaki chicken and fried noodles served vegetarian, with chicken, or with shrimp. Produce from nearby gardens and fish fresh off the chef's own hook are among the highlights. Hawaiian music wafts through Bamboo from 6:30pm to closing on weekends.

Hwy. 270, Hawi. © **808/889-5555.** Reservations recommended. Main courses $7.95–$18 lunch, $13–$38 dinner (full- and half-size portions available at dinner). MC, V. Tues–Sat 11:30am–2:30pm and 6–8:30pm; Sun 11:30am–2:30pm (brunch).

Kohala Rainbow Cafe *Value* GOURMET DELI   This place is known for its healthful fare and made-with-care wraps. It serves fresh soups, giant salads, and homemade sandwiches and burgers, but the wraps are most popular—herb-garlic flatbread filled with local organic baby greens and vine-ripened organic tomatoes, cheese, and various fillings. The Kamehameha Wrap features *kalua* pork, two different cheeses, and a Maui onion dressing. My favorite is the Mexican veggie wrap: greens, tomatoes, avocado, roasted peppers, cheese, and refried beans. There are a few seats outdoors next to a striking mural.

Hwy. 270, Kapaau, in front of the King Kamehameha Statue. © **808/889-0099.** Main courses under $10. MC, V. Mon–Fri 11am–5pm.

Tropical Dreams of Ice Cream

Tropical Dreams ice creams have spread out over the island but got their start in North Kohala. Across the street from Bamboo, **Kohala Coffee Mill and Tropical Dreams Ice Cream,** Highway 270, Hawi (© **808/889-5577**), serves upscale ice creams along with sandwiches, pastries, and a selection of Island coffees. The Tahitian vanilla and litchi ice creams are local legends, but I also love the macadamia-nut torte and *lilikoi* bars, made by a local pastry chef. Jams, jellies, herb vinegars, Hawaiian honey, herbal salts, and macadamia-nut oils are among the gift items for sale. It's open Monday to Friday from 6am to 6pm, and Saturday and Sunday from 7am to 5:30pm.

5 Waimea

Note: You'll find the following restaurants on the "Where to Stay & Dine in North Kohala & Waimea" map on p. 51.

EXPENSIVE

Daniel Thiebaut Restaurant 🌟🌟 FRENCH-ASIAN   This restaurant features Big Island products (Kamuela Pride beef, Kahua Ranch lettuces, Hirabara Farms field greens, herbs and greens from Adaptations in South Kona) as interpreted by the French-trained Thiebaut, formerly executive chef at Mauna Kea Beach Resort. Highlights include a Hunan-style rack of lamb, wok-fried scallops, vegetarian specials (such as crispy avocado spring rolls with a smoked tomato coulis), and fresh fish. The recently remodeled restaurant is full of intimate enclaves and has a gaily lit plantation-style veranda. In recent years, unfortunately, the quality of this once-sterling restaurant has varied wildly. If Chef Daniel is in, you will most likely get an excellent meal, but if he is not cooking that night, service may suffer. My other complaint is the alarming rise in prices and simultaneous decrease in the amount of food on your plate.

65–1259 Kawaihae Rd. (the Historic Yellow Building). © **808/887-2200.** www.danielthiebaut.com. Reservations recommended. Entrees $25–$50. AE, DISC, MC, V. Daily 3:30–9pm; Sun brunch 10am–1:30pm.

Merriman's 🌟🌟 HAWAII REGIONAL   Merriman's is peerless. Although founder/owner/chef Peter Merriman now commutes between the Big Island and Maui, where he runs the Hula Grill, he manages to maintain the sizzle that has made Merriman's a premier

Hawaii attraction. Order anything from Chinese short ribs to a goat-cheese-and-eggplant sandwich for lunch; at dinner, choose from the signature wok-charred ahi, kung pao shrimp, lamb from nearby Kahua Ranch, and a noteworthy vegetarian selection. Among my many favorites are the Caesar salad with sashimi, Pahoa corn and shrimp fritters, and the sautéed, sesame-crusted fresh catch with spicy *lilikoi* sauce. *Kalua* pig quesadillas and the famous platters of seafood and meats are among the many reasons this is still the best, and busiest, dining spot in Waimea.

In Opelu Plaza, Hwy. 19. ℂ **808/885-6822.** Reservations recommended. Main courses $12–$24 lunch, $23–$45 dinner (market price for ranch lamb or ahi). AE, MC, V. Mon–Fri 11:30am–1:30pm; daily 5:30–9pm.

INEXPENSIVE

Tako Taco Taqueria HEALTHY MEXICAN   Once a tiny "hole in the wall" with the most delicious (and healthy) Mexican food, Tako Taco recently moved to the other side of Waimea into bigger quarters and added margaritas, beer, and wine to the menu. Alas, the food is not what it once was. There's plenty of room to eat there, or you can take out. Most items fall between $6.50 and $12. The fresh fish burrito (with beans, rice, cheese, guacamole, sour cream, slaw, and salsa) is a hot deal at $8.50. There are plenty of vegetarian selections. If the Mexican wedding cookies or chocolate chip cookies are available, grab one (they're huge and only $1 each).

64–1066 Mamalahoa Hwy., Waimea. ℂ **808/887-1717.** All items $14 and under. AE, MC, V. Mon–Sat 11am–9pm, Sun noon–9pm.

6 The Hamakua Coast

Cafe Il Mondo ⊕ PIZZA/ESPRESSO BAR   A tiny cafe with a big spirit has taken over the Andrade Building in the heart of Honokaa. Tropical watercolors and local art, the irresistible aromas of garlic sauces and pizzas, and a 1924 koa bar meld gracefully in Sergio and Dena Ramirez's tribute to the Old World. A classical and flamenco guitarist, Sergio occasionally plays solo guitar in his restaurant while contented diners tuck into the stone oven–baked pizzas. Try the Sergio pizza—pesto with marinated artichokes and mushrooms—or one of the calzones. Sandwiches come cradled in fresh French, onion, or rosemary buns. There's fresh soup daily, roasted chicken, and other specials; all greens are fresh, local, and organic.

Mamane St., Honokaa. ℂ **808/775-7711.** Pizzas $10–$19; sandwiches $6.50; pasta $12. No credit cards. Tues–Sat 10am–8pm.

Jolene's Kau Kau Korner AMERICAN/LOCAL   This place is nothing fancy, but it's homey and friendly, with eight tables and windows overlooking a scene much like an Old Western town but for the cars. Choose from saimin, stir-fried tempeh with vegetables, sandwiches (including a good vegetarian tempeh burger), plate lunches (mahimahi, fried chicken, shrimp, beef stew), and familiar selections of local food.

At Mamane St. and Lehua, Honokaa. (℗ **808/775-9498.** Plate lunches $7–$9.50; dinner main courses $8.95–$19. No credit cards. Mon, Wed, and Fri 10am–8pm; Tues and Thurs 10am–3pm.

Simply Natural 𝒦 (𝑉𝑎𝑙𝑢𝑒) HEALTH FOOD/SANDWICH SHOP Simply Natural is a superb find on Honokaa's main street. I love this charming deli with its friendly staff, wholesome food, and vintage interior. It offers a counter and a few small tables with bright table-cloths and fresh anthuriums. Don't be fooled by the unpretentious-ness of the place; I had the best smoked-chicken sandwich I've ever tasted here. The owner's mother proudly displayed the gloriously plump whole chicken, smoked by her neighbor in Honokaa, before slicing and serving it on freshly baked onion bread from the Big Island Bakery. The wholesome menu features flavorful items such as sautéed mushroom-onion sandwich (on squaw, onion, or rosemary bread), tempeh burgers, and breakfast delights that include taro-banana pancakes. Top it off with premium ice cream by Hilo Homemade (another favorite) or a smoothie. The mango-pineapple-banana-strawberry version is sublime.

Mamane St., Honokaa. (℗ **808/775-0119.** Deli items $3.50–$7.95. No credit cards. Mon–Sat 8am–3:30pm.

Tex Drive In & Restaurant AMERICAN/LOCAL ETHNIC When Ada Lamme bought the old Tex Drive In, she made signifi-cant changes, such as improving upon an ages-old recipe for Por-tuguese *malassadas,* a cakelike doughnut without a hole. Tex sells tens of thousands of these sugar-rolled morsels a month, including ones filled with pineapple/papaya preserves, pepper jelly, or Bavar-ian cream. The menu has a local flavor and features ethnic special-ties: Korean chicken, teriyaki meat, *kalua* pork with cabbage, and Filipino specials. New on the menu are Tex wraps, served with homemade sweet-potato chips. With its gift shop and visitor center, Tex is a roadside attraction and a local hangout; residents have been gathering here for decades over early morning coffee and breakfast.

Hwy. 19, Honokaa. (℗ **808/775-0598.** Main courses $7.95–$12. DC, DISC, MC, V. Daily 6:30am–8:30pm.

What's Shakin' ☆ *(Finds)* HEALTH FOOD   Look for the cheerful, plantation-style, wooden house in yellow and white with a green roof, 2 miles north of the Hawaii Tropical Botanical Garden. Many of the bananas and papayas from Patsy and Tim Withers's 20-acre farm end up here, in fresh-fruit smoothies like the Papaya Paradise, an ambrosial blend of pineapples, coconuts, papayas, and bananas. If you're in the mood for something more substantial, try the blue-corn tamale with homemade salsa, the teriyaki-ginger tempeh burger, or one of the wraps. There are several lunch specials daily, and every plate arrives with fresh fruit and a green salad topped with Patsy's Oriental sesame dressing. You can sit outdoors in the garden and enjoy the staggering ocean view.

27–999 Old Mamalahoa Hwy. (on the 4-mile scenic drive), Pepeekeo. ℂ **808/964-3080.** Most items less than $8.50; smoothies all $5.75. MC, V. Daily 10am–5pm.

7 Hilo

Note: You'll find the following restaurants on the "Hilo" map on p. 59.

EXPENSIVE

Harrington's ☆ SEAFOOD/STEAK   This is arguably the prettiest location in Hilo, on a clear rocky pool teeming with koi (carp) at Reeds Bay, close to the waterfront but not on it. The house specialty, thinly sliced Slavic steak swimming in butter and garlic, is part of the old-fashioned steak-and-seafood formula that makes the Harrington's experience a predictable one. But the Caesar salad is zesty and noteworthy, and for those oblivious to calories, the escargots—baked en casserole on a bed of spinach and topped with lightly browned cheeses—are a rewarding choice. The meunière-style fresh catch, sautéed in white wine and topped with a lightly browned lemon-butter sauce, is also popular. The strongest feature of Harrington's is the tranquil beauty of Reeds Pond (also known as Ice Pond), one of Hilo's visual wonders. The open-air restaurant perches on the pond's shores, creating a sublime ambience.

135 Kalanianaole Ave. ℂ **808/961-4966.** Reservations recommended. Lunch main courses $9.95–$16; dinner main courses $17 to market price. MC, V. Mon–Fri 11am–2pm; Mon–Sun 5:30–9pm.

Pescatore ☆ SOUTHERN ITALIAN   In a town of ethnic eateries and casual mom-and-pop diners, this is a special-occasion restaurant, dressier and pricier than most Hilo choices. It's ornate, especially for Hilo, with gilded frames on antique paintings, chairs

Moments   **A Lunch for All Five Senses**

Hidden in the tall eucalyptus trees outside of the old plantation community of Paauilo lies the **Hawaiian Vanilla Company,** on Paauilo Mauka Road, (© **808/776-1771; www.hawaiivanilla.com).** Located next to a gulch, surrounded by wild coffee, guava, loquats, and avocado trees, the company hosts one of the truly sensuous experiences on the Big Island—a multicourse Vanilla Luncheon. Before you even enter the huge Vanilla Gallery and Kitchen, you will be embraced by the heavenly sent of vanilla. You'll see vanilla orchid vines, and if you're truly lucky, you may see the elusive blossoms. One of the real treats is listening to owner Jim Reddekopp's presentation (and video) on how vanilla is grown, how it's used in the meal you will be eating, and just about everything else you ever wanted to know about this magical orchid and bean. The four-course, 2-hour lunch is $39 and worth every penny. The lunch is usually offered Wednesday and Thursday, and also sometimes on Tuesday and Friday; reservations are required. Other activities at the Hawaiian Vanilla Company are formal tea service, vanilla tastings, brunch, or just wandering through the mill. Myriad vanilla products, from beans to extracts, teas to lotions, are for sale.

of vintage velvet, koa walls, and a tile floor. The fresh catch is offered in several preparations, including reduced-cream and Parmesan or capers and wine. The paper-thin ahi carpaccio is garnished with capers, red onion, garlic, lemon, olive oil, and shaved Parmesan—and it's superb. Chicken, veal, and fish Marsala; a rich and garlicky scampi Alfredo; and the *fra diavolo* (a spicy seafood marinara) are among the dinner offerings, which come with soup or salad. Lighter fare, such as simple pasta marinara and chicken Parmesan, prevails at lunch. Breakfast is terrific, too.

235 Keawe St. © **808/969-9090.** Reservations recommended for dinner. Breakfast $5–$8; lunch main courses $5–$12; dinner main courses $16–$29. AE, DC, DISC, MC, V. Mon–Fri 8:30am–2pm and 5–9pm; Sat–Sun 7:30am–2pm and 5–9pm.

Restaurant Kaikodo 𝕬𝕬 ECLECTIC Hilo's most elegant restaurant is housed in a 100-year-old Toyama Building (listed on the National Register of Historic Buildings) that was transformed by owners Howard and Mary Ann Rogers into a light-filled space with such historic details as a 19-foot mahogany bar from England and 100-year-old cut-glass doors from China. Chef Shae Catrett's menu ranges from meat (filet mignon, spice-crusted rack of lamb or grilled pork chop) to fish (blackened ahi), to vegetarian (eggplant stuffed with a medley of vegetables with chile rice cake).

60 Keawe St., Hilo. ℂ 808/961-2558. www.restaurantkaikodo.com. Reservations recommended. Main courses lunch $9.50–$17, dinner $14–$34. AE, MC, V. Mon–Fri 11am–2pm; dinner Sun–Thurs 5:30–9pm, Fri–Sat 5:30–9:30pm.

MODERATE

Hilo Bay Café ⭐⭐ (Finds) PACIFIC RIM *Foodie alert:* In the midst
of a suburban shopping mall is this upscale, elegant eatery. It was created by the people from the Island Naturals Market and Deli, located on the other side of the shopping center. When you enter, the cascade of orchids sitting on the marble bar is the first thing you see. Mellow jazz wafts from speakers, and plush chairs at low tables fill out the room. The creative menu ranges from house-made ravioli (stuffed with artichoke hearts, roasted garlic, and cream cheese) to potato-crusted fresh catch, to grilled pork loin with bordelaise sauce. Lunch features salads (such as seared ahi Caesar), sandwiches (think grilled free-range chicken breast), and entrees (such as flaky-crust vegetarian potpie, slow-cooked pork barbecue ribs, and crispy spanakopita). There's also a terrific wine list and great martinis. Don't miss eating here.

Waiakea Center, 315 Makaala St. ℂ 808/935-4939. Reservations recommended for dinner. Lunch $8–$15; dinner entrees $9–$26. AE, DISC, MC, V. Mon–Sat 11am–9pm; Sun 5–9pm.

Nihon Restaurant & Cultural Center ⭐ (Value) JAPANESE This
restaurant offers a beautiful view of Hilo Bay on one side and the soothing green sprawl of Liliuokalani Gardens on the other. This is a magnificent part of Hilo that's often overlooked because of its distance from the central business district. The menu features steak-and-seafood combination dinners and selections from the sushi bar, including the innovative poke and lomi salmon hand rolls. The "Businessman's Lunch," a terrific deal, comes with sushi, potato salad, soup, vegetables, and two choices from the following: butterfish, shrimp tempura, sashimi, chicken, and other morsels. This isn't inexpensive dining, but the value is sky-high, with a presentation that matches the serenity of the room and its stunning view of the bay.

Overlooking Liliuokalani Gardens and Hilo Bay, 123 Lihiwai St. ℂ 808/969-1133. Reservations recommended. Main courses $9–$20; combination dinner $19. AE, DC, DISC, MC, V. Mon–Sat 11am–1:30pm and 5–8pm.

Ocean Sushi Deli ⚡ *Finds* SUSHI Hilo's nexus of affordable sushi: Local-style specials stretch purist boundaries but are so much fun: lomi salmon, oyster nigiri, opihi nigiri, unagi avocado hand roll, ahi poke roll, and special new rolls that use thin sheets of tofu skins and cooked egg. For traditionalists, there are ample shrimp, salmon, *hamachi,* clam, and other sushi delights—a long menu of them, including handy ready-to-cook sukiyaki and *shabu-shabu* sets.

239 Keawe St. ⓒ **808/961-6625.** Sushi boxes $4.75–$50; sushi family platters $20–$50. MC, V. Mon–Sat 10:30am–2pm and 5–9pm.

Queen's Court Restaurant AMERICAN/BUFFET Many of those with a "not me!" attitude toward buffets have been disarmed by the Hilo Hawaiian's generous and well-rounded offerings at budget-friendly prices. A la carte menu items are offered Monday through Thursday, but it's the Hawaiian, seafood, and Dungeness crab/prime rib buffets throughout the week that draw throngs of local families. Lovers of Hawaiian food also come for the Friday Hawaiian lunch buffet.

In the Hilo Hawaiian Hotel, 71 Banyan Dr. ⓒ **808/935-9361.** Reservations recommended. Fri Hawaiian lunch buffet $16; Mon–Thurs prime rib/crab buffet $27; Fri–Sun seafood buffet $30. AE, DC, DISC, MC, V. Mon–Sat 6:30–9:15am and 11:15am–1:15pm; Sun 6:30–9:15am and 10:30am–1:30pm (brunch); daily 5:30–9pm.

Restaurant Miwa ⚡ JAPANESE Come to the Hilo Shopping Center to discover sensational seafood in a quintessential neighborhood sushi bar. This self-contained slice of Japan is a pleasant surprise in an otherwise unremarkable mall. *Shabu-shabu* (you cook your own ingredients in a heavy pot), tempura, fresh catch, and a full sushi selection are among the offerings. At dinner, you can splurge on the steak and lobster combination without dressing up. The haupia (coconut pudding) cream-cheese pie is a Miwa signature but is not offered daily; blueberry cream cheese is the alternative.

In the Hilo Shopping Center, 1261 Kilauea Ave. ⓒ **808/961-4454.** Reservations recommended. Main courses $9–$37 (most $10–$15). AE, DC, DISC, MC, V. Mon–Sat 11am–2pm and 5–10pm; Sun 5–9pm.

Seaside Restaurant ⚡⚡ STEAK/SEAFOOD This is a casual local favorite—a Hilo signature with a character all its own. The mullet and *aholehole* (a silvery mountain bass) are fished out of the pond shortly before you arrive—you can't get much fresher than that. The restaurant has large windows overlooking the glassy ponds that spawned your dinner. Colin Nakagawa and his family cook the fish in two unadorned styles: fried or steamed in ti leaves with lemon juice and onions. Daily specials include steamed opakapaka, onaga (snapper), steak and lobster, *paniolo*-style prime rib, salmon encrusted with a nori-wasabi sprinkle, New York steak, and shrimp. If you are here on Wednesday through Sunday, they serve very fresh sushi. *Note:* If you want fish from the pond, *you must call ahead.* The outdoor tables are fabulous at dusk when the light reflects on the ponds with an otherworldly glow.

1790 Kalanianaole Ave. (C) **808/935-8825.** Reservations recommended. Main courses $15–$30. AE, DC, MC, V. Tues–Thurs and Sun 5–8:30pm; Fri–Sat 5–9pm.

INEXPENSIVE

Cafe Pesto Hilo Bay 🅐🅐 PIZZA/PACIFIC RIM   Cafe Pesto's Italian brick oven burns many bushels of ohia and kiawe wood to turn out its toothsome pizzas, topped with fresh organic herbs and island-grown produce. The high-ceilinged 1912 room looks out over Hilo's bay. It's difficult to resist the wild mushroom–artichoke pizza or the chipotle and tomato-drenched Southwestern. But go with the Four Seasons, dripping with prosciutto, bell peppers, and mushrooms—it won't disappoint. Some of my other favorites are the Milolii, a crab-shrimp-mushroom sandwich with basil pesto; the chile-grilled shrimp pizza; and the flash-seared poke and spinach salad.

In the S. Hata Building, 308 Kamehameha Ave. (C) **808/969-6640.** Pizzas $8.95–$18. AE, DC, DISC, MC, V. Sun–Thurs 11am–9pm; Fri–Sat 11am–10pm.

Ken's House of Pancakes AMERICAN/LOCAL   The only 24-hour coffee shop on the Big Island, Ken's fulfills basic dining needs simply and efficiently, with a good dose of local color. Lighter servings and a concession toward health-conscious meals and salads have been added to the menu, a clever antidote to the numerous pies available. Omelets, pancakes, French toast made with Portuguese sweet bread, saimin, sandwiches, and soup stream out of the busy kitchen. Other affordable selections include fried chicken, steak, prime rib, and grilled fish. Tuesday is taco night, Wednesday is prime-rib night, Thursday is Hawaiian plate, and Sunday is all-you-can-eat-spaghetti night. Very local, very Hilo.

1730 Kamehameha Ave. (C) **808/935-8711.** Most items less than $8. AE, DC, DISC, MC, V. Daily 24 hr.

Kuhio Grille AMERICAN/HAWAIIAN   The "home of the 1-pound *laulau*" is quite the local hangout, a coffee/saimin shop with a few tables outdoors and a bustling business indoors. Taro and taro leaves from Waipio Valley are featured in the popular Hawaiian plate, but there are other local specialties: saimin, miso-saimin, taro-corned-beef hash, chicken yakitori, burgers, and their famous fried rice. The "Kanak Atak" is a 1-pound lau and includes *kalua* pig, lomi salmon, pickled onions, haupia, rice, and poi, all for $17. Habitués make a beeline for the counter, where breakfast is served all day.

In Prince Kuhio Plaza. ℂ 808/959-2336. Main courses $7–$20. AE, DISC, MC, V. Sun–Thurs 6am–10pm; Fri–Sat 6am–midnight.

Miyo's JAPANESE Often cited by local publications as the island's "best Japanese restaurant," Miyo's offers home-cooked, healthy food (no MSG) served in an open-air room on Wailoa Pond, where curving footpaths and greenery fill the horizon. Sliding shoji doors bordering the dining area are left open so you can take in the view, which includes Mauna Kea on clear days. The sesame chicken (deep-fried and boneless with a spine-tingling sesame sauce) is a bestseller, but the entire menu is appealing. For vegetarians, there are specials such as vegetable tempura, vegetarian *shabu-shabu* (cooked in a chafing dish at your table, then dipped in a special sauce), and noodle and seaweed dishes. Other choices include mouthwatering sashimi, beef teriyaki, fried oysters, tempura, ahi *donburi* (seasoned and steamed in a bowl of rice), sukiyaki, and generous combination dinners. All orders are served with rice, soup, and pickled vegetables. The miso soup is a wonder, and the ahi tempura plate is one of Hilo's best buys. Special diets (low-sodium, sugarless) are cheerfully accommodated.

In Waiakea Villas, 400 Hualani St. ℂ 808/935-2273. Lunch main courses $6–$13, combinations $9–$11; dinner main courses $6–$13, combinations $10–$15. MC, V. Mon–Sat 11am–2pm and 5:30–8:30pm.

Naung Mai 𝒱𝒶𝓁𝓊ℯ THAI This quintessential hole in the wall has gained an extra room, but even with 26 seats, it fills up quickly. In a short time, Naung Mai has gained the respect of Hilo residents for its curries and pad Thai noodles, and its use of fresh local ingredients. The flavors are assertive, the produce comes straight from the Hilo Farmers Market, and the prices are good. The four curries—green, red, yellow, and Mussaman (Thai Muslim)—go with the jasmine, brown, white, and sticky rice. The pad Thai rice noodles, served with tofu and fresh vegetables, come with a choice of chicken, pork, or shrimp, and are sprinkled with fresh peanuts. You can order your curry Thai-spicy (incendiary) or American-spicy (moderately hot), but even mild, the flavors are outstanding. Owner-chef Jirawan Onmai also makes wonderful spring rolls and a Tom Yum spicy soup that is legendary. Lunch specials are a steal. Naung Mai is obscured behind the Garden Exchange, so it may take some seeking out.

86 Kilauea Ave. ⓒ 808/934-7540. Reservations recommended. Main dishes $10–$14. MC, V. Mon–Fri 11am–2pm; Mon–Thurs 5–8:30pm; Fri–Sat 5–9pm.

Nori's Saimin & Snacks ⓡ (Finds) SAIMIN/NOODLE SHOP

Like Naung Mai, Nori's requires some searching out, but it's worth it. Unmarked and not visible from the street, it's located across from the Hilo Lanes bowling alley, down a short driveway into an obscure parking lot. You'll wonder what you're doing here, but stroll into the tiny noodle house with the neon sign of chopsticks and a bowl, grab a plywood booth or Formica table, and prepare to enjoy the best saimin on the island. Saimin comes fried or in a savory homemade broth—the key to its success—with various embellishments, from seaweed to won-ton dumplings. Ramen, soba, udon, and *mundoo* (a Korean noodle soup) are among the 16 varieties of noodle soups. Barbecued chicken or beef sticks are smoky and marvelous. Plate lunches (teriyaki beef, ahi, Korean short ribs) and sandwiches give diners ample choices from morning to late night, but noodles are the star. The "big plate" dinners feature ahi, barbecued beef, fried noodles, kal bi ribs, and salad—not for junior appetites. The desserts at Nori's are also legendary, with its signature haupia and sweet-potato pies flying out the door almost as fast as the famous chocolate mochi cookies and cakes.

688 Kinoole St. ⓒ 808/935-9133. Most items less than $8.50; "big plate" dinner for 2 $19. AE, DC, MC, V. Mon 10:30am–3pm; Tues–Sat 10:30am–3pm and 4pm–midnight; Sun 10:30am–10pm.

Royal Siam Thai Restaurant ⓡ THAI   A popular neighbor-

hood restaurant, the Royal Siam serves consistently good Thai curries in a simple room just off the sidewalk. Fresh herbs and vegetables from the owner's gardens add an extra zip to the platters of noodles, soups, curries, and specialties, which pour out of the kitchen in clouds of spicy fragrance. The Buddha Rama, a wonderful concoction of spinach, chicken, and peanut sauce, is a scene-stealer and a personal favorite. The Thai garlic chicken, in sweet basil with garlic and coconut milk, is equally superb.

70 Mamo St. ⓒ 808/961-6100. Main courses $9–$13. AE, DC, DISC, MC, V. Mon–Sat 11am–2pm and 5–9pm; Sun 5–9pm.

8 Hawaii Volcanoes National Park

Note: You'll find the following restaurants on the "Where to Stay & Dine in the Volcano Area" map on p. 63.

EXPENSIVE

Kiawe Kitchen PIZZA/MEDITERRANEAN   Although it has a somewhat limited menu, this small eatery is a great place to stop for hot soup or fresh salad after viewing the volcano, and, recently, they added a full bar. The pizza is excellent (all fresh ingredients) but pricey; I'd recommend the insalada caprese and a bowl of soup for lunch. Dinners include lamb (both rack and shank), pasta dishes, a vegetarian item, and usually beef. The menu changes daily (whatever they can get fresh that day). There's an interesting beer list (all from Hawaii) and yummy espresso drinks (including Kona coffees). You can eat on the lanai or inside the restaurant.

19–4005 Haunani Rd., Volcano. ✆ 808/967-7711. Main courses lunch $10–$13, dinner $16–$25. MC, V. Daily noon–2:30pm and 5:30–9:30pm.

Kilauea Lodge & Restaurant ✦ CONTINENTAL   Diners travel long distances to escape from the crisp upland air into the warmth of this high-ceilinged lodge. The decor is a cross between chalet-cozy and volcano-rugged; the sofa in front of the 1938 fireplace is especially inviting when a fire is roaring. The European cooking is a fine culinary act. Favorites include the fresh catch, hasenpfeffer, potato-leek soup (all flavor and no cream), and Alsatian soup. All dinners come with soup, a loaf of freshly baked bread, and salad.

Hwy. 11 (Volcano Village exit). ✆ 808/967-7366. Reservations recommended. Main courses $20–$40. AE, MC, V. Daily 5:30–9pm.

INEXPENSIVE

Lava Rock Cafe ✦ ECLECTIC/LOCAL   Volcano Village's newest favorite spot is a cheerful, airy oasis with tables and booths indoors and semi-outdoors, under a clear corrugated-plastic ceiling. The cross-cultural menu includes everything from chow fun to fajitas. The choices include three-egg omelets and pancakes with wonderful house-made *lilikoi* butter, teriyaki beef and chicken, serious desserts (like mango cheesecake), fresh catch, T-bone steak, and steak-and-shrimp combos. The lunchtime winners are the "seismic sandwiches" (which the cafe will pack for hikers), chili, quarter-pound burgers, salads, plate lunches, and "volcanic" heavies such as Southern-fried chicken and grilled meats.

Hwy. 11 (Volcano Village exit, next to Kilauea Kreations). ℰ **808/967-8526.** Main courses $4.50–$9 lunch, $7–$18 dinner. MC, V. Sun 7:30am–4pm; Mon 7:30am–5pm; Tues–Sat 7:30am–9pm.

Thai Thai Restaurant THAI   Volcano's first Thai restaurant adds warming curries to the chill of upcountry life. The menu features spicy curries (five types, rich with coconut milk and spices), satays, coconut-rich soups, noodles and rice, and sweet-and-sour stir-fries of fish, vegetables, beef, cashew chicken, and garlic shrimp. A big hit is the green papaya salad made with tomatoes, crunchy green beans, green onions, and a heap of raw and roasted peanuts—a full symphony of color, aroma, texture, and flavor.

19–4084 Old Volcano Rd. ℰ **808/967-7969.** Main courses $9–$15. AE, DISC, MC, V. Daily 5–9pm.

Volcano Golf & Country Club AMERICAN/LOCAL   One of the first two eateries in the area, this golf-course clubhouse has a reputation as a low-key purveyor of local favorites. The food ranges from okay to good, while the room—looking out over a fairway—is cordial. It's not as clichéd as it sounds, especially when the mists are rolling in and the greens and grays assume an eye-popping intensity; I've even seen nene geese from my table. In the typically cool Volcano air, local favorites such as chicken or fish sandwiches, hamburgers, pastas, saimin, and Hawaiian stew with rice become especially comforting. Also featured are teriyaki beef or chicken, and stir-fry.

Hwy. 11 (at mile marker 30). ℰ **808/967-8228.** Reservations recommended for large groups. Breakfast items under $9; lunch items under $9.75. AE, DC, DISC, MC, V. Mon–Fri 8am–3pm; Sat–Sun 7am–3pm.

9 Naalehu/South Point

Shaka Restaurant *(Kids)* AMERICAN/LOCAL   You can't miss the Shaka sign from the highway. This welcome addition to the Naalehu restaurant scene has white tile floors, long tables, an espresso machine, and a friendly, casual atmosphere. The serviceable menu of plate lunches and American fare will seem like gourmet cuisine after a long drive through the Ka'u desert. The servings are humongous, and the prices are kind to your wallet. Locals come here for the plate lunches, sandwiches (the Shaka burger is very popular), and honey-dipped fried chicken, and for the fresh catch at dinner—grilled, deep-fried, or prepared in a special panko crust with a ginger-mango sauce. Bring the kids; they'll love the pizza.

Hwy. 11. Naalehu. ℰ **808/929-7404.** Main courses $4.50–$8.95 lunch, $4.50–$22 dinner. MC, V. Daily 10am–9pm.

4

Fun On & Off the Beach

This is why you've come to Hawaii—the sun, the sand, and the surf. In this chapter, we'll tell you about the best beaches, from where to soak up the rays to where to plunge beneath the waves for a fish's-eye of the underwater world. We've covered a range of ocean activities on the Big Island, as well as our favorite places and outfitters for these marine adventures. Also in this chapter are things to do on dry land, including the best spots for hiking and camping and the greatest golf courses.

1 Beaches

Too young geologically to have many great beaches, the Big Island instead has a collection of unusual ones: brand-new black-sand beaches, green-sand beaches, salt-and-pepper beaches, and even a rare (for this island) white-sand beach.

THE KONA COAST
KAHALUU BEACH PARK 🌟🌟
This is the most popular beach on the Kona Coast; these reef-protected lagoons attract 1,000 people a day almost year-round. Kahaluu is the best all-around beach on Alii Drive, with coconut trees lining a narrow salt-and-pepper sand shore that gently slopes to turquoise pools. The schools of brilliantly colored tropical fish that weave in and out of the reef make this a great place to snorkel. In summer, it's also an ideal spot for children and beginning snorkelers; the water is so shallow that you can just stand up if you feel uncomfortable. But in winter, there's a rip current when high surf rolls in; look for the lifeguard warnings.

Kahaluu isn't the biggest beach on the island, but it's one of the best equipped, with off-road parking, beach-gear rentals, a covered pavilion, restrooms, barbecue pits, and a food concession. It gets crowded, so come early to stake out a spot.

KEKAHA KAI STATE PARK (KONA COAST STATE PARK) 𝒜

This beach is about 2 miles north of the airport on Queen Kaahumanu Highway; turn left at a sign pointing improbably down a bumpy road. You won't need a four-wheel-drive vehicle to make it down here—just drive slowly and watch out for potholes. At the end you'll find 5 miles of shoreline with a half-dozen long, curving beaches and a big cove on Mahaiula Bay, as well as archaeological and historical sites. The series of well-protected coves is excellent for swimming, and there's great snorkeling and diving offshore; the big winter waves attract surfers.

Facilities include restrooms, picnic tables, and barbecue pits; you'll have to bring your own drinking water. The beach is open daily from 8am to 8pm (the closing is strictly enforced, and there's no overnight camping).

WHITE SANDS BEACH 𝒜

Don't blink as you cruise Alii Drive, or you'll miss White Sands Beach. This small, white-sand pocket beach about 4½ miles south of Kailua-Kona is sometimes called Disappearing Beach because it does just that, especially at high tide or during storms. It vanished completely when Hurricane Iniki hit in 1991, but it's now back in place (at least, it was the last time I looked). On calm days, the water is perfect for swimming and snorkeling. Locals use the elementary waves to teach their children how to surf and boogie-board. In winter the waves swell to expert levels, attracting surfers and spectators. Facilities include restrooms, showers, lifeguards, and a small parking lot.

THE KOHALA COAST
ANAEHOOMALU BAY (A-BAY) 𝒜𝒜

The Big Island makes up for its dearth of beaches with a few spectacular ones, like Anaehoomalu, or A-Bay, as the locals call it. This popular gold-sand beach, fringed by a grove of palms and backed by royal fish ponds still full of mullet, is one of Hawaii's most beautiful. It fronts the Waikoloa Beach Marriott Resort and is enjoyed by guests and locals alike (it's busier in summer but doesn't ever get truly crowded). The beach slopes gently from shallow to deep water; swimming, snorkeling, diving, kayaking, and windsurfing are all excellent here. Equipment rental and snorkeling, scuba, and windsurfing instruction are available at the north end of the beach. At the far edge of the bay, snorkelers and divers can watch endangered green sea turtles line up

Beaches & Outdoor Activities on the Big Island

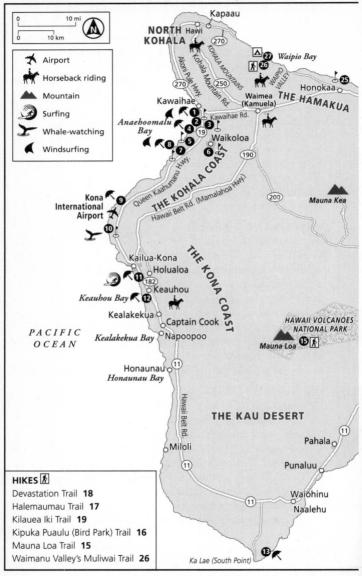

Map legend:

- ✈ Airport
- 🐎 Horseback riding
- ▲ Mountain
- 🏄 Surfing
- 🐋 Whale-watching
- 🏄 Windsurfing

Scale: 0 — 10 mi / 0 — 10 km

Labels on map: Kapaau, NORTH KOHALA, Hawi, Akoni Pule Hwy., Kohala Mountain Rd, Kohala Mountain Rd (250), (270), KOHALA MOUNTAINS, Waipio Bay, WAIPIO VALLEY, 27, 26, 25, Honokaa, THE HAMAKUA, Waimea (Kamuela), Kawaihae, Kawaihae Rd., Anaehoomalu Bay, 1, 2, 3, 4, 5, 6, 7, 8, Waikoloa, (19), (190), THE KOHALA COAST, Queen Kaahumanu Hwy., Hawaii Belt Rd. (Mamalahoa Hwy.), (200), Mauna Kea ▲, Kona International Airport, 9, 10, Kailua-Kona, Holualoa, 11, (182), Keauhou, 12, Keauhou Bay, Kealakekua, Captain Cook, Napoopoo, Kealakekua Bay, THE KONA COAST, HAWAII VOLCANOES NATIONAL PARK, Mauna Loa ▲, 15, Honaunau, Honaunau Bay, (11), PACIFIC OCEAN, Hawaii Belt Rd., THE KAU DESERT, Miloli, Pahala, Punaluu, Waiohinu, Naalehu, 13, Ka Lae (South Point)

HIKES 🏃

- Devastation Trail **18**
- Halemaumau Trail **17**
- Kilauea Iki Trail **19**
- Kipuka Puaulu (Bird Park) Trail **16**
- Mauna Loa Trail **15**
- Waimanu Valley's Muliwai Trail **26**

BEACHES
Anaehoomalu Bay (A-Bay) **8**
Green Sand (Papakolea) Beach **13**
Hapuna Beach **4**
Kahaluu Beach Park **12**
Kaunaoa (Mauna Kea) Beach **1**
Kekaha Kai State Park **9**
Leleiwi Beach Park **23**
White Sands Beach **11**

CABINS & CAMPGROUNDS
Halape Shelter **14**
Kilauea Military Camp **21**
Namakani Paio Campground **16**
Waimanu Valley Campsites **27**

PACIFIC OCEAN

COAST

(19)

○ Laupahoehoe

(220) ○ Honomu

(19)

Hilo Bay

(200) Saddle Rd.

Hilo ○

Stainback Hwy.

Mountain View ○

○ Keaau

(130)

Pahoa

THE PUNA REGION

KAHAUALEA NATURAL AREA RESERVE

(130) (137) (132)

Kilauea Caldera ■ **Volcano**

Chain of Craters Rd.

HAWAII VOLCANOES NATIONAL PARK

24
23
22
21 20 19 16 18 17 14

Hilo International Airport

GOLF COURSES
Hamakua Country Club **25**
Hapuna Golf Course **3**
Hilo Municipal Golf Course **22**
Hualalai Golf Course **10**
Mauna Kea Golf Course **2**
Mauna Lani Frances I'i Brown Championship Courses **5**
Naniloa Country Club **24**
Volcano Golf and Country Club **20**
Waikoloa Beach Course **7**
Waikoloa Kings' Course **7**
Waikoloa Village Golf Club **6**

and wait their turn to have small fish clean them. Facilities include restrooms, showers, picnic tables, and plenty of parking.

HAPUNA BEACH ✿✿✿

Just off Queen Kaahumanu Highway, south of the Hapuna Beach Prince Hotel, lies this crescent of gold sand—big, wide, and ½ mile long. In summer, when the beach is widest, the ocean calmest, and the crowds biggest, this is the island's best beach for swimming, snorkeling, and bodysurfing. But beware of Hapuna in winter, when its thundering waves, strong rip currents, and lack of lifeguards can be dangerous. Facilities include A-frame cabins for camping, pavilions, restrooms, showers, and plenty of parking.

KAUNAOA BEACH (MAUNA KEA BEACH) ✿✿✿

Everyone calls this gold-sand beach Mauna Kea Beach (it's at the foot of Mauna Kea Beach Hotel), but its real name is Hawaiian for "native dodder," a lacy, yellow-orange vine that once thrived on the shore. A coconut grove sweeps around this golden crescent, where the water is calm and protected by two black-lava points. The sandy bottom slopes gently into the bay, which often fills with tropical fish, sea turtles, and manta rays, especially at night, when the hotel lights flood the shore. Swimming is excellent year-round, except in rare winter storms. Snorkelers prefer the rocky points, where fish thrive in the surge. Facilities include restrooms, showers, and ample parking, but there are no lifeguards.

HILO
LELEIWI BEACH PARK ✿

Hilo's beaches may be few, but Leleiwi is one of Hawaii's most beautiful. This unusual cove of palm-fringed black-lava tide pools fed by freshwater springs and rippled by gentle waves is a photographer's delight—and the perfect place to take a plunge. In winter, big waves can splash these ponds, but the shallow pools are generally free of currents and ideal for families with children, especially in the protected inlets at the center of the park. Leleiwi often attracts endangered sea turtles, making this one of Hawaii's most popular snorkeling spots. The beach is 4 miles out of town on Kalanianaole Avenue. Facilities include restrooms, showers, lifeguards, picnic pavilions, and paved walkways. There's also a marine-life exhibit here.

SOUTH POINT
GREEN SAND BEACH (PAPAKOLEA BEACH) ✿

Hawaii's famous green-sand beach is located at the base of Puu o Mahana, an old cinder cone spilling into the sea. The place has its problems: It's difficult to reach; the open bay is often rough; there are no facilities, fresh water, or shade from the relentless sun; and howling winds scour the point. Nevertheless, each year the unusual green sands attract thousands of oglers, who follow a well-worn four-wheel-drive-only road for 2½ miles to the top of a cliff, which you have to climb down to reach the beach. The sand is crushed olivine, a green semiprecious mineral found in eruptive rocks and meteorites. If the surf's up, check out the beach from the cliff's edge; if the water's calm, it's generally safe to swim.

To get to Green Sand Beach from the boat ramp at South Point, follow the four-wheel-drive trail; even if you have a four-wheel-drive vehicle, you may want to walk because the trail is very, very bad in parts. Make sure you have appropriate closed-toed footwear: tennis shoes or hiking boots. The trail is relatively flat, but you're usually walking into the wind as you head toward the beach. The beginning of the trail is lava. After the first 10 to 15 minutes of walking, the lava disappears and the trail begins to cross pastureland. After about 30 to 40 minutes more, you'll see an eroded cinder cone by the water; continue to the edge, and there lie the green sands below.

The best way to reach the beach is to go over the edge from the cinder cone. (It looks like walking around the south side of the cone would be easier, but it's not.) From the cinder cone, go over the overhang of the rock, and you'll see a trail.

Going down to the beach is very difficult and treacherous, as you'll be able to see from the top. You'll have to make it over and around big lava boulders, dropping down 4 to 5 feet from boulder to boulder in certain spots. And don't forget that you'll have to climb back up. Look before you start; if you have any hesitation, don't go down (you get a pretty good view from the top anyway).

Warning: When you get to the beach, watch the waves for about 15 minutes and make sure they don't break over the entire beach. If you walk on the beach, always keep one eye on the ocean and stick close to the rock wall. There can be strong rip currents here, and it's imperative to avoid them. Allow a minimum of 2 to 3 hours for this entire excursion.

2 Watersports

If you want to rent beach toys, like snorkel gear or boogie boards, the beach concessions at all the big resorts, as well as tour desks and dive shops, offer equipment rentals and sometimes lessons for beginners. The cheapest place to get great rental equipment is **Snorkel Bob's,** in the parking lot of Huggo's Restaurant at 75–5831 Kahakai Rd., at Alii Drive, Kailua-Kona (© **808/329-0770**; www.snorkelbob.com).

BOATING

For fishing charters, see "Sportfishing: The Hunt for Granders," later in this chapter.

Body Glove Cruises 🐠🐠   The *Body Glove*, a 55-foot trimaran that carries up to 100 passengers, runs an adventurous sail-snorkel-dive cruise at a reasonable price. You'll be greeted with fresh Kona coffee, fruit, and breakfast pastries; you'll then sail north of Kailua to Pawai Bay, a marine preserve where you can snorkel, scuba-dive, swim, or just hang out on the deck for a couple of hours. After a buffet deli lunch spread, you might want to take the plunge off the boat's waterslide or diving board before heading back to Kailua Pier. The boat departs daily from the pier at 9am and returns at 1:30pm. The only thing you need to bring is a towel; snorkeling equipment (and scuba equipment, if you choose to dive) is provided. *Money-saving tip:* The afternoon trip is cheaper.

Kailua Pier. © **800/551-8911** or 808/326-7122. Morning cruise $112 adults, $72 children 6–12, free for children 5 or under; afternoon cruise $73 adults, $53 children 6–12, free for children 5 or under; additional $59 for certified scuba divers with own equipment ($69 without own equipment) and $79 additional for introductory scuba; whale-watching (Dec–Apr) $73 adults, $53 children 6–12, free for children 5 or under.

Captain Beans' Cruises   Captain Beans' runs Kona's most popular dinner cruise on a 150-foot catamaran, which can accommodate about 290 passengers. The 2-hour cruise includes dinner, cocktails, dancing, and Hawaiian entertainment.

Kailua Pier. © **800/831-5541** or 808/329-2955. www.robertshawaii.com. $61 adults, $34 children ages 4–11.

Captain Dan McSweeney's Year-Round Whale-Watching Adventures 🐠🐠🐠   Hawaii's most impressive visitors—45-foot humpback whales—return to the waters off Kona every winter. Capt. Dan McSweeney, a whale researcher for more than 25 years, works daily with the whales, so he has no problem finding them. Frequently, he drops an underwater microphone into the water so you can listen to their songs, or uses an underwater video camera to show you what's going on. In humpback season—roughly December to April—Dan makes two 3-hour trips daily. From July 1 to December 20, he schedules one morning trip on Tuesday, Thursday, and Saturday to look for pilot, sperm, false killer, melon-headed, pygmy killer, and beaked whales. Captain Dan guarantees a sight-ing, or he'll take you out again for free. No cruises in May and June.

Honokohau Harbor. ℂ **888/WHALE6** or 808/322-0028. www.ilovewhales.com. $70 adults, $60 children under 11.

Captain Zodiac   If you'd prefer to take a **snorkel cruise to Kealakekua Bay** in a small boat, go in Captain Zodiac's 16-passen-ger, 24-foot inflatable rubber life raft. The boat takes you on a wild ride 14 miles down the Kona Coast to Kealakekua, where you'll spend about an hour snorkeling in the bay and then enjoy snacks and beverages at the picnic snorkel site. Trips are twice daily, from 8am to 12:15pm and from 12:45 to 5pm. *Warning:* Pregnant women and those with bad backs should avoid this often-bumpy ride.

Gentry's Marina, Honokohau Harbor. ℂ 808/329-3199. www.captainzodiac.com. $87 adults, $72 children 3–12 (book on the Internet for better rates).

Fair Wind Snorkeling and Diving Adventures 🐠🐠🐠 *Kids*   One of the best ways to snorkel Kealakekua Bay, the marine-life preserve that's one of the best snorkel spots in Hawaii, is on Fair Wind's half-day **sail-and-snorkel cruise to Kealakekua.** Recently the company has added the latest (state-of-the-art) luxury 55-foot foil-assist catama-ran (the first on the Big Island) for an upscale experience that promises a faster and smoother ride on a boat full of luxury. We recommend the *Hula Kai* cruise, a 5-hour morning snorkel and dive cruise that includes a light breakfast, a gourmet barbecue lunch, two snorkeling sites, a guided tour, and optional scuba diving for $149 adults (mini-mum age 8). Hula Kai also has an afternoon snorkeling and sunset bar-becue for $125 (minimum age 8). Fair Wind also has a 60-foot catamaran that holds up to 100 passengers. The morning cruise leaves from Keauhou Bay at 9am and returns at 1:30pm, and includes a light breakfast, lunch, snorkel gear, and lessons; it goes for $115 for adults, $69 for kids 4 to 12 years, and $29 for toddlers. The afternoon snack cruise is a little shorter and a little cheaper: It runs from 2 to 5:30pm and includes snacks, sailing, and snorkeling, at a cost of $75 for adults, $45 for 4–12 year olds, and free for kids 3 and under. During whale season, the *Hula Kai* has a 3-hour whale-watching trip for $69.

78-7130 Kaleiopapa St., Kailua-Kona. ℂ **800/677-9461** or 808/322-2788. www. fair-wind.com. Snorkel cruises $65–$139 adults, $39–$59 children 4–12 (prices vary depending on cruise).

Kamanu Charters 🐠🐠   This sleek catamaran, 36 feet long and 22 feet wide, provides a laid-back sail-snorkel cruise from Honoko-hau Harbor to Pawai Bay. The 3½-hour trip includes a tropical lunch (deli sandwiches, chips, fresh island fruit, and beverages), snorkeling gear, and personalized instruction for first-time snorkelers. The *Kamanu* sails Monday through Saturday (weather permitting) at 9am and 1:30pm; it can hold up to 24 people.

Honokohau Harbor. © **800/348-3091** or 808/329-2021. www.kamanu.com. $75 adults, $45 children under 12.

BODY BOARDING (BOOGIE BOARDING) & BODYSURFING

On the Kona side of the island, the best beaches for body boarding and bodysurfing are **Hapuna Beach, White Sands Beach,** and **Kekaha Kai State Park.** On the east side, try **Leleiwi Beach.**

KAYAKING

OCEAN KAYAKING   Imagine sitting at sea level, eye to eye with a turtle, a dolphin, even a whale—it's possible in an oceangoing kayak. Anyone can kayak in calm waters: Just get in, find your balance, and paddle. After a few minutes of instruction and a little practice in a calm area (like the lagoon in front of the **King Kamehameha's Kona Beach Hotel**), you'll be ready to explore. Beginners can practice their skills in **Kailua** and **Kealakekua bays;** intermediates might try paddling from **Honokohau Harbor** to **Kekaha Kai Beach Park;** the **Hamakua Coast** is a challenge for experienced kayakers.

You can rent one- and two-person kayaks (and other ocean toys) from **Aloha Kayak** ✦✦✦ (© **877/322-1441** or 808/322-2868; www.alohakayak.com) for $20 for a half-day single and $30 double ($25 for a full-day single and $40 for a full-day double). They also have a unique tour from Keauhou Bay and the Captain Cook Monument, with Hawaiian guides showing you sea caves and snorkeling areas full of fish and turtles. The tours are either 4 hours ($65 adults, $33 for children ages 12 and under) or 2½ hours ($50 adults, $25 children ages 12 and under) and include all equipment, beverages, snorkeling gear, and snacks.

PARASAILING

Get a bird's-eye view of Hawaii's pristine waters with **UFO Parasail** (© **800/FLY-4UFO** or 808/325-5836; www.ufoparasail.net). UFO offers parasail rides daily from 8am to 2pm from Kailua Pier. The cost is $56 for the standard flight of 7 minutes of air time at 400 feet, and $65 for a deluxe 10-minute ride at 800 feet. You can go up alone or with a friend; no experience is necessary. *Tip:* Take the early-bird special (when the light is fantastic and the price is right) at 8am for just $51 (for 400 ft.) and $61 (for 800 ft.).

SCUBA DIVING

The Big Island's leeward coast offers some of the best diving in the world; the water is calm, warm, and clear. Want to swim with fast-moving game fish? Try **Ulua Cave** at the north end of the Kohala Coast. There are nearly two dozen dive operators on the west side of the Big Island, plus a couple in Hilo. They offer everything from scuba-certification courses to guided boat dives.

"This is not your mother or father's dive shop," says Jeff Kirschner, of the newly opened **BottomTime,** 74–5590 Luhia St. (© **866/GO-DIVEN** or 808/331-1858; www.bottomtimehawaii.com). "This is a dive shop for today's diver." Kirschner claims that what sets Bottom-Time apart is their willingness to take their 34-foot catamaran (complete with showers, TV, and restrooms) to unusual dive sites, and "not those sites just 2 minutes from the mouth of the harbor." Bottom-Time also offers introductory dives in enriched air (Nitrox) for $170 and two-tank dives for $130.

One of Kona's oldest dive shops, **Jack's Diving Locker,** 75–5819 Alii Dr. (© **800/345-4807** or 808/329-7585; www.jacksdivinglocker. com), has recently purchased another longtime dive shop, Kona Coast Divers, and has combined the two businesses into one. Plus, it has expanded its former 600-square-foot retail store into an 8,000-square-foot dive center with swimming pool (with underwater viewing windows), retail store, classrooms, full-service rentals, and a full-service sports diving and technical diving facility. They offer the classic two-tank dive for $125 and a two-tank manta ray night dive for $145.

HOT-LAVA DIVES   Hilo's **Nautilus Dive Center,** 382 Kamehameha Ave., between Open Market and the Shell Gas Station (© **808/935-6939;** www.nautilusdivehilo.com), offers a very unusual opportunity for advanced divers: diving where the lava flows into the ocean. "Sometimes you can feel the pressure from the sound waves as the lava explodes," owner Bill De Rooy says. "Sometimes you have perfect visibility to the color show of your life." As we went to press, these hot lava dives were on hold (an unstable collapse of a recent lava field sent 20 acres of lava into the ocean; fortunately, no one was injured). Call to see if the dives have resumed ($150–$200 for a two-tank dive).

NIGHT DIVING WITH MANTA RAYS 🐟🐟   A little less risky—but still something you'll never forget—is swimming with manta rays on a night dive. These giant, harmless creatures, with wingspans that reach up to 14 feet, glide gracefully through the water to feed on plankton. **Jack's Diving Locker,** 75–5819 Alii Dr.

(© 800/345-4807 or 808/329-7585; www.jacksdivinglocker.com) offers a "Manta Ray Madness" dive for $145 for a two-tank dive and $95 for snorkelers. Everyone from beginners through experts will love this dive. They do not guarantee that these wild creatures will show up every night, but they do boast a more than 90% sightings record. If they are booked, try **Sandwich Isle Divers,** 75–5729 Alii Dr., in the back of the Kona Market Place (© 888/743-3483 or 808/329-9188; www.sandwichisledivers.com). It offers one-tank nighttime manta dives for $85, including equipment ($75 if you have your own gear), and two tanks for $100 if you have all your gear or $115 if you need to rent gear.

WEEKLONG DIVES   If you're looking for an all-diving vacation, you might think about spending a week on the 80-foot *Kona Aggressor II* (© 800/344-5662 or 808/329-8182; www.aggressor.com), a live-aboard dive boat that promises to provide you with unlimited underwater exploration, including day and night dives, along 85 miles of the Big Island's coastline. You might spot harmless 70-foot whale sharks, plus not-so-harmless tiger and hammerhead sharks, as well as dolphins, whales, monk seals, and sea turtles. Ten divers are accommodated in five staterooms. Guided dives are available, but as long as you're certified, just log in with the dive master and you're free to follow the limits of your dive computer. It's $2,295 for 7 days (without gear), double occupancy, which includes excellent accommodations and all meals. Rental gear, from cameras (starting at $100 a week) to dive gear ($120) to computers ($125), is available.

SNORKELING

If you come to Hawaii and don't snorkel, you'll miss half the fun. The year-round calm waters along the Kona and Kohala coasts are home to spectacular marine life. Some of the best snorkeling areas on the Kona-Kohala coasts include **Hapuna Beach Cove,** at the foot of the Hapuna Beach Prince Hotel, a secluded little cove where you can snorkel with schools of yellow tangs, needlefish, and green sea turtles. But if you've never snorkeled in your life, **Kahaluu Beach Park** is the best place to start. Just wade in and look down at the schools of fish in the bay's black-lava tide pools. Another "hidden" snorkeling spot is off the rocks north of the boat launch ramp at **Honaunau Bay.** Other great snorkel sites include **White Sands Beach, Kekaha Kai State Park,** and **Ho'okena, Honaunau, Puako,** and **Spencer** beach parks.

In addition to **Snorkel Bob's,** mentioned in the intro to this section, you can rent gear from **Kona Coast Divers** ☆, Honokohau Marina, Kailua-Kona (© **808/329-8802;** www.konacoastdivers.com).

SNORKELING CRUISES TO KEALAKEKUA BAY ☆☆☆ Probably the best snorkeling for all levels can be found in **Kealakekua Bay.** The calm waters of this underwater preserve teem with a wealth of marine life. Coral heads, lava tubes, and underwater caves all provide an excellent habitat for Hawaii's vast array of tropical fish, making mile-wide Kealakekua the Big Island's best accessible spot for snorkeling and diving. Without looking very hard, you can see octopuses, free-swimming moray eels, parrotfish, and goat fish; once in a while, a pod of spinner dolphins streaks across the bay. Kealakekua is reachable only by boat; in addition to **Fair Wind** (p. 101) and **Captain Zodiac** (p. 101), check out **Sea Quest Snorkeling and Rafting Adventures** (© **808/329-RAFT;** www.seaquesthawaii.com), which offers unique coastal adventures through sea caves and lava tubes on the Kona Coast, as well as snorkeling plunges into the ocean at the Historic Place of Refuge in Honaunau and at the Captain Cook Monument at Kealakekua. The six-passenger, rigid-hull, inflatable rafts can go where larger boats can't. The 4-hour morning tour is $85 adults and $72 children, while the 3-hour afternoon tour goes for $64 adults and $54 children. During whale season, they have a 3-hour whale-watching cruise for $53 adults and children. They do not allow children under 6 years old, pregnant women, or people with bad backs.

SNUBA

If you're not quite ready to make the commitment to scuba but you want more time underwater than snorkeling allows, **Big Island Snuba Tours** (© **808/326-7446;** www.snubabigisland.com) may be the answer. Just like in scuba, the diver wears a regulator and mask; however, the tank floats on the surface on a raft and is connected to the diver's regulator by a hose that allows the diver to go 20 to 25 feet down. You need only 15 minutes of instruction before you're ready to go. Snuba can actually be easier than snorkeling, as the water is calmer beneath the surface. It costs $79 for a 1½-hour dive from the beach, $125 for one dive from a boat, and $150 for two dives from a boat; children must be at least 8 years old.

SPORTFISHING: THE HUNT FOR GRANDERS ☆☆

If you want to catch fish, it doesn't get any better than the Kona Coast, known internationally as the marlin capital of the world. Big-game fish, including gigantic blue marlin and other Pacific billfish, tuna, mahimahi, sailfish, swordfish, ono (also known as wahoo), and giant trevallies (ulua), roam the waters here. When anglers here catch marlin that weigh 1,000 pounds or more, they call them *granders;* there's even a "wall of fame" on Kailua-Kona's Waterfront Row, honoring 40 anglers who've nailed more than 20 tons of fighting fish.

Nearly 100 charter boats with professional captains and crew offer fishing charters out of **Keauhou, Kawaihae, Honokohau,** and **Kailua Bay harbors.** If you're not an expert angler, the best way to arrange a charter is through a booking agency like the **Charter Desk at Honokohau Marina** (© 888/KONA-4-US or 808/329-5735; www.charterdesk.com) or **Charter Services Hawaii** (© 800/567-2650 or 808/334-1881; www.konazone.com). Either one will sort through the more than 40 different types of vessels, fishing specialties, and personalities to match you with the right boat. Prices range from $590 to $1,200 or so for a full-day exclusive charter (you and up to five of your friends have the entire boat to yourselves), or for $80 you can share a boat with others and rotate your turn at pulling in the big one.

Serious sportfishers should call the boats directly. They include *Anxious* (© 808/326-1229; www.alohazone.com), *Marlin Magic* (© 808/325-7138; www.marlinmagic.com), and *Ihu Nui* (© 808/325-1513; www.charterdesk.com/ihunui.html). If you aren't into hooking a 1,000-pound marlin or 200-pound tuna and just want to go out to catch some smaller fish and have fun, I recommend **Reel Action Light Tackle Sportfishing** ✸✸ (© 808/325-6811; www.charternet.com/flyfish/hawaii.html). Light-tackle anglers and saltwater fly-fishermen should contact *Sea Genie II* ✸✸ (© 808/325-5355; www.seageniesportfishing.com), which has helped several anglers set world records. All of the above outfitters operate out of Honokohau Harbor.

Most big-game charter boats carry six passengers max, and the boats supply all equipment, bait, tackle, and lures. No license is required. Many captains now tag and release marlins; other fish caught belong to the boat (not to you, the charter)—that's Island style. If you want to eat your catch or have your trophy marlin mounted, arrange it with the captain before you go.

SUBMARINE DIVES

This is the stuff movies are made of: venturing 100 feet below the sea in a high-tech, 65-foot submarine. On a 1-hour trip, you'll be able to explore a 25-acre coral reef that's teeming with schools of colorful tropical fish. Look closely and you might catch glimpses of moray eels—or even a shark—in and around the reef. On selected trips, you'll watch as divers swim among these aquatic creatures, luring them to the view ports for face-to-face observation. Call **Atlantis Submarines** *&*, 75–5669 Alii Dr. (across the street from Kailua Pier), Kailua-Kona (*©* **800/548-6262;** www.atlantisadventures.com). Trips leave daily between 10am and 3pm. The cost is $84 for adults and $42 for children under 12, or book on the website for $76 adults and $38 kids. *Note:* The ride is safe for everyone, but skip it if you suffer from claustrophobia.

SURFING

Most surfing off the Big Island is for the experienced only. As a general rule, the beaches on the north and west shores of the island get northern swells in winter, while those on the south and east shores get southern swells in summer. Experienced surfers should check out the waves at **Pine Trees** (north of Kailua-Kona), **Lyman's** (off Alii Dr. in Kailua-Kona), and **Banyan's** (also off Alii Dr.); reliable spots on the east side of the island include **Honolii Point** (outside Hilo), **Hilo Bay Front Park,** and **Keaukaha Beach Park.** But there are a few sites where beginners can catch a wave, too: You might want to try **Kahuluu Beach,** where the waves are manageable most of the year, other surfers are around to give you pointers, and there's a lifeguard on shore.

Ocean Eco Tours (*©* **808/324-SURF;** www.oceanecotours.com), owned and operated by veteran surfers, is one of the few companies on the Big Island that teaches surfing. Private lessons cost $150 per person (including all equipment) and usually last a minimum of 2 hours; 2- to 3-hour group lessons go for $95 (also including all equipment), with a maximum of four students. Both teachers love this ancient Hawaiian sport, and their enthusiasm is contagious. The minimum age is 8, and you must be a fairly good swimmer.

Your only Big Island choice for surfboard rentals is **Pacific Vibrations,** 75–5702 Likana Lane (just off Alii Dr., across from the pier), Kailua-Kona (*©* **808/329-4140;** www.laguerdobros.com/pacvib/ pacificv.html), where they rent short boards for $10 for 24 hours and long boards for $10 to $20.

WINDSURFING

The constant 5- to 25-knot winds blowing toward the beach make **Anaehoomalu Bay (A-Bay),** on the Kohala Coast, one of the best beaches for windsurfing. If you get into trouble, the wind brings you back to shore instead of taking you out to sea. **Ocean Sports,** at the Waikoloa Beach Marriott Resort (© **808/885-5555;** www.hawaiioceansports.com), starts beginners on a land simulator to teach them how to handle the sail and "come about" (turn around and come back). Instruction is $60 an hour; after a half-hour or so of instruction on land, you're ready to hit the water. If you already know how to windsurf, equipment rental is $30 an hour. Advanced windsurfers should head to **Puako** and **Hilo Bay.**

3 Hiking & Camping

For information on camping and hiking, contact **Hawaii Volcanoes National Park,** P.O. Box 52, Hawaii National Park, HI 96718 (© **808/985-6000;** www.nps.gov/havo); **Puuhonua O Honaunau National Historic Park,** Honaunau, HI 96726 (© **808/328-2288;** www.nps.gov/puho); the **State Division of Forestry and Wildlife,** P.O. Box 4849, Hilo, HI 96720 (© **808/947-4221;** www.hawaii. gov); the **State Division of Parks,** P.O. Box 936, Hilo, HI 96721 (© **808/974-6200;** www.hawaii.gov); the **County Department of Parks and Recreation,** 25 Aupuni St., Hilo, HI 96720 (© **808/ 961-8311;** www.hawaii-county.com); or the **Hawaii Sierra Club** (© **808/959-0452;** www.hi.sierraclub.org).

Camping equipment is *not* available for rent on the Big Island. Plan to bring your own or buy it at **Hilo Surplus Store** (© **808/ 935-6398**).

GUIDED DAY HIKES   A guided day hike is a great way to discover natural Hawaii without having to sleep under a tree to do it. Call the following outfitters ahead of time (before you arrive) for a schedule of trips; they fill up quickly.

A longtime resident of Hawaii, Dr. Hugh Montgomery of **Hawaiian Walkways** ✿, Honokaa (© **800/457-7759** or 808/775-0372; www.hawaiianwalkways.com), former "Tour Operator of the Year" by the Hawaii Ecotourism Association of Hawaii, offers a variety of options, ranging from excursions that skirt the rim of immense valleys to hikes through the clouds on the volcano. Hikes are $95 for adults, $75 for kids, to $135 for adults and $95 for kids. Custom hikes are available for $95 each for six hikers. Prices include food, beverages, and equipment.

Naturalist and educator Rob Pacheco of **Hawaii Forest & Trail** ✿✿, 74–5035-B Queen Kaahumanu Hwy. (behind the Chevron Station), Kailua-Kona (© **800/464-1993** or 808/331-8505; www. hawaii-forest.com), offers day trips to some of the island's most remote, pristine, natural areas, some of which he has exclusive access to. Rob's fully trained staff narrates the entire trip, offering extensive natural, geological, and cultural commentary (and more than a little humor). Tours are limited to 10 people and are highly personalized to meet the group's interests and abilities. Options include waterfall adventures, rainforest discovery hikes, birding tours, volcanoes, and even an off-road adventure in a 6×6 Pinzgauer Scrambler that allows you to explore hard-to-reach places. Each tour involves 2 to 4 hours of easy-to-moderate walking, over terrain manageable by anyone in average physical condition. Half-day trips, including snacks, beverages, water, and gear, range from $109 to $165 for adults, $89 to $115 for children ages 8 to 12.

GUIDED NIGHT HIKES For an off-the-beaten-track experience, **Arnott's Lodge,** 98 Apapane Rd., Hilo (*Ⓒ* **808/969-7097;** www.arnottslodge.com), offers a daylong tour of Hawaii Volcanoes National Park, followed by a night lava hike right up to the fiery flow. The 9½-hour tour leaves the lodge at noon and spends most of the afternoon in the park. The lava hike (a 4-hr., somewhat strenuous round-trip hike) takes place as the sun is setting, so you can see the glow of the flow both during and after sunset. The cost is $80.

HAWAII VOLCANOES NATIONAL PARK 🌀🌀🌀

This national park is a wilderness wonderland. Miles of trails not only lace the lava, but also cross deserts, rainforests, beaches, and, in winter, snow at 13,650 feet. Trail maps (highly recommended) are sold at park headquarters. Check conditions before you head out. Come prepared for sun, rain, and hard wind any time of year. Always wear sunscreen and bring plenty of drinking water.

Warning: If you have heart or respiratory problems or if you're pregnant, don't attempt any hike in the park; the fumes will bother you.

TRAILS IN THE PARK

KILAUEA IKI TRAIL You'll experience the work of the volcano goddess, Pele, firsthand on this hike. The 4-mile trail begins at the visitor center, descends through a forest of ferns into still-fuming Kilauea Iki Crater, and then crosses the crater floor past the vent where a 1959 lava blast shot a fountain of fire 1,900 feet into the air for 36 days. Allow 2 hours for this fair-to-moderate hike.

HALEMAUMAU TRAIL This moderate 3.5-mile hike starts at the visitor center, goes down 500 feet to the floor of Kilauea Crater, crosses the crater, and ends at Halemaumau Overlook.

DEVASTATION TRAIL Up on the rim of Kilauea Iki Crater, you can see what an erupting volcano did to a once-flourishing ohia forest. The scorched earth with its ghostly tree skeletons stands in sharp contrast to the rest of the lush forest. Everyone can take this .5-mile hike on a paved path across the eerie bed of black cinders. The trail head is on Crater Rim Road at Puu Puai Overlook.

KIPUKA PUAULU (BIRD PARK) TRAIL This easy, 1.5-mile, hour-long hike lets you see native Hawaiian flora and fauna in a little oasis of living nature in a field of lava. For some reason, the once red-hot lava skirted this miniforest and let it survive. At the trail head on Mauna Loa Road is a display of plants and birds you'll see on the walk. Go early in the morning or in the evening (or, even better, just after a rain) to see native birds like the *apapane* (a small, bright-red bird with black wings and tail) and the iiwi (larger and orange-vermilion colored, with a curved orange bill). Native trees along the trail include giant ohia, koa, soapberry, kolea, and mamani.

MAUNA LOA TRAIL Probably the most challenging hike in Hawaii, this trail goes 7.5 miles from the lookout to a cabin at 10,035 feet and then 12 more miles up to the primitive Mauna Loa summit cabin at 13,250 feet, where the climate is subarctic and overnight temperatures are below freezing year-round. This 4-day round-trip requires advance planning, great physical condition, and registration at the visitor center. Call ℗ **808/985-6000** for maps and details. The trail head begins where Mauna Loa Road ends, 14 miles north of Highway 11.

CAMPGROUNDS & WILDERNESS CABINS IN THE PARK

The only park campground accessible by car is **Namakani Paio,** which has a pavilion with picnic tables and a fireplace (no wood is provided). Tent camping is free; no reservations are required. Stays are limited to 7 days per year. Backpack camping at hiker shelters and cabins is available on a first-come, shared basis, but you must register at the visitor center.

   Kilauea Military Camp, a mile from the visitor center, is a rest-and-recreation camp for active and retired military personnel. Facilities include 75 one- to three-bedroom cabins with fireplaces (some with a Jacuzzi), cafeteria, bowling alley, bar, general store, weight room, and tennis and basketball courts. Rates are based on rank, ranging from $73 to $159 a night. Call ℗ **808/967-8333** on the Big Island, or 808/438-6707 on Oahu (www.kmc-volcano.com).

The following cabins and campgrounds are the best of what the park and surrounding area have to offer:

HALAPE SHELTER   This backcountry site, about 7 miles from the nearest road, is the place for those who want to get away from it all and enjoy their own private white-sand beach. The small, three-sided stone shelter, with a roof but no floor, can accommodate two people comfortably, but four's a crowd. You could pitch a tent inside, but if the weather is nice, you're better off setting up outside. There's a catchment water tank, but check with rangers on the water situation before hiking in (sometimes they don't have accurate information on the water level; bring extra water just in case). The only other facility is a pit toilet. Go on weekdays if you're really looking for an escape. It's free to stay here, but you're limited to 3 nights. Permits are available at the visitor center on a first-come, first-served basis, no earlier than noon on the day before your trip. For more information, call © **808/985-6000.**

NAMAKANI PAIO CAMPGROUNDS & CABINS   Just 5 miles west of the park entrance is a tall eucalyptus forest where you can pitch a tent in an open grassy field. The trail to Kilauea Crater is just ½ mile away. No permit is needed, but stays are limited to 7 days. Facilities include pavilions with barbecues and a fireplace, picnic tables, outdoor dish-washing areas, restrooms, and drinking water. There are also 10 cabins that accommodate up to four people each. Each cabin has a covered picnic table at the entrance and a fireplace with a grill. Toilets, sinks, and hot showers are available in a separate building. You can get groceries and gas in the town of Volcano, 4 miles away. Make cabin reservations through **Volcano House,** P.O. Box 53, Hawaii National Park, HI 96718 (© **808/967-7321**); the cost is $40 per night for two adults (and two children), $48 for three adults, and $56 for four adults.

WAIMANU VALLEY'S MULIWAI TRAIL

This difficult 2- to 3-day backpacking adventure—only for the hardy—takes you to a hidden valley some call Eden, with virgin waterfalls and pools and spectacular views. The trail, which goes from sea level to 1,350 feet and down to the sea again, takes more than 9 hours to hike in and more than 10 hours to hike out. Be prepared for clouds of bloodthirsty mosquitoes, and look out for wild pigs. If it's raining, forget it: You'll have 13 streams to cross before you reach the rim of Waimanu Valley, and rain means flash floods.

You must get permission to camp in Waimanu Valley from the **Division of Forestry and Wildlife,** P.O. Box 4849, Hilo, HI 96720-0849 (© **808/974-4221**). Permits to the nine designated campsites are assigned by number. They're free, but you're limited to a 7-day stay. Facilities are limited to two composting pit toilets. The best water in the valley is from the stream on the western wall, a 15-minute walk up a trail from the beach. All water must be treated before drinking. The water from the Waimanu Stream drains from a swamp, so skip it. Be sure to pack out what you take in.

To get to the trail head, take Highway 19 to the turnoff for Honokaa; drive 9½ miles to the Waipio Valley Lookout. Unless you have four-wheel-drive, this is where your hike begins. Walk down the road and wade the Wailoa Stream; then cross the beach and go to the northwest wall. The trail starts here and goes up the valley floor, past a swamp, and into a forest before beginning a series of switch-backs that parallel the coastline. These switchbacks go up and down about 14 gulches. At the ninth gulch, about two-thirds of the way along the trail, is a shelter. After the shelter, the trail descends into Waimanu Valley, which looks like a smaller version of Waipio Valley but without a sign of human intrusion.

4 Golf & Other Outdoor Activities

The not-for-profit group **Friends for Fitness,** P.O. Box 1671, Kailua-Kona, HI 96745 (© **808/322-0033**), offers a free brochure on physical activities (from aerobics to yoga) in West Hawaii; they will gladly mail it to you upon request.

GOLF

For last-minute and discount tee times, call **Stand-by Golf** (© **888/645-BOOK** or 808/322-BOOK) between 7am and 11pm. Stand-by Golf offers discounted (10%–40%), guaranteed tee times for same-day or next-day golfing.

If your game's a little rusty, head for the **Swing Zone,** 74–5562 Makala Blvd. (corner of Kuikuni Hwy., by the Old Airport Park), Kailua-Kona (© **808/329-6909**). The driving range has 27 mats and 10 grass tee spaces, the practice putting green and chipping area is free with a bucket of balls (60 balls for $6), and the pro shop sells limited supplies (rental clubs are available, too, for just $2). For $6, including a putter and a ball, you can play a round on the 18-hole, all-grass putting course built in the shape of the Big Island.

In addition to the courses below, I love the fabulous **Hualalai Golf Course** 🌺🌺🌺 at Four Seasons Resort Hualalai (p. 41). Unfortunately, it's open only to resort guests—but for committed golfers, this Jack Nicklaus–designed championship course is reason enough to pay the sky-high rates.

THE KOHALA COAST

Hapuna Golf Course 🌺🌺🌺   Since its opening in 1992, this 18-hole championship course has been named the most environmentally sensitive course by *Golf* magazine, as well as "Course of the Future" by the U.S. Golf Association. Designed by Arnold Palmer and Ed Seay, this 6,027-yard, links-style course extends from the shoreline to 700 feet above sea level, with views of the pastoral Kohala Mountains and the Kohala coastline. The elevation changes on the course keep it challenging (and windy at the higher elevations). There are a few elevated tee boxes and only 40 bunkers. Facilities include putting greens, driving ranges, lockers, showers, a pro shop, and restaurants.

Hapuna Beach Prince Hotel, off Hwy. 19 (near mile marker 69). ✆ 808/880-3000. www.hapunabeachprincehotel.com. Greens fees $145 ($120 for resort guests).

Mauna Kea Golf Course 🌺🌺🌺   This breathtakingly beautiful par-72, 7,114-yard championship course, designed by Robert Trent Jones, Jr., is consistently rated one of the top golf courses in the United States. The signature 3rd hole is 175 yards long; the Pacific Ocean and shoreline cliffs stand between the tee and the green, giving every golfer, from beginner to pro, a real challenge. Another par-3 that confounds duffers is the 11th hole, which drops 100 feet from tee to green and plays down to the ocean, into the steady trade winds. When the trades are blowing, 181 yards might as well be 1,000 yards. The Mauna Kea Beach Hotel, which fronts the golf course, is temporarily closed for repairs due to the 2006 earthquake, but facilities currently open include putting greens, a driving range, lockers and showers, a pro shop, and a restaurant. Book ahead; the course is very popular, especially for early weekend tee times.

Mauna Kea Beach Resort, Hwy. 19 (near mile marker 68). ✆ 808/882-5400. www.maunakeabeachhotel.com. Greens fees $210 ($150 for resort guests).

Mauna Lani Frances I'i Brown Championship Courses 🌺🌺🌺
The **Mauna Lani South Course,** a 7,029-yard par-72, has an unforgettable ocean hole: the downhill, 221-yard, par-3 7th, which is bordered by the sea, a salt-and-pepper sand dune, and lush kiawe trees. The **North Course** may not have the drama of the oceanfront holes,

but because it was built on older lava flows, the more extensive indigenous vegetation gives the course a Scottish feel. The hole that's cursed the most is the 140-yard, par-3 17th: It's absolutely beautiful but plays right into the surrounding lava field. Facilities include two driving ranges, a golf shop (with teaching pros), a restaurant, and putting greens.

Mauna Lani Dr., off Hwy. 19 (20 miles north of Kona Airport). © 808/885-6655. www.maunalani.com. Greens fees $205 ($140 for resort guests); twilight rates $90.

Waikoloa Beach Course ⚑ This pristine 18-hole, par-70 course certainly reflects the motto of designer Robert Trent Jones, Jr.: "Hard par, easy bogey." Most golfers remember the par-5, 505-yard 12th hole, a sharp dogleg left with bunkers in the corner and an elevated tee surrounded by lava. Facilities include a golf shop, restaurant, and driving range.

1020 Keana Place (adjacent to the Waikoloa Beach Marriott Resort and Hilton Waikoloa Village), Waikoloa. © 877/WAIKOLOA or 808/886-6060. www.waikoloa golf.com. Greens fees: $195 ($130 for resort guests); twilight rates $75.

Waikoloa Kings' Course ⚑ This sister course to the Waikoloa Beach Course is about 500 yards longer. Designed by Tom Weiskopf and Jay Morrish, the 18-hole links-style tract features a double green at the 3rd and 6th holes, and several carefully placed bunkers that often come into play due to the ever-present trade winds. Facilities include a pro shop and showers.

600 Waikoloa Beach Dr. (adjacent to the Waikoloa Beach Marriott Resort and Hilton Waikoloa Village), Waikoloa. © 877/WAIKOLOA or 808/886-7888. www.waikoloa beachresort.com. Greens fees: $175 ($125 for resort guests); twilight rates $75.

Waikoloa Village Golf Club This semiprivate 18-hole course, with a par-72 for each of the three sets of tees, is hidden in the town of Waikoloa and usually overshadowed by the glamour resort courses along the Kohala Coast. Not only is it a beautiful course with great views, but it also offers some great golfing. The wind can play havoc with your game here (like most Hawaii golf courses). Robert Trent Jones, Jr., designed this challenging course, inserting his trademark sand traps, slick greens, and great fairways. I'm particularly fond of the 18th hole: This par-5, 490-yard thriller doglegs to the left, and the last 75 yards up to the green are water, water, water. Enjoy the fabulous views of Mauna Kea and Mauna Loa, and—on a very clear day—Maui's Haleakala in the distance.

Waikoloa Rd., Waikoloa Village, off Hwy. 19 (18 miles north of Kona Airport). © 808/ 883-9621. www.waikoloa.org. Greens fees: $75. Turn left at the Waikoloa sign; it's about 6 miles up, on your left.

Improve Your Golf Game in 2½ Hours

Darrin Gee's Spirit of Golf Academy (★★★, P.O. Box 2308, Kohala (✆ **866-GOLF-433** or 808/887-6800; www.spiritof golfhawaii.com), has developed a program for the inner, mental game of golf that will improve your score in just 2½ hours, whether you're a beginner or you've been swinging clubs for years. Unlike the majority of golf schools, which focus on the mechanics of the golf swing, for just $250 you will learn how to improve your mental game, using his Seven Principals of golf, which means learning how to increase your focus and concentration, how to relax under pressure, and how to play to your potential. The small clinics (four players to one instructor) are available at championship golf courses on the Big Island.

THE HAMAKUA COAST

Hamakua Country Club (Value   As you approach the sugar town of Honokaa, you can't miss this funky 9-hole course, built in the 1920s on a very steep hill overlooking the ocean. It's a par-33, 2,520-yard course. Architect Frank Anderson managed to squeeze in 9 holes by crisscrossing holes across fairways—you may never see a layout like this again. But the best part about Hamakua is the price—just $20 for 18 holes (you play the course twice). The course is open to nonmembers on weekdays only; you don't need a tee time. Just show up, and if no one's around, drop your $20 in the box and head out. Carts aren't allowed because of the steep hills.

On the ocean side of Hwy. 19 (41 miles from Hilo), Honokaa. ✆ **808/775-7244.** Greens fees: $20 for 18 holes (you play the 9-hole course twice).

HILO

Hilo Municipal Golf Course   This is a great course for the casual golfer: It's flat, scenic, and often fun. *Warning:* Don't go after a heavy rain (especially in winter), when the fairways can get really soggy and play can slow way down. The rain does keep the course green and beautiful, though. Wonderful trees (monkeypods, coconuts, eucalyptus, banyans) dot the grounds, and the views—of Mauna Kea on one side and Hilo Bay on the other—are breathtaking. There are four sets of tees, with a par-71 from all; the back tees give you 6,325 yards of play. Getting a tee time can be a challenge; weekdays are your best bet.

340 Haihai St. (between Kinoole and Iwalani sts.), Hilo. ℂ **808/959-7711.** Greens fees: $29 weekdays; $34 Sat–Sun and holidays. From Hilo, take Hwy. 11 toward Volcano; turn right at Puainako St. (at Prince Kuhio Shopping Center), left on Kinoole, and then right on Haihai St.

Naniloa Country Club   At first glance, this semiprivate, 9-hole course looks pretty flat and short, but once you get beyond the 1st hole—a wide, straightforward 330-yard par-4—things get challenging. The tree-lined fairways require straight drives, and the huge lake on the 2nd and 5th holes is sure to haunt you. This course is very popular with locals and visitors alike. Rental clubs are available.

120 Banyan Dr. (at the intersection of Hwy. 11 and Hwy. 19). ℂ **808/935-3000.** Greens fees: $25 ($15 Naniloa Hotel guests) Mon–Fri; $35 ($25 Naniloa Hotel guests) Sat–Sun (if you can get a tee time); twilight rates are $10 less.

VOLCANO VILLAGE
Volcano Golf and Country Club   Located at an altitude of 4,200 feet, this public course got its start in 1922, when the Blackshear family put in a green using old tomato cans for the holes. It now has three sets of tees to choose from, all with a par of 72. The course is unusually landscaped, making use of the pine and ohia trees scattered throughout. It's considered challenging by locals. *Some tips from the regulars:* Because the course is at such a high altitude, the ball travels farther than you're probably used to, so club down. If you hit the ball off the fairway, take the stroke—you don't want to look for your ball in the forest and undergrowth. Also, play a pitch-and-run game—the greens are slick.

Hwy. 11, on the right side, just after the entrance to Hawaii Volcanoes National Park. ℂ **808/967-7331.** www.volcanogolfshop.com. Greens fees: $64.

BICYCLING & MOUNTAIN BIKING
For mountain-bike and cross-training bike rentals in Kona, go to **Dave's Bike and Triathlon Shop,** 75–5669 Alii Dr., across from the Kailua Pier, behind Atlantis Submarine (ℂ **808/329-4522**). Dave rents brand-name mountain bikes (with full suspension) for $15 a day or $60 a week (including helmet and water bottle). Feel free to ask Dave for route advice and local weather reports. You can also rent a bike rack for your car ($10 a week).

   Hawaiian Pedals ℱ, Kona Inn Shopping Village, Alii Drive, Kailua-Kona (ℂ **808/329-2294**), and **Hawaiian Pedals Bike Works,** Hale Hana Centre, 74–5583 Luhia St., Kailua-Kona (ℂ **808/326-2453;** www.hawaiianpedals.com), have a huge selection of bikes: cruisers ($20 a day), mountain bikes and hybrids ($35 a day), and racing bikes and front-suspension mountain bikes ($45 a day). Bike racks go for $5 a day, and you pay only for the days you actually use it (the honor system): If you have the rack for a week but use it for only 2 days, you'll be charged just $10. The folks at the shops are friendly and knowledgeable about cycling routes all over the Big Island.

GUIDED TOURS   **Kona Coast Cycling** (© 877/592-BIKE or 808/327-1133; www.cyclekona.com) offers half-day (3–4 hr.) and full-day (4–6 hr.) bicycling tours, ranging from a casual ride to intense mountain biking at its best. The locations are diverse, from the rolling hills of a Kona coffee farm to awesome views of the Waipio Valley Lookout. Most tours include round-trip transportation from hotels, van support, tour guide, helmets, gloves, water, snacks, and lunch on the full-day trips. Prices range from $70 to $230 for adults and $60 to $100 for children (ages 6–15).

Contact the **Big Island Mountain Bike Association,** P.O. Box 6819, Hilo, HI 96720 (© 808/961-4452; www.interpac.net/~ mtbike), for its free brochure, *Big Island Mountain Biking,* which has useful safety tips on biking as well as great off-road trails for both beginner and advanced riders.

BIRDING

Native Hawaiian birds are few—and dwindling. But Hawaii still offers extraordinary birding for anyone nimble enough to traverse tough, mucky landscape. And the best birding is on the Big Island; birders the world over come here hoping to see three Hawaiian birds, in particular: akiapolaau, a woodpecker wannabe with a war club–like head; nukupuu, an elusive little yellow bird with a curved beak, one of the crown jewels of Hawaiian birding; and alala, the critically endangered Hawaiian crow that's now almost impossible to see in the wild.

Good spots to see native Hawaiian and other birds include the following:

HAWAII VOLCANOES NATIONAL PARK   The best places for accomplished birders to go on their own are the ohia forests of this national park, usually at sunrise or sunset, when the little forest birds seem to be most active. The Hawaiian nene goose can be spotted at the park's Kipuka Nene Campground, a favorite nesting habitat. Geese and pheasants sometimes appear on the Volcano Golf Course in the afternoon.

HAKALAU FOREST NATIONAL WILDLIFE REFUGE   The first national wildlife refuge established solely for forest bird management is on the eastern slope of Mauna Kea above the Hamakua

Coast. It's open for birding on Saturday, Sunday, and state holidays, using the public access road only. You must call ahead of time to get the gate combinations of the locked gates and to register. Contact Refuge Manager Richard Wass, Hakalau Forest, 154 Waianuenue Ave., Room 219, Hilo, HI 96720 (© **808/933-6915;** Richard_Wass@ mail.fws.gov).

HILO PONDS   Ducks, coots, herons (night and great blue), cattle egrets, and even Canada and snow geese fly into these popular coastal wetlands in Hilo, near the airport. Take Kalanianaole Highway about 3 miles east, past the industrial port facilities to Loko Waka Pond and Waiakea Pond.

BIRDING TOURS

If you don't know an apapane from a nukupuu, go with someone who does. Contact **Hawaii Forest & Trail,** 74–5035-B Queen Kaahumanu Hwy. (behind the Chevron Station), Kailua-Kona (© **800/ 464-1993** or 808/331-8505; www.hawaii-forest.com), to sign up for the **Rainforest and Dry Forest Adventure tour** ☆☆, led by naturalist Rob Pacheco. On this tour you'll venture into pristine rainforest to see rare and endangered Hawaiian birds. Immersed in this world of giant ferns and crisp mountain air, the guide will also point out Hawaii's unique botany and evolution. This full-day tour costs $155 and includes pickup, midmorning snack with coffee, lunch, beverages, daypacks, binoculars, walking sticks, and rain gear.

HORSEBACK RIDING

Kohala Na'alapa ☆, on Kohala Mountain Road (Hwy. 250) at mile marker 11 (ask for directions to the stables at the security-guard station; © **808/889-0022;** www.naalapastables.com), offers unforgettable journeys into the rolling hills of Kahua and Kohala ranches, past ancient Hawaiian ruins, through lush pastures with grazing sheep and cows, and along mountaintops with panoramic coastal views. The horses and various riding areas are suited to everyone from first-timers to experienced equestrians. There are two trips a day: a 2½-hour tour at 9am for $89 and a 1½-hour tour at 1:30pm for $68. No riders over 230 pounds, no pregnant riders, and no children under 8 permitted.

Experienced riders should sign up for a trip with **King's Trail Rides, Tack, and Gift Shop** ☆☆, Highway 11 at mile marker 111, Kealakekua (© **808/323-2388;** www.konacowboy.com). These 4-hour trips, with 2 hours of riding, are limited to four people. The trip heads down the mountain along Monument Trail to the Captain

Cook Monument in Kealakekua Bay, where you'll stop for lunch and an hour of snorkeling. The $135 weekday ($150 weekends) price tag includes lunch and gear.

To see Waipio Valley on horseback, call **Waipio Na'alapa Trail Rides** ✯ (© **808/775-0419;** www.naalapastables.com). The 2½-hour tours of this gorgeous tropical valley depart Monday through Saturday at 9:30am and 1pm (don't forget your camera). The guides are well versed in Hawaiian history and provide running commentary as you move through this historic place. The cost is $89 for adults. No kids under 8, pregnant riders, or riders over 230 pounds.

RIDING PARKER RANCH   Visitors can explore **Parker Ranch** (© **808/885-7655;** www.parkerranch.com/horseback.html) and its vast 175,000-acre working cattle ranch. You'll learn firsthand about Parker Ranch, its history, and its variety of plant life, and you may even catch glimpses of pheasant, francolins, or wild pigs. Rides (suitable for beginners) are available three times daily at 8:15am, 12:15pm, and a sunset ride at 4pm for $79 per person. Morning and noon rides are 2 hours, and the sunset ride is 1½ hours. Kids must be at least 7 years old. Riders will feel like Hawaiian *paniolo* (cowboys) as they ride through stone corrals where up to 5,000 Hereford cattle were rounded up after being brought down from the slopes of Mauna Kea. A visit to the racetrack where Parker Ranch thoroughbreds were trained and still hold the record for speed is included in the excursion. The rides all begin at the Blacksmith Shop on Pukalani Road.

TENNIS

You can play for free at any Hawaii County tennis court; for a detailed list of all courts on the island, contact **Hawaii County Department of Parks and Recreation,** 25 Aupuni St., Hilo, HI 96720 (© **808/ 961-8720;** www.hawaii-county.com/parks/parks.htm). The best courts in Hilo are at the Hoolulu Tennis Stadium, located next to the Civic Auditorium on Manono Street. Most resorts in the Kona-Kohala area do not allow nonguests to use their tennis facilities.

5

Seeing the Sights

If you want nothing more than a fabulous beach to lie on and a perfectly mixed mai tai, you're going to the right place. But if you want more out of your vacation, read on. On the Big Island, you can visit fascinating historic sites, hunt for petroglyphs, climb to the top of Mauna Kea, learn about the local flora at a botanical garden or national park, and much more. This chapter will help you get the most from your Big Island experience.

1 The Kona Coast

GUIDED WALKING TOURS   The **Kona Historical Society** (© 808/323-2005; www.konahistorical.org) hosts two historical walking tours in the Kona region. All walks must be booked in advance; call for reservations and departure locations. The 75-minute **Historic Kailua Village Walking Tour** ✸ (© 808/323-3222; www.konahistorical.org/tours/walking.shtml) is the most comprehensive tour of the Kona Coast. It takes you all around Kailua-Kona, from King Kamehameha's last seat of government to the summer palace of the Hawaiian royal family and beyond, with lots of Hawaiian history along the way. Tickets are $20 for adults, $10 for children ages 5 to 12.

The 1-hour **Living History Tour** takes you through the everyday life of a Japanese family on the Uchida Coffee Farm during the 1920s to 1940s. Interact with costumed interpreters as they go about life on a coffee farm. The tour is offered Monday through Friday on the hour from 9am to 3pm, for $15 adults and $7.50 kids ages 5 to 12. Meet at the Kona Historical Society office, 81–6551 Mamalahoa Hwy. (next to Kona Specialty Meats), across from mile marker 110, Kealakekua. Call ahead for reservations (© 808/323-2006).

SELF-GUIDED DRIVING TOURS   **Big Island Audio Tour** (© 808/896-4275; www.bigislandaudiotour.com), a self-guided audio tour on CD, features 36 tracks of information, including directions to the well-known sites plus tracks on beaches, short hikes, side trips, and information on Hawaiian language, history, and culture. The cost is $20 plus $2 for shipping.

If you're interested in seeing how your morning cup of joe goes from beans to brew, get a copy of the **Coffee Country Driving Tour.** This self-guided drive will take you farm by farm through Kona's famous coffee country; it also features a fascinating history of the area, the lowdown on coffee-making lingo, some insider tips on how to make a great cup, and even a recipe for Kona coffee macadamia-nut chocolate-chunk pie (goes great with a cup of java). The free brochure is available at the **Big Island Visitors Bureau,** 250 Waikoloa Beach Dr., Waikoloa, HI 96738 (© **808/886-1652;** www.gohawaii.com/bigisland).

IN & AROUND KAILUA-KONA ☆☆☆

Ellison S. Onizuka Space Center (Kids   This small museum has a real moon rock and memorabilia in honor of Big Island–born astronaut Ellison Onizuka, who died in the 1986 *Challenger* space shuttle disaster. Displays include a gravity well, which illustrates orbital motion, and an interactive rocket-propulsion exhibit, where you can launch your own miniature space shuttle.

At Kona International Airport, Kailua-Kona. © **808/329-3441.** www.hawaiimuseums. org/mc/ishawaii_astronaut.htm. Admission $3 adults, $1 children 18 and under. Daily 8:30am–4:30pm. Parking in airport lot, $2 per hour.

Hulihee Palace ☆☆   This two-story New England–style mansion of lava rock and coral mortar, built in 1838 by the Big Island's governor, John Adams Kuakini, overlooks the harbor at Kailua-Kona. The largest, most elegant residence on the island when it was erected, Hulihee became a home to Hawaii's royalty, making it the other royal palace in the United States (the most famous being Oahu's Iolani Palace). Now run by Daughters of Hawaii, it features many 19th-century mementos and gorgeous koa furniture. You'll get lots of background and royal lore on the guided tour. No photography is allowed. There was some damage to this historic structure in the 2006 earthquake, but by the time you read this, all is scheduled to be repaired.

The palace hosts 12 **Hawaiian music and hula concerts** a year, each dedicated to a Hawaiian monarch, at 4pm on the last Sunday of the month (except June and Dec, when the performances are held in conjunction with King Kamehameha Day and Christmas).

Across the street is **Mokuaikaua Church** (© **808/329-1589**), the oldest Christian church in Hawaii. It's constructed of lava stones, but its architecture is New England style all the way. The 112-foot steeple is still the tallest man-made structure in Kailua-Kona.

75–5718 Alii Dr., Kailua-Kona. ℂ **808/329-1877.** www.huliheepalace.org. Admission $6 adults, $4 seniors, $1 children. Daily 9am–4pm. Daily tours held throughout the day (arrive at least an hour before closing).

Kailua Pier   This is action central for water adventures. Fishing charters, snorkel cruises, and party boats all come and go here. Stop by around 4pm, when the captains weigh in with the catch of the day, usually huge marlin—the record-setters often come in here. It's also a great place to watch the sunset.

On the waterfront outside Honokohau Harbor, Kailua-Kona. ℂ **808/329-7494.**

Kamehameha's Compound at Kamakahonu Bay 🌟🌟   On the ocean side of the Kona Beach Hotel is a restored area of deep spiritual meaning to Hawaiians. This was the spot that King Kamehameha the Great chose to retreat to in 1812 after conquering the Hawaiian Islands. He stayed until his death in 1819. The king built a temple, **Ahuena Heiau,** and used it as a gathering place for his kahuna (priests) to counsel him on governing his people in times of peace. In 1820 it was on this sacred ground that Kamehameha's son Liholiho, as king, sat down to eat with his mother, Keopuolani, and Kamehameha's principal queen, Kaahumanu, thus breaking the ancient *kapu* (taboo) against eating with women; this act established a new order in the Hawaiian kingdom. The temple grounds are now just a third of their original size, but still impressive. You're free to come and wander the grounds, envisioning the days when King Kamehameha appealed to the gods to help him rule with the spirit of humanity's highest nature.

On the grounds of King Kamehameha's Kona Beach Hotel, 75–5660 Palani Rd., Kailua-Kona. ℂ **808/329-2911.** www.konabeachhotel.com/history.cfm. Free admission. Daily 9am–4pm; guided tours Mon–Fri at 1:30pm.

Kona Brewing Co. and Brewpub   This microbrewery is the first of its kind on the Big Island. Spoon and Pops, a father-and-son duo from Oregon, brought their brewing talents here and now produce about 25 barrels (about 124,000 gal.) per year. Drop by any time during their business hours and take a quick, informal tour of the brewery, after which you get to taste the product. A brewpub on the property serves gourmet pizza, salads, and fresh-brewed Hawaiian ales.

75–5629 Kuakini Hwy., Kailua-Kona. (Entry on Pawai Place: Turn north on Kuakini Hwy. [from Palani Rd.] and drive approximately ½ mile to the first stop sign, Kaiwi Street, and turn right. Take your first right on Pawai Place and follow it until it ends at the brewery parking lot. Watch for directional signs along the way.) ℂ **808/334-BREW.** www.konabrewingco.com. Free tours and tastings. Tours Mon–Fri 10:30am and 3pm.

Kailua-Kona Town

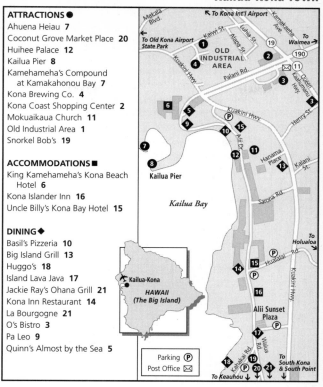

ATTRACTIONS ●
Ahuena Heiau **7**
Coconut Grove Market Place **20**
Huihee Palace **12**
Kailua Pier **8**
Kamehameha's Compound
  at Kamakahonou Bay **7**
Kona Brewing Co. **4**
Kona Coast Shopping Center **2**
Mokuaikaua Church **11**
Old Industrial Area **1**
Snorkel Bob's **19**

ACCOMMODATIONS ■
King Kamehameha's Kona Beach
  Hotel **6**
Kona Islander Inn **16**
Uncle Billy's Kona Bay Hotel **15**

DINING ◆
Basil's Pizzeria **10**
Big Island Grill **13**
Huggo's **18**
Island Lava Java **17**
Jackie Ray's Ohana Grill **21**
Kona Inn Restaurant **14**
La Bourgogne **21**
O's Bistro **3**
Pa Leo **9**
Quinn's Almost by the Sea **5**

Natural Energy Laboratory of Hawaii Authority (NELHA)

Technology buffs should consider a visit to NELHA, where the hot tropical sun, in combination with a complex pumping system that brings 42°F (6°C) ocean water from 2,000 feet deep up to land, is used to develop innovations in agriculture, aquaculture, and ocean conservation. The interesting 1½-hour tour takes in all areas of the high-tech ocean science and technology park, including the seawater delivery system, the energy-conversion process, and some of the park's more interesting tenants, from Maine lobsters to giant clams.

73–4460 Queen Kaahumanu Hwy. (at mile marker 94), Kailua-Kona. ℭ 808/329-8073. www.nelha.org. Public presentation tours $8 adults, free for children 8 and under. Tues–Thurs 10am; reservations required.

UPCOUNTRY KONA: HOLUALOA 🌺🌺

On the slope of Hualalai volcano above Kailua-Kona sits the small village of Holualoa, which attracts travelers weary of super-resorts. Here you'll find a little art and culture—and shade.

This funky upcountry town, centered on two-lane Mamalahoa Highway, is nestled amid a lush, tropical landscape where avocados grow as big as footballs. Little more than a wide spot in the road, Holualoa is a cluster of brightly painted, tin-roofed plantation shacks enjoying a revival as B&Bs, art galleries, and quaint shops (see chapter 6 for details). In 2 blocks, it manages to pack in two first-rate galleries, a frame shop, a potter, a glassworks, a goldsmith, an old-fashioned general store, a vintage 1930s gas station, a tiny post office, a Catholic church, and the **Kona Hotel,** a hot-pink clapboard structure that looks like a Western movie set—you're welcome to peek in, and you should.

The cool up-slope village is the best place in Hawaii for a coffee break. That's because Holualoa is in the heart of the coffee belt, a 20-mile-long strip at an elevation of between 1,000 and 1,400 feet, where all the Kona coffee in the world is grown in the rich volcanic soil of the cool uplands. Everyone's backyard seems to teem with glossy green leaves and ruby-red cherries (which contain the seeds, or beans, used to make coffee), and the air smells like an espresso bar. The **Holuakoa Cafe,** on Mamalahoa Highway (Hwy. 180) in Holualoa (© 808/322-2233), is a great place to get a freshly brewed cup.

To reach Holualoa, follow narrow, winding Hualalai Road up the hill from Highway 19; it's about a 15-minute drive.

SOUTH KONA 🌺🌺🌺

Kona Historical Society Museum 🌺🌺   This well-organized museum is housed in the historic Greenwell Store, built in 1875 by Henry Nicholas Greenwell out of native stone. Antiques, artifacts, and photos tell the story of this fabled coast. The museum is filled with items that were common to everyday life here when coffee growing and cattle raising were the main industries. Stocked with accurate reproductions of goods that filled the shelves and hung from the ceiling joists, the store will offer a glimpse of the past, complete with storekeepers, dressed in period costumes, offering visitors St. Jacobs Oil to cure your arthritis or rheumatism. Before you leave, the shopkeeper may share some gossip about local people and events. The Historical Society has another project in the works: the Kona Heritage Ranch, an outdoor museum on the daily life of a rancher in 1890, which will be located next door to the Greenwell

Store. As part of the project, the Kona Historical Society has created a replica of an 1890 Portuguese Stone Oven, the first of several structures and programs planned for the Kona Heritage Ranch. Portuguese from the Azores or Madeira started coming to Kona in the 1870s to help develop and manage dairies, a key phase of the ranching industry in Hawaii. The outdoor hive-type oven, made with cemented stone, was a constant presence wherever the Portuguese dairymen (and sugar industry workers) settled. They brought with them both their knowledge of dairying on tropical islands and their love of freshly baked stone-oven bread. An informal group gathers every Thursday to learn about wood-fired baking techniques. Coming is a $1-million visitor center to be completed by the end of 2008. Serious history buffs should sign up for one of the museum's walking tours; see "Guided Walking Tours," above.

Hwy. 11, between mile markers 111 and 112, Kealakekua. ⓒ **808/323-3222** or 808/ 323-2006. www.konahistorical.org. Free admission (donations accepted). Mon–Fri 9am–3pm. Parking on grassy area next to Kona Specialty Meats parking lot.

Kula Kai Caverns and Lava Tubes 𝒢𝒢 (Finds)   Before you trudge up to Pele's volcanic eruption, take a look at her underground handiwork. Ric Elhard and Rose Herrera have explored and mapped out the labyrinth of lava tubes and caves, carved out over the past 1,000 years or so, that crisscross their property on the southwest rift zone on the slopes of Mauna Loa near South Point. Tour choices range from an easy half-hour tour on a well-lit underground route ($15 for adults, $8 for children ages 5–12) to a more adventuresome 2-hour caving trip ($65 per person; recommended minimum age is 8). Helmets, lights, gloves, and knee pads are all included. Sturdy shoes are recommended for caving.

Off Hwy. 11, Ocean View. ⓒ **808/929-7539.** www.kulakaicaverns.com. Half-hour tour $15 adults, $8 children 5–12; 2-hr. tour $65 adults and children; 3-hr. tour $95. Tours by appointment. Between mile markers 79 and 78 off Hwy. 11.

The Painted Church 𝒢 (Finds)   Oh, those Belgian priests—what a talented lot. In the late 1800s, Father John Berchman Velghe borrowed a page from Michelangelo and painted biblical scenes inside St. Benedict's Catholic Church so the illiterate Hawaiians could visualize the white man's version of creation.

Hwy. 19, Honaunau. ⓒ **808/328-2227.**

Puuhonua O Honaunau National Historical Park 𝒢𝒢𝒢   With its fierce, haunting idols, this sacred site on the black-lava Kona Coast certainly looks forbidding. To ancient Hawaiians, however, Puuhonua

O Honaunau served as a 16th-century place of refuge, providing sanctuary for defeated warriors and *kapu* (taboo) violators. A great rock wall—1,000 feet long, 10 feet high, and 17 feet thick—defines the refuge where Hawaiians found safety. On the wall's north end is Hale O Keawe Heiau, which holds the bones of 23 Hawaiian chiefs. Other archaeological finds include burial sites, old trails, and a portion of an ancient village. On a self-guided tour of the 180-acre site—which has been restored to its precontact state—you can see and learn about reconstructed thatched huts, canoes, and idols, and feel the *mana* (power) of old Hawaii.

A cultural festival, usually held in June, allows you to join in games, learn crafts, sample Hawaiian food, see traditional hula, and experience life in precontact Hawaii. Every Labor Day weekend, one of Hawaii's major outrigger canoe races starts here and ends in Kailua-Kona. Call for details on both events.

Hwy. 160 (off Hwy. 11 at mile marker 104), Honaunau. ℂ 808/328-2288. www. nps.gov/puho. Admission $5 per vehicle, good for 7 days. Visitor center daily 8am–4:30pm; park Mon–Thurs 6am–8pm, Fri–Sun 6am–11pm. From Hwy. 11, it's 3½ miles to the park entrance.

2 South Point: Land's End ⭐⭐⭐

At the end of 11 miles of bad road that peters out at Kaulana Bay, in the lee of a jagged, black-lava point, you'll find Land's End—the tail end of the United States. From the tip (beware of the big waves that lash the shore if you walk out there), the nearest continental landfall is Antarctica, 7,500 miles away.

It's a 2½-mile four-wheel-drive trip and a hike down a cliff from South Point to the anomaly known as **Green Sand Beach** ⭐ (see chapter 4).

Back on the Mamalahoa Highway (Hwy. 11), about 20 miles east, is the small town of Pahoa; turn off the highway and travel about 5 miles through this once-thriving sugar plantation and beyond to the **Wood Valley Temple and Retreat Center** ⭐ (ℂ 808/928-8539; www.nechung.org), also known as *Nechung Drayang Ling* ("Island of Melodious Sound"). It's an oasis of tranquillity tucked into the rainforest. Built by Japanese sugar-cane workers, the temple, retreat center, and surrounding gardens were rededicated by the Dalai Lama in 1980 to serve as a spiritual center for Tibetan Buddhism. You can walk the beautiful grounds, attend services, and breathe in the quiet mindfulness of this serene area.

3 The Kohala Coast ⓐⓐⓐ

Puukohola Heiau National Historic Site ⓐⓐⓐ   This seacoast temple, called "the hill of the whale," is the single most imposing and dramatic structure of the ancient Hawaiians. It was built by Kamehameha I from 1790 to 1791. The temple stands 224 feet long by 100 feet wide, with three narrow terraces on the seaside and an amphitheater to view canoes. Kamehameha built this temple after a prophet told him he would conquer and unite the islands if he did so; 4 years later, he fulfilled his kingly goal. The site also includes an interactive visitor center, the house of John Young, a trusted advisor of Kamehameha, and, offshore, the submerged ruins of Hale O Ka Puni, a shrine dedicated to the shark gods.

Hwy. 270, near Kawaihae Harbor. ⓒ 808/882-7218. www.nps.gov/puhe. Free admission. Tours $2. Daily 7:30am–4pm. The visitor center is on Hwy. 270; the *heiau* is a short walk away. The trail is closed when it's too windy, so call ahead if you're in doubt.

ANCIENT HAWAIIAN FISH PONDS

Like their Polynesian forebears, Hawaiians were among the first aquaculturists on the planet. Scientists still marvel at the ways they used the brackish ponds along the shoreline to stock and harvest fish. There are actually two different types of ancient fish ponds (or *loko iʻa*). Closed ponds, located inshore, were closed off from the ocean. Open ponds used rock walls as a barrier to the ocean and sluice gates that connected the ponds to the ocean. The gates were woven vines, with just enough room for juvenile fish to swim in at high tide while keeping the bigger, fatter fish from swimming out. Generally, the Hawaiians kept and raised mullet, milkfish, and shrimp in these open ponds; juvenile manini, papio, eels, and barracuda occasionally found their way in, too.

The **Kalahuipuaa Fish Ponds,** at Mauna Lani Resort (ⓒ **808/ 885-6622**), are great examples of both types of ponds in a lush tropical setting. South of the Mauna Lani Resort are **Kuualii** and **Kahapapa Fish Ponds,** at the Waikoloa Beach Marriott Resort (ⓒ **808/ 885-6789**). Both resorts have taken great pains to restore the ponds to their original states and to preserve them for future generations; call ahead to arrange a free guided tour.

KOHALA COAST PETROGLYPHS

The Hawaiian petroglyphs are a great enigma of the Pacific—no one knows who made them or why. They appear at 135 different sites on six inhabited islands, but most of them are found on the Big Island.

At first glance, the huge slate of pahoehoe looks like any other smooth black slate of lava on the seacoast of the Big Island—until gradually, in slanting rays of the sun, a wonderful cast of characters leaps to life before your eyes. You might see dancers and paddlers, fishermen and chiefs, hundreds of marchers all in a row. Pictures of the tools of daily life are everywhere: fish hooks, spears, poi pounders, canoes. The most common representations are family groups. There are also post–European contact petroglyphs of ships, anchors, horses, and guns.

The largest concentration of these stone symbols in the Pacific lies within the 233-acre **Puako Petroglyph Archaeological District** ✿, near Mauna Lani Resort. The 1.5-mile **Malama Trail** starts north of Mauna Lani Resort; take Highway 19 to the resort turnoff and drive toward the coast on North Kaniku Drive, which ends at a parking lot; the trail head is marked by a sign and interpretive kiosk. Go in the early morning or late afternoon, when it's cool. A total of 3,000 designs have been identified.

The **Kings' Shops** (✆ **808/886-8811**), at the Waikoloa Beach Resort, offers a free tour of the surrounding petroglyphs Tuesday through Friday at 10:30am and Saturday at 8:30am; it meets in front of the Food Pavilion. For the best viewing, go Saturday morning.

Visitors with disabilities, as well as others, can explore petroglyphs at **Kaupulehu Petroglyphs** ✿ in the **Kona Village Resort,** Queen Kaahumanu Highway (✆ **808/325-5555**). Free guided tours are offered three times a week, but reservations are required (or you won't get past the gatehouse). Here you can see some of the finest images in the Hawaiian Islands. There are many petroglyphs of sails, canoes, fish, and chiefs in headdresses, plus a burial scene. Kite motifs—rare in rock art—similar to those found in New Zealand are also here. This is Hawaii's only ADA-accessible petroglyph trial.

Warning: The petroglyphs are thousands of years old and easily destroyed. Do not walk on them or attempt to take a "rubbing" (there's a special area in the Puako Preserve for doing so). The best way to capture a petroglyph is with a photo in the late afternoon, when the shadows are long.

4 North Kohala ✿✿✿

Lapakahi State Historical Park ✿ (Kids)   This 14th-century fishing village, on a hot, dry, dusty stretch of coast, offers a glimpse into the lifestyle of the ancients. Lapakahi is the best-preserved fishing village in Hawaii. Take the self-guided 1-mile loop trail past stone platforms, fish

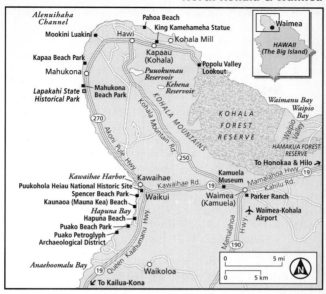

shrines, rock shelters, salt pans, and restored *hale* (houses) to a coral-sand beach and the deep blue sea (good snorkeling). Wear good hiking shoes or tennies; it's a hearty 45-minute walk. Go early in the morning or late in the afternoon to beat the heat.

Hwy. 270, Mahukona. ☏ **808/889-5566.** www.hawaii.gov/dlnr/dsp/hawaii.html. Free admission. Daily 8am–4pm. Guided tours by appointment.

Mo'okini Luakini Heiau ☆☆ *Moments* The 1,500-year-old Mo'okini Heiau, once used by kings to pray and offer human sacrifices, is Hawaii's oldest, largest, and most sacred religious site (and now a national historic landmark). The massive three-story stone temple, dedicated to Ku, the Hawaiian god of war, was erected in A.D. 480; each stone is said to have been passed hand to hand from Pololu Valley, 14 miles away, by 18,000 men who worked from sunset to sunrise. Kamehameha, born nearby under Halley's Comet, sought spiritual guidance here before embarking on his campaign to unite Hawaii. You can see the temple only on the third Saturday of every month, when volunteers pull weeds and clean up property surrounding the temple. If you'd like to help out, call the Mo'okini Preservation Foundation, on Oahu (☏ **808/373-8000**).

On the north shore, near Upolu Point Airport.

The Original King Kamehameha Statue 𝓚𝓚 Here stands King Kamehameha the Great, right arm outstretched, left arm holding a spear, as if guarding the seniors who have turned a century-old New England–style courthouse into an airy center for their golden years. The center is worth a stop just to meet the town elders, who are quick to point out the local sights, hand you a free *Guide to Historic North Kohala,* and give you a brief tour of the courthouse, whose walls are covered with the faces of innocent-looking local boys killed in World War II, Korea, and Vietnam.

But the statue's main attraction here. There's one just like it in Honolulu, across the street from Iolani Palace, but this is the original: an 8-foot, 6-inch bronze by Thomas R. Gould, a Boston sculptor. It was cast in Europe in 1880 but was lost at sea on its way to Hawaii. A sea captain eventually recovered the statue, which was placed here, near Kamehameha's Kohala birthplace, in 1912.

Kamehameha was born in 1750, became ruler of Hawaii in 1810, and died in Kailua-Kona in 1819. His burial site remains a mystery.

Hwy. 270, Kapaau.

Pololu Valley Lookout 𝓚𝓚𝓚 At this end-of-the-road scenic lookout, you can gaze at the vertical jade-green cliffs of the Hamakua Coast and two islets offshore. The view may look familiar once you get here—it often appears on travel posters. Linger if you can; adventurous travelers can take a switchback trail (a good 45-min. hike) to a secluded black-sand beach at the mouth of a wild valley once planted in taro; bring water and bug spray.

At the end of Hwy. 270, Makapala.

Pua Mau Place (𝓚𝒾𝒹𝓈) Perched on the sun-kissed western slopes of the Kohala Mountains and dotted with deep, craggy ravines lies one of Hawaii's most unusual botanical gardens, Pua Mau Place, a 45-acre oasis with breathtaking views of both the ocean and the majestic mountains. It's dedicated to plants that are "ever blooming," an expansive collection of continuously flowering tropical flowers, trees, and shrubs. The gardens also have an aviary of exotic birds and a unique hibiscus maze planted with some 200 varieties of hibiscus. This is a great place for families (children are invited to feed the birds in the aviary). Visitors can take the self-guided tour (along with a booklet filled with the names and descriptions of all the plants) along mulched pathways meandering through the gardens, where every plant is clearly marked.

10 Ala Kahua, Kawaihae. ℰ **808/882-0888.** www.puamau.com. Admission $10 adults, $8 seniors and students, free for children 12 and under. Daily 9am–4pm. Located off Hwy. 270 on Ala Kahua Dr. (in Kohala Estates) just north of Kawaihae. Turn at the 6-mile marker, ½ mile up the hill to the gate at a lava rock wall.

5 Waimea (Kamuela) ★★★

Kamuela Museum   It takes only about an hour to explore tiny Kamuela Museum. Its eclectic collection includes an early Hawaiian dogtooth death cup, a piece of rope used on the *Apollo* mission, and ancient artifacts from the royal family.

At the junction of Hwy. 19 and Hwy. 250, Waimea. ℰ **808/885-4724.** www.hawaii museums.org/mc/ishawaii_kamuela.htm. Admission $5 adults, $2 children under 12. Daily 8am–5pm.

Parker Ranch ℛ   The *paniolo* (cowboy) tradition began here in 1809, when John Parker, a 19-year-old New England sailor, jumped ship and rounded up wild cows for King Kamehameha. There's some evidence that Hawaiian cowboys were the first to be taught by the great Spanish horsemen, the *vaqueros;* they were cowboying 40 years before their counterparts in California, Texas, and the Pacific Northwest. The Parker Ranch, after six generations of cowboys, is smaller today than in its glory, but it still is a working ranch; some 12 cowboys work 250 horses and over 30,000 head of cattle on 175,000 acres.

The **Visitor Center,** located at the Parker Ranch Shopping Center on Highway 190 (ℰ **808/885-7655**), is open daily from 9am to 5pm and houses the **Parker Ranch Museum,** which displays items that have been used throughout the ranch's history and illustrates six generations of Parker family history. An interesting video captures the essence of day-to-day life on a working ranch.

You can also tour two historic homes on the ranch. In 1989 the late Richard Smart—a sixth-generation heir—opened his 8,000-square-foot yellow Victorian home, **Puuopelu,** to art lovers. The French Regency gallery here includes original works by Renoir, Degas, Dufy, Corot, Utrillo, and Pissarro. Next door is **Mana Hale,** a little New England saltbox built from koa wood 140 years ago.

If you want to get out and see the ranch itself, take the 45-minute narrated **Kohala Carriage Tour** (Tues–Sat), which takes place in an old-fashioned wagon pulled by two large Belgian draft horses, with seating for 20, roll-down protection from the elements, and warm blankets for the upcountry temperatures. The tour rolls past ancient Hawaiian artifacts, 19th-century stone corrals (still in use), and miles of vast rolling hills; it stops at a working cowboy station, where visitors can get out, take photos, and stretch their legs.

See "Horseback Riding," under "Golf & Other Outdoor Activities" in chapter 4, for details on riding tours of Parker Ranch. Allow about 1½ hours to see the ranch.

Parker Ranch Center, Waimea. (© **808/885-7655** for visitor center. www.parker ranch.com. Admission to museum $7 adults, $4.50 children younger than 12; tour of ranch homes $8.50 adults, $6 children; Kohala Carriage Tour $15 adults, $12 children. Visitor center and museum Mon–Sat 9am–5pm. If you're seeing the museum only, you can arrive as late as 4pm; the last museum/ranch homes tickets are sold at 4pm; the final museum/carriage tour tickets are sold at 2pm.

6 Mauna Kea ✦✦✦

The summit of Mauna Kea, the world's tallest mountain if measured from its base on the ocean floor, is the best place on earth for astronomical observations because its mid-Pacific site is near the Equator and because it enjoys clear, pollution-free skies and pitch-black nights with no urban light to interfere. That's why Mauna Kea is home to the world's largest telescope, but the stargazing from here is fantastic even with the naked eye.

SETTING OUT   You'll need a four-wheel-drive vehicle to climb to the peak, **Observatory Hill.** A standard car will get you as far as the visitor center, but check your rental agreement before you go; some agencies prohibit you from taking your car on the Saddle Road, which is narrow and rutted, and has a soft shoulder.

SAFETY TIPS   Always check the weather and Mauna Kea road conditions before you head out (© **808/969-3218**). Dress warmly; the temperatures drop into the 30s (around 0°C) after dark. Drink as much liquid as possible, avoiding alcohol and coffee, in the 36 hours surrounding your trip to avoid dehydration. Don't go within 24 hours of scuba diving—you could get the bends. The day before you go, avoid gas-producing foods, such as beans, cabbage, onions, soft drinks, or starches. If you smoke, take a break for 48 hours before to allow the carbon monoxide in your bloodstream to dissipate—you need all the oxygen you can get. Wear dark sunglasses to avoid snow blindness, and use lots of sunscreen and lip balm. Pregnant women and anyone under 13 or with a heart condition or lung ailment are advised to stay below. Once you're at the top, don't overexert yourself; it's bad for your heart. Take it easy up here.

ACCESS POINTS & VISITOR CENTERS   It's about an hour from Hilo or Waimea to the visitor center and another 30 to 45 minutes from here to the summit. Take the Saddle Road (Hwy. 200) from Highway 190; it's about 19 miles to Mauna Kea State Recreation Area, a good place to stop and stretch your legs. Go another 9 miles to the unmarked Summit Road turnoff, at mile marker 28 (about 9,300 ft.), across from the Hunter's Check-in Station. People usually start getting lightheaded after the 9,600-foot marker (about 6¼ miles up the Summit Rd.), the site of the last comfort zone and the **Onizuka Visitor Information Station** (© **808/961-2180;** www. ifa.hawaii.edu/info/vis). Named in memory of Hawaii's fallen astronaut, a native of the Big Island and a victim of the *Challenger* explosion, the center is open daily from 9am to 10pm.

TOURS & PROGRAMS   If you'd rather not go it alone to the top, you can caravan up as part of a **free summit tour,** offered Saturday and Sunday at 1pm from the visitor center (returns at 5pm). You must be 16 or older and in good health (no cardiopulmonary problems), not be pregnant, and have a four-wheel-drive vehicle. The tours explain the development of the facilities on Mauna Kea and include a walking tour of an observatory at 13,796 feet. Call © **808/961-2180** if you'd like to participate.

Every night from 6 to 10pm, you can do some serious **stargazing** from the **Onizuka Visitor Information Station.** There's a free lecture at 6pm, followed by a video, a question-and-answer session, and your chance to peer through 11-inch, 14-inch, and 16-inch telescopes. Bring a snack and, if you've got them, your own telescope or binoculars, along with a flashlight (with a red filter). Dress for 30° to 40°F (–1° to 4°C) temperatures, but call for the weather report first (© **808/961-5582**). Families are welcome.

Another telescope tour is offered, free, during the day, by the **Subaru Telescope** (© **808/934-5056;** www.subarutelescope.org). You must book the 30-minute tour a week in advance, as they offer only 15 tours a month: Monday through Friday, at 10:30am, 11:30am, and 1:30pm on a first-to-sign-up basis. The Subaru Telescope is 1 of 13 world-class telescopes on the summit of Mauna Kea. You will need a four-wheel-drive car to make the trip up. They recommend that you stop for at least 30 minutes at the Onizuka Visitor Center at 9,000 feet to acclimate. Because of the risk of altitude sickness, the 30-minute tour is closed to pregnant women, children under 16, and anyone with health concerns that could be aggravated by the high altitude. Scuba divers are advised to schedule dives on a day separate from the tour.

At the **Keck Telescope Control Center,** 65–1120 Mamalahoa Hwy. (Hwy. 19), across from the North Hawaii Community Hospital,

Experiencing Where the Gods Live

"The ancient Hawaiians thought of the top of Mauna Kea as heaven, or at least where the gods and goddess lived," according to Monte "Pat" Wright, owner and chief guide of **Mauna Kea Summit Adventures.**

Wright, the first guide to take people up to the top of the Mauna Kea, world's tallest mountain when measured from the base and an astonishing 13,796 feet when measured from sea level, says he fell in love with this often-snow-capped peak the first time he saw it.

Mauna Kea Summit Adventures offers a luxurious trip to the top of the world. The 7- to 8-hour adventure begins midafternoon, when guests are picked up along the Kona-Kohala coast in a brand-new $65,000 custom four-wheel-drive turbo-diesel van.

As the passengers make the drive up the mountain, the extensively trained guide discusses the geography, geology, natural history, and Hawaiian culture along the way.

The first stop is at the Onizuka Visitor Information Station, at 9,000 feet.

"We let people out to stretch, get acclimatized to the altitude, and eat dinner," Wright says.

As guests gear up with Mauna Kea Summit's heavy, arctic-style hooded parkas and gloves (30°F/–1°C is the average temperature on the mountain), the guide describes why the world's largest telescopes are located on Mauna Kea and also tells stories about the lifestyle of astronomers who live for a clear night sky.

After a dinner of gourmet sandwiches, vegetarian onion soup, and hot chocolate, coffee, or tea, everyone climbs back into the van for the half-hour ride to the summit.

Waimea (© **808/885-7887**; www.keckobservatory.org), you can see a model of the world's largest telescope, which sits atop Mauna Kea. The center is open Monday through Friday from 8am to 4:30pm. A 12-minute video explains the Keck's search for objects in deep space.

The W.M. Keck Observatory does not offer tours at the summit, but it does provides a visitor's gallery with a 12-minute video, informational panels on the observatory layout and science results, two

As the sun sinks into the Pacific nearly 14,000 feet below, the guide points out the various world-renowned telescopes as they rotate into position for the night viewing.

After the last trace of sunset colors has disappeared from the sky, the tour again descends down to midmountain, where the climate is more agreeable, for stargazing. Each tour has Celestron Celestar 8 deluxe telescopes, which are capable of 30-175× magnification and gather up to 500 times more light than the unaided eye.

Wright does caution people to book the adventure early in their vacation.

"Although we do cancel about 25 trips a year due to weather, we want to be able to accommodate everyone," he says. If guests book at the beginning of their holiday and the trip is canceled due to weather, then Mauna Kea Summit will attempt to reschedule another day.

Wright also points out that due to the summit's low oxygen level (40% less oxygen than sea level) and the diminished air pressure (also 40% less air pressure than sea level), the lack of oxygen can be a serious problem for people with heart or lung problems or for scuba divers who have been diving in the previous 24 hours.

Pregnant woman, children under 13, and obese people should not travel to the summit due to the decreased oxygen. Because the roads to the summit are bumpy, anyone with a bad back might want to opt out.

The cost for this celestial adventure is $185 including tax (15% discounted if you book online at www.maunakea.com, 2 weeks in advance). For more information, call ℂ 888/322-2366 or 808/322-2366, or go to www.maunakea.com.

public restrooms, and a viewing area with partial views of the Keck telescope and dome. Gallery hours are 10am to 4pm Monday to Friday.

MAKING THE CLIMB   If you're heading up on your own, stop at the visitor center for about a half-hour to get acquainted with the altitude. Walk around, eat a banana, and drink some water before you press onward and upward in low gear, engine whining. It takes about 30 to 45 minutes to get to the top from here. The trip is a mere 6 miles, but you climb from 9,000 to nearly 14,000 feet.

AT THE SUMMIT   Up here, 11 nations, including Japan, France, and Canada, have set up peerless infrared telescopes to look into deep space. Among them sits the **Keck Telescope,** the world's largest. Developed by the University of California and the California Institute of Technology, it's eight stories high, weighs 150 tons, and has a 33-foot-diameter mirror made of 36 perfectly attuned hexagon mirrors, like a fly's eye, rather than one conventional lens.

Also at the summit, up a narrow footpath, is a cairn of rocks; from it, you can see across the Pacific Ocean in a 360-degree view that's beyond words and pictures. When it's socked in, you get a surreal look at the summits of Mauna Loa and Maui's Haleakala poking through the puffy white cumulus clouds beneath your feet.

Inside a cinder cone just below the summit is **Lake Waiau,** the only glacial lake in the mid-Pacific, and at 13,020 feet above sea level, one of the highest lakes in the world. The lake never dries up, even though it gets only 15 inches of rain a year and sits in porous lava where there are no springs. Nobody quite knows what to make of this, but scientists suspect the lake is replenished by snowmelt and permafrost from submerged lava tubes. You can't see the lake from Summit Road; you must take a brief high-altitude hike. But it's easy: On the final approach to the summit area, upon regaining the blacktop road, go about 200 yards to the major switchback and make a hard right turn. Park on the shoulder of the road (which is at 13,200 ft.). No sign points the way, but there's an obvious .5-mile trail that goes down to the lake about 200 feet across the lava. Follow the base of the big cinder cone on your left; you should have the summit of Mauna Loa in view directly ahead as you walk.

7 The Hamakua Coast ✸✸✸

The sugar industry's rich 117-year history, along the scenic 45-mile coastline from Hilo to Hamakua, comes alive in the interpretive *Hilo-Hamakua Heritage Coast* drive guide, produced by the **Hawaii Island Economic Development Board,** 117 Kiawe St., Hilo, HI 96720 (© **808/935-2180;** www.hiedb.org).

The free guide not only points out the historic sites and museums, scenic photo opportunities, restaurants and stores, and even restrooms along the Hawaii Belt Road (Hwy. 19), but also has corresponding brown-and-white points-of-interest signs on the highway.

Visitor information centers anchored at either end in Hilo and in Hamakua offer additional information on the area.

NATURAL WONDERS ALONG THE COAST

Akaka Falls 🎝🎝🎝   See one of Hawaii's most scenic waterfalls via an easy 1-mile paved loop through a rainforest, past bamboo and ginger, and down to an observation point. You'll have a perfect view of 442-foot Akaka and nearby Kahuna Falls, which is a mere 100-footer. Keep your eyes peeled for rainbows. The noise you hear is the sound of coqui frogs, an alien frog from Puerto Rico that has become a pest on the Big Island.

On Hwy. 19, Honomu (8 miles north of Hilo). Turn left at Honomu and head 3½ miles inland on Akaka Falls Rd. (Hwy. 220).

Hawaii Tropical Botanical Garden 🎝🎝   More than 1,800 species of tropical plants thrive in this little-known Eden by the sea. The 40-acre garden, nestled between the crashing surf and a thundering waterfall, has the world's largest selection of tropical plants growing in a natural environment, including torch gingers (which tower on 12-ft. stalks), a banyan canyon, an orchid garden, a banana grove, a bromeliad hill, and a golden bamboo grove, which rattles like a jungle drum in the trade winds. Some endangered Hawaiian specimens, such as the rare *Gardenia remyi,* are flourishing in this habitat. The gardens are seldom crowded; you can wander around by yourself all day.

Off Hwy. 19 on the 4-mile Scenic Rte., Onomea Bay (8 miles north of Hilo). © **808/ 964-5233.** www.htbg.com. Admission $15 adults, $5 children 6–16, free for children 5 and younger. Daily 9am–4pm.

Laupahoehoe Beach Park 🎝   This idyllic place holds a grim reminder of nature's fury. In 1946 a tidal wave swept across the village that once stood on this lava-leaf (that's what *laupahoehoe* means) peninsula and claimed the lives of 20 students and four teachers. A memorial in this pretty little park recalls the tragedy. The land here ends in black sea stacks that resemble tombstones. It's not a place for swimming, but the views are spectacular.

Laupahoehoe Point exit off Hwy. 19.

World Botanical Garden 🎝🎝   Just north of Hilo is Hawaii's largest botanical garden, with some 5,000 species. When the fruits are in season, the staff hands out free chilled juices. One of the most spectacular sites is the .25-mile rainforest walk (wheelchair accessible) along a stream on a flower-lined path to the viewing area of the three-tiered, 300-foot Umauma Falls. Parents will appreciate the large children's maze, where the "prize" is a playing field near the exit. The mock-orange hedge, which defines the various paths in the maze, is only 5 feet tall, so most parents can peer over the edge to keep an eye on their *keiki*. Other terrific walks include one through a wellness garden with medicinal Hawaiian plants and the "rainbow walk" (an ethno-botanical garden rainbow walk). There's also an arboretum. Still under construction as we went to press is a phylogenetic garden with plants and trees arranged in roughly the same sequence they first appeared on earth.

Off Hwy. 19 near the 16-mile marker in Umauma. P.O. Box 411, Honomu, HI 96728. ℭ 808/963-5427. www.worldbotanicalgardens.com. Admission $13 adults, $6 teens 13–19 years, $3 children 5–12 years, free for children under 5. Guided tours $40 adults, $30 teens, $20 children. Daily 9am–5:30pm.

HONOKAA 𝕬𝕬𝕬

Honokaa is worth a visit to see the remnants of plantation life, when sugar was king. This is a real place that hasn't yet been boutiqued into a shopping mall; it looks as if someone has kept it in a bell jar since 1920. There's a real barbershop, a real Filipino store, some good shopping (see chapter 6), and a hotel with creaky floorboards that dishes up hearty food. The town also serves as the gateway to spectacular Waipio Valley (see below).

Honokaa has no attractions, per se, but you might want to check out the **Katsu Goto Memorial,** next to the library at the Hilo end of town. Katsu Goto, one of the first indentured Japanese immigrants, arrived in Honokaa in the late 1800s to work on the sugar plantations. He learned English, quit the plantation, and aided his fellow immigrants in labor disputes with American planters. On October 23, 1889, he was hanged from a lamppost in Honokaa, a victim of local-style justice.

THE END OF THE ROAD: WAIPIO VALLEY 𝕬𝕬𝕬

Long ago, this lush, tropical place was the valley of kings, who called it the valley of "curving water" (which is what *Waipio* means). From the black-sand bay at its mouth, Waipio sweeps 6 miles between sheer, cathedral-like walls that reach almost a mile high. Once 40,000 Hawaiians lived here, amid taro, red bananas, and wild guavas in an area etched by streams and waterfalls. Only about 50 Hawaiians live in the valley today, tending taro, fishing, and soaking up the ambience of this old Hawaiian place.

The sacred valley is steeped in myth and legend. Many of the ancient royals are buried here; some believe they rise up to become Marchers of the Night, whose chants reverberate through the valley.

The caskets of Hawaiian chiefs Liloa and Lono Ika Makahiki, stolen from the Bishop Museum, are believed to have been brought here by Hawaiians.

To get to Waipio Valley, take Highway 19 from Hilo to Honokaa, and then Highway 240 to **Waipio Valley Lookout** ⟨⭑⭑⭑⟩, a grassy park on the edge of Waipio Valley's sheer cliffs with splendid views of the wild oasis below. This is a great place for a picnic; you can sit at old redwood picnic tables and watch the white combers race along the black-sand beach at the mouth of the valley.

From the lookout, you can hike down into the valley. *Warning:* Do not attempt to drive your rental car down into the valley (even if you see someone else doing it). The problem is not so much going down as coming back up. Every day, rental cars have to be "rescued" and towed back up to the top, at great expense to the driver. Instead, take the **Waipio Valley Shuttle** (✆ **808/775-7121**) on a 90- to 120-minute guided tour (Mon–Sat 9am–4pm). Get your tickets at **Waipio Valley Art Works,** on Highway 240, 2 miles from the lookout (✆ **808/775-0958**). Tickets are $45 for adults, $20 for kids 11 and under.

You can also explore the valley on a narrated 90-minute **Waipio Valley Wagon Tour** (✆ **808/775-9518;** www.waipiovalleywagontours.com), a historical ride by mule-drawn surrey. Tours are offered Monday through Saturday at 9:30am, 11:30am, 1:30pm, and 3:30pm. It costs $55 for adults, $50 for seniors, $25 for children ages 4 to 12; call for reservations.

If you want to spend more than a day in the valley, plan ahead. A few simple B&Bs are situated on the ridge overlooking the valley and require advance reservations (see chapter 2).

8 Hilo ⟨⭑⭑⭑⟩

Contact or stop by the **Downtown Hilo Improvement Association,** 252 Kamehameha Ave., Hilo, HI 96720 (✆ **808/935-8850;** www.downtownhilo.com), for a copy of its very informative self-guided walking tour of Hilo, which focuses on 18 historical sites dating from the 1870s to the present.

ON THE WATERFRONT

Old banyan trees shade **Banyan Drive** ⟨⭑⭑⟩, the lane that curves along the waterfront to the Hilo Bay hotels. Most of the trees were planted in the mid-1930s by memorable visitors like Cecil B. DeMille (who was here in 1933 filming *Four Frightened People*), Babe Ruth (his tree is in front of Hilo Hawaiian Hotel), King

George V, Amelia Earhart, and other celebrities whose fleeting fame didn't last as long as the trees themselves.

It's worth a stop along Banyan Drive—especially if the coast is clear and the summit of Mauna Kea is free of clouds—to make the short walk across the concrete-arch bridge in front of the Naniloa Hotel to **Coconut Island** ✸, if only to gain a panoramic sense of the place.

Also along Banyan Drive is **Liliuokalani Gardens** ✸✸, the largest formal Japanese garden this side of Tokyo. This 30-acre park, named for Hawaii's last monarch, Queen Liliuokalani, is as pretty as a postcard, with bonsai, carp ponds, pagodas, and a moon-gate bridge. Admission is free; open 24 hours.

OTHER HILO SIGHTS

Lyman Museum & Mission House ✸ *Kids*
The oldest wood-frame house on the island was built in 1839 by David and Sarah Lyman, a missionary couple who arrived from New England in 1832. This hybrid combined New England– and Hawaiian-style architecture and is built of hand-hewn koa planks and native timbers. Here the Lymans received such guests as Mark Twain and Hawaii's monarchs. The well-preserved house is the best example of missionary life and times in Hawaii. You'll find lots of artifacts from the 19th century, including furniture and clothing from the Lymans and one of the first mirrors in Hilo.

The **Earth Heritage Gallery** in the complex next door continues the story of the islands with geology and volcanology exhibits, a mineral rock collection that's rated one of the best in the country, and a section on local flora and fauna. The **Island Heritage Gallery** features displays on Hawaiian culture, including a replica of a grass *hale* (house), as well as on other cultures transplanted to Hawaii's shores. A special exhibit gallery features changing exhibits on the history, art, and culture of Hawaii.

276 Haili St. (at Kapiolani St.), Hilo. ✆ 808/935-5021. www.lymanmuseum.org. Admission $10 adults, $8 seniors over 60, $3 children 6–17, $21 per family. Mon–Sat 9:30am–4:30pm. Tours 10am, 11am, 1pm, 2pm, and 3pm.

Maunaloa Macadamia Nut Factory
Explore this unique factory to learn how Hawaii's favorite nut is grown and processed. And, of course, you'll want to try a few samples.

Macadamia Nut Rd. (8 miles from Hilo, off Hwy. 11), Hilo. ✆ 888/MAUNA LOA or 808/966-8618. www.maunaloa.com. Free admission; self-guided factory tours. Daily 8:30am–5pm. From Hwy. 11, turn on Macadamia Nut Rd.; go 3 miles down the road to the factory.

Moments   Imiloa: Exploring the Unknown

Absolutely do *not* miss the recently opened **Imiloa: Astronomy Center of Hawaii.** The 300 exhibits in the 12,000-square-foot gallery make the connection between the Hawaiian culture and its explorers, who discovered the Hawaiian Islands, and the astronomers who explore the heavens from the observatories atop Mauna Kea. *Imiloa,* which means "explorer" or "seeker of profound truth," is the perfect name for this architecturally stunning center, located on 9.1 landscaped acres overlooking Hilo Bay in the University of Hawaii at Hilo Science and Technology Park campus, 600 Imiloa Pl. (© **808/969-9700;** www.imiloa hawaii.org). Plan to spend at least a couple of hours here; a half a day would be better, to allow time to browse the excellent interactive exhibits as well as take in one of the planetarium shows, which boast a state-of-the-art digital projection system. Open Tuesday to Sunday from 9am to 4pm; admission is $15 for adults and $7.50 for children ages 4 to 12.

Mokupapa: Discovery Center for Hawaii's Remote Coral Reef *Kids Value*   This 4,000-square-foot center is perfect for kids, who can explore the Northwest Hawaiian Islands coral reef ecosystem. Through interactive displays, engaging three-dimensional models, and an immersion theater, the kids can learn natural science, culture, and history while having a great time. A 2,500-gallon saltwater aquarium provides a habitat for a collection of fish from the Northwest Hawaiian Islands reefs. Lots of fun at a terrific price: free!

308 Kamehameha Ave., Suite 109, Hilo. © **808/933-8198.** www.hawaiireef.noaa. gov. Free admission. Tues–Sat 9am–4pm.

Naha Stone   This 2½-ton stone was used as a test of royal strength: Ancient legend said that whoever could move the stone would conquer and unite the islands. As a 14-year-old boy, King Kamehameha the Great moved the stone—and later fulfilled his destiny. The Pinao stone, next to it, once guarded an ancient temple.

In front of Hilo Public Library, 300 Waianuenue Ave.

A Desert Crossing

If you follow Highway 11 counterclockwise from Kona to the Volcano, you'll get a preview of what lies ahead in the national park: hot, scorched, quake-shaken, bubbling-up new/dead land. This is the great Kau Desert, layer upon layer of lava flows, fine ash, and fallout. As you traverse the desert, you cross the Great Crack and the Southwest Rift Zone, a major fault zone that looks like a giant groove in the earth, before you reach Kilauea Volcano.

Nani Mau Gardens 🛪 Just outside Hilo is Nani Mau ("forever beautiful"), where Makato Nitahara, who turned a 20-acre papaya patch into a tropical garden, claims to have every flowering plant in Hawaii. His collection includes more than 2,000 varieties, from fragile hibiscus, whose blooms last only a day, to durable red anthuriums imported from South America. There are also Japanese gardens, an orchid walkway, a botanical museum, a house full of butterflies, and a restaurant that's open for lunch and dinner.

421 Makalika St., Hilo. ℂ **808/959-3500.** www.nanimau.com. Admission $10 adults, $5 children 4–10. Tram tours $5 extra for adults, $3 extra for children. Daily 9am–4:30pm. Go 3 miles south of Hilo Airport on Hwy. 11, turn on Makalika St., and continue ¾ mile.

Pacific Tsunami Museum 🛪 The most interesting artifacts here are not the exhibits, but the volunteers who survived Hawaii's most deadly "walls of water" in 1946 and 1960, both of which reshaped the town of Hilo. Visitors can listen to their stories of terror and view a range of exhibits, from interactive computers to a children's section, to a display on what happens when a local earthquake triggers a seismic wave, as it did in 1975 during the Big Island's last tsunami.

130 Kamehameha Ave., Hilo. ℂ **808/935-0926.** www.tsunami.org. Admission $7 adults, $6 seniors, $5 ages 6–17 years, 5 and under free. Mon–Sat 9am–4pm.

Panaewa Rainforest Zoo 🛪 *Kids* This 12-acre zoo, nestled in the heart of the Panaewa Forest Reserve south of Hilo, is the only outdoor rainforest zoo in the United States. Some 50 species of animals from rainforests around the globe call Panaewa home—including several endangered Hawaiian birds. All of them are exhibited in a natural setting. This is one of the few zoos where you can observe Sumatran tigers, Brazilian tapirs, and the rare pygmy hippopotamus, an endangered "minihippo" found in Western Africa.

Stainback Hwy. (off Hwy. 11), Hilo. ℂ **808/959-7224.** www.hilozoo.com. Free admission. Daily 9am–4pm. Petting zoo Sat 1:30–2:30pm; tiger feeding 3:30pm daily.

Rainbow Falls ⊛ (*Moments*)   Go in the morning, around 9 or 10am, just as the sun comes over the mango trees, to see Rainbow Falls at its best. The 80-foot falls spill into a big round natural pool surrounded by wild ginger. According to legend, Hina, the mother of Maui, lives in the cave behind the falls. Unfortunately, swimming in the pool is no longer allowed.

West on Waianuenue Ave., past Kaumana Dr.

9 Hawaii Volcanoes National Park ⊛⊛⊛

Yellowstone, Yosemite, and other national parks are spectacular, no doubt about it. But in my opinion, they're all ho-hum compared to this one: Here nothing less than the miracle of creation is the daily attraction.

In the 19th century, before tourism became Hawaii's middle name, the islands' singular attraction for world travelers wasn't the beach, but the volcano. From the world over, curious spectators gathered on the rim of Kilauea's Halemaumau crater to see one of the greatest wonders of the globe. Nearly a century after it was named a national park (in 1916), Hawaii Volcanoes remains the state's premier natural attraction.

Hawaii Volcanoes has the only rainforest in the U.S. National Park system—and it's the only park that's home to an active volcano. Most people drive through the park (it has 50 miles of good roads, some of them often covered by lava flows) and call it a day. But it takes at least 3 days to explore the whole park, including such oddities as **Halemaumau Crater** ⊛⊛⊛, a still-fuming pit of steam and sulfur; the intestinal-looking **Thurston Lava Tube** ⊛⊛⊛; **Devastation Trail** ⊛⊛⊛, a short hike through a desolated area destroyed by lava; and, finally, the end of **Chain of Craters Road** ⊛⊛⊛, where lava regularly spills across the man-made two-lane blacktop to create its own red-hot freeway to the sea. In addition to some of the world's weirdest landscapes, the park has hiking trails, rainforests, campgrounds, a historic old hotel on the crater's rim, and that spectacular, still-erupting volcano.

NOTES ON THE ERUPTING VOLCANO   Volcanologists refer to Hawaii's volcanic eruptions as "quiet" eruptions because gases escape slowly instead of building up and exploding violently all at once. Hawaii's eruptions produce slow-moving, oozing lava that provides excellent, safe viewing most of the time.

Even so, the volcano has still caused its share of destruction. Since the current eruption of Kilauea began on January 3, 1983, lava has covered some 16,000 acres of lowland and rainforest, threatening rare hawks, honeycreeper birds, spiders, and bats, while destroying power and telephone lines and eliminating water service possibly forever. Some areas have been mantled repeatedly and are now buried underneath 80 feet of lava. At last count, the lava flow had destroyed nearly 200 homes and businesses, wiped out Kaimu Black Sand Beach (once Hawaii's most photographed beach) and Queen's Bath, obliterated entire towns and subdivisions (Kalapana, Royal Gardens, Kalapana Gardens, and Kapaahu Homesteads), and buried natural and historic landmarks (a 12th-c. *heiau,* the century-old Kalapana Mauna Kea Church, Wahaulu Visitor Center, and thousands of archaeological artifacts and sites). The cost of the destruction—so far—is estimated at $100 million. But how do you price the destruction of a 700-year-old temple or a 100-year-old church?

However, Kilauea hasn't just destroyed parts of the island; it has also added to it—more than 560 acres of new land. The volume of erupted lava over the last 2 decades measures nearly 2 billion cubic yards—enough new rock to pave a two-lane highway 1¼ million miles long, circling the earth some 50 times. Or, as a spokesperson for the park puts it: "Every 5 days, there is enough lava coming out of Kilauea volcano's eruption to place a thin veneer over Washington, D.C.—all 63 square miles."

The most prominent vent of the eruption has been Puu Oo, a 760-foot-high cinder-and-spatter cone. The most recent flow—the one you'll be able to see, if you're lucky—follows a 7-mile-long tube from the Puu Oo vent area to the sea. This lava flow has extended the Big Island's shoreline seaward and added hundreds of acres of new land along the steep southern slopes. Periodically, the new land proves unstable, falls under its own weight, and slides into the ocean. (These areas of ground gained and lost are not included in the tally of new acreage—only the land that sticks counts.)

Scientists are also keeping an eye on Mauna Loa, which has been swelling since its last eruption in 1983. If there's a new eruption, there could be a fast-moving flow down the southwest side of the island, possibly into South Kona or Kau.

WHAT YOU'RE LIKELY TO SEE   With luck, the volcano will still be streaming rivers of red lava when you visit the park, but a continuous eruption of this length (more than 2 decades) is setting new ground, so to speak. Kilauea continues to perplex volcanologists because most major eruptions in the past have ended abruptly after only several months.

Hawaii Volcanoes National Park

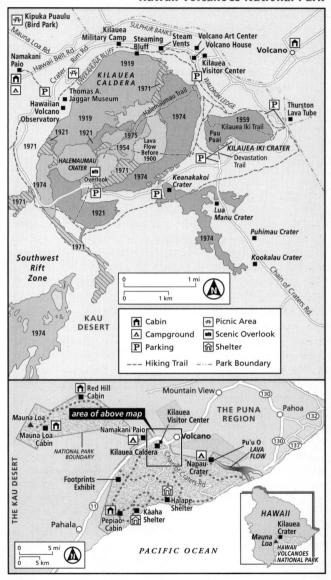

Kipuka Puaulu (Bird Park)

Mauna Loa Rd.

Hawaii Belt Rd.

Crater Rim Rd.

Namakani Paio

Hawaiian Volcano Observatory

Kilauea Military Camp

SULPHUR BANKS

Steaming Bluff

Steam Vents

Volcano Art Center

Volcano House

Volcano

Kilauea Visitor Center

UWEKAHUNA BLUFF

KILAUEA CALDERA

Thomas A. Jaggar Museum

Halemaumau Trail

WALDRON LEDGE

Thurston Lava Tube

1919

1971

1919

1971

1921

1921

1921

1974

1975

1954

Lava Flow Before 1900

HALEMAUMAU CRATER

Overlook

1971

1974

Keanakakoi Crater

1959

Kilauea Iki Trail

Puu Puai

KILAUEA IKI CRATER

Devastation Trail

1971

1974

1974

1971

1974

Lua Manu Crater

Puhimau Crater

Kookalau Crater

Southwest Rift Zone

KAU DESERT

1974

Chain of Craters Rd.

0 — 1 mi
0 — 1 km

N

Cabin
Campground
Parking
--- Hiking Trail

Picnic Area
Scenic Overlook
Shelter
Park Boundary

Red Hill Cabin

Mountain View

THE PUNA REGION

Pahoa

Mauna Loa

Mauna Loa Cabin

NATIONAL PARK BOUNDARY

area of above map

Namakani Paio

Kilauea Caldera

Kilauea Visitor Center

Volcano

Pu'u O LAVA FLOW

Napau Crater

Chain of Craters Rd.

THE KAU DESERT

Footprints Exhibit

Halape Shelter

Pepiao Cabin

Kaaha Shelter

Pahala

PACIFIC OCEAN

0 — 5 mi
0 — 5 km

N

HAWAII

Mauna Loa

Kilauea Crater

HAWAII VOLCANOES NATIONAL PARK

145

(Tips **A Volcano-Visiting Tip**

Thanks to its higher elevation and windward (rainier) location, this neck of the woods is always colder than it is at the beach. If you're coming from the Kona side of the island in summer, expect it to be at least 10° to 20° cooler at the volcano; bring a sweater or light jacket. In the winter months, expect temperatures to be in the 40s or 50s (single digits to midteens Celsius), and dress accordingly. Always have rain gear on hand, especially in winter.

But neither Mother Nature nor Madame Pele (the volcano goddess) runs on a schedule. The volcano could be shooting fountains of lava hundreds of feet into the air on the day you arrive, or it could be completely quiet—there are no guarantees. On many days, the lava flows right by accessible roads, and you can get as close as the heat will allow; sometimes, however, the flow is in underground tubes where you can't see it, or miles away from the nearest access point, visible only in the distance. Always ask the park rangers for advice before you set out on any lava-viewing expeditions.

VOLCANO VOCABULARY   The volcano has its own unique, poetic vocabulary that describes in Hawaiian what cannot be said so well in English. The lava that looks like swirls of chocolate cake frosting is called **pahoehoe** (pa-*hoy*-hoy); it results from a fast-moving flow that curls artistically as it moves. The big, blocky, jumbled lava that looks like a chopped-up parking lot is called **aa** (ah-ah); it's caused by lava that moves slowly, pulling apart as it overruns itself.

Newer words include **vog,** which is volcanic smog made of volcanic gases and smoke from forests set on fire by aa and pahoehoe. **Laze** results when sulfuric acid hits the water and vaporizes and mixes with chlorine to become, as any chemistry student knows, hydrochloric acid. Both vog and laze sting your eyes and can cause respiratory illness; don't expose yourself to either for too long. Anyone with heart or breathing trouble, or women who are pregnant, should avoid both vog and laze.

JUST THE FACTS
WHEN TO GO   The best time to go is when Kilauea is really pumping. If you're lucky, you'll be in the park when the volcano is active and there's a fountain of lava; mostly, the lava runs like a red river downslope into the sea. If you're on another part of the island

and hear a TV news bulletin that the volcano is acting up, head to Hilo to see the spectacle. You won't be sorry—and your favorite beach will still be there when you get back.

ACCESS POINTS Hawaii Volcanoes National Park is 29 miles from Hilo, on Hawaii Belt Road (Hwy. 11). If you're staying in Kailua-Kona, it's 100 miles, or about a 2½-hour drive, to the park. At press time, admission was still $10 per vehicle, but the park was proposing to double that to $20 per car in 2008; once you pay the fee, you can come and go as often as you want for 7 days. Hikers and bicyclists pay $5; bikes are allowed only on roads and paved trails.

VISITOR CENTERS & INFORMATION Contact **Hawaii Volcanoes National Park,** P.O. Box 52, Hawaii Volcanoes National Park, HI 96718 (© **808/985-6000;** www.nps.gov/havo). **Kilauea Visitor Center** is at the entrance to the park, just off Highway 11; it's open daily from 7:45am to 5pm.

ERUPTION UPDATES Everything you wanted to know about Hawaii's volcanoes, from what's going on with the current eruptions to where the next eruption is likely to be, is now available on the Hawaiian Volcano Observatory's new website, **http://hvo.wr.usgs. gov/kilauea/update/main.html**. The site is divided into areas on Kilauea (the currently erupting volcano), Mauna Loa (which last erupted in 1984), and Hawaii's other volcanoes. Each section provides photos, maps, eruption summaries, and historical information.

You can also get the latest on volcanic activity in the park by calling the park's **24-hour hot line** (© **808/985-6000**). Updates on volcanic activity are also posted daily on the bulletin board at the visitor center.

HIKING & CAMPING IN THE PARK Hawaii Volcanoes National Park offers a wealth of hiking and camping possibilities. See "Hiking & Camping," in chapter 4, for details.

ACCOMMODATIONS IN & AROUND THE PARK If camping isn't your thing, don't worry. There's a hotel, **Volcano House,** within the park boundary, on the rim of Halemaumau Crater. Volcano Village, just outside the park, has plenty of comfortable and convenient hotels and restaurants (see chapters 2 and 3).

SEEING THE HIGHLIGHTS

Your first stop should be **Kilauea Visitor Center** ⚡⚡, a rustic structure in a shady grove of trees just inside the entrance to the park. Here you can get up-to-the-minute reports on the volcano's activity, learn how volcanoes work, see a film showing blasts from the past, get information on hiking and camping, and pick up the obligatory postcards.

Filled with a new understanding of volcanology and the volcano goddess, Pele, you should then walk across the street to **Volcano House;** go through the lobby and out the other side, where you can get a look at **Kilauea Caldera** ★★★, a 2½-mile wide, 500-foot-deep pit. The caldera used to be a bubbling pit of fountaining lava; today you can still see wisps of steam that might, while you're standing there, turn into something more.

Now get out on the road and drive by the **Sulphur Banks** ★, which smell like rotten eggs, and the **Steam Vents** ★★★, where trails of smoke, once molten lava, rise from within the inner reaches of the earth. This is one of the places where you feel that the volcano is really alive. Stop at the **Thomas A. Jaggar Museum** ★★★ (open daily 8:30am–5pm; free admission) for a good look at Halemaumau Crater, which is ½ mile across and 1,000 feet deep. On a clear day, you might also see Mauna Loa, 20 miles to the west. The museum shows video from days when the volcano was really spewing, explains the Pele legend in murals, and monitors earthquakes (a precursor of eruptions) on a seismograph.

Once you've seen the museum, drive around the caldera to the south side, park, and take the short walk to Halemaumau Crater's edge, past stinky sulfur banks and steam vents, to stand at the overlook and stare in awe at this once-fuming old fire pit, which still generates ferocious heat out of vestigial vents.

If you feel the need to cool off now, go to the **Thurston Lava Tube** ★★★, the coolest place in the park. You'll hike down into a natural bowl in the earth, a forest preserve the lava didn't touch—full of native birds and giant tree ferns. Then you'll see a black hole in the earth; step in. It's all drippy and cool here, with bare roots hanging down. You can either resurface into the bright daylight or, if you have a flashlight, poke on deeper into the tube, which goes for another ½ mile or so.

If you're still game for a good hike, try **Kilauea Iki Crater** ★, a 4-mile, 2-hour hike across the floor of the crater, which became a bubbling pool of lava in 1959 and sent fountains of lava 1,900 feet in the air, completely devastating a nearby ohia forest and leaving another popular hike ominously known as **Devastation Trail** ★★★. This .5-mile walk is a startling look at the powers of a volcanic eruption on the environment. (See "Hiking & Camping," in chapter 4, for details on these and other park hikes.)

Check out ancient Hawaiian art at the **Puu Loa Petroglyphs** ★, around mile marker 15 down Chain of Craters Road. Look for the stack of rocks on the road. A brief .5-mile walk will bring you to a circular boardwalk where you can see thousands of mysterious Hawaiian petroglyphs carved in stone. *Warning:* It's very easy to destroy these ancient works of art. Do not leave the boardwalk, and do not walk on or around the petroglyphs. Rubbings of petroglyphs will destroy them; the best way to capture them is by taking a photo.

This area, Puu Loa, was a sacred place for generations. Fathers came here to bury their newborns' umbilical cords in the numerous small holes in the lava, thus ensuring a long life for the child.

THE VOLCANO AFTER DARK   If the volcano is erupting, be sure to see it after dark. Brilliant red lava snakes down the side of the mountain and pours into the sea, creating a vivid display you'll never forget. About 1½ hours before sunset, head out of the park and back down Volcano Highway (Hwy. 11). Turn onto Highway 130 at Keaau; go past Pahoa to the end of the road. (The drive takes the better part of an hour.) From here (depending on the flow), it's about a mile walk over sharp crusted lava; park rangers will tell you how to get to the best viewing locations, or you can call ahead (© 808/985-6000) to check where the current eruption is and how to get there. Be forewarned that the flow changes constantly and, on some days, may be too far from the road to hike, in which case you'll have to be content with seeing it from a distance. Be sure to heed the rangers: In the past, a handful of hikers who ignored these directions died en route; new lava can be unstable and break off without warning. Take water, a flashlight, and your camera, and wear sturdy shoes.

A BIRD'S-EYE VIEW   The best way to see Kilauea's bubbling caldera is from on high, in a helicopter. This bird's-eye view puts the enormity of it all into perspective. I recommend **Blue Hawaiian Helicopter** ⟨⟨⟨ (© 800/745-BLUE or 808/886-1768; www.blue hawaiian.com), a professionally run, locally based company with an excellent safety record; comfortable, top-of-the-line copters; and pilots who are extremely knowledgeable about everything from volcanology to Hawaii lore. The company flies out of both Hilo and Waikoloa (Hilo is cheaper because it's closer). From Hilo, the 45-minute **Circle of Fire tour** ⟨⟨ takes you over the boiling volcano and then on to a bird's-eye view of the destruction the lava has caused and remote beaches ($210 per person, or $169 online). From Waikoloa, the 2-hour **Big Island Spectacular** ⟨⟨⟨ stars the volcano, tropical valleys, Hamakua Coast waterfalls, and the Kohala Mountains (from $424, or $364 online, but worth every penny).

6

Shops & Galleries

While chefs and farmers tout this island as fertile ground for crops and food, artists point to its primal, volcanic energy as a boost to their creative endeavors. Art communities and galleries are sprinkled across the Big Island, in villages like Holualoa and Volcano, where fine works in pottery, wood-turning, handmade glass, and other two- and three-dimensional media are sold in serene settings.

Although the visual arts are flourishing on this island, the line between shop and gallery can often be too fine to determine. Too many self-proclaimed "galleries" sell schlock or a mixture of arts, crafts, and tacky souvenirs. T-shirts and Kona coffee mugs are a souvenir staple in many so-called galleries.

The galleries and shops below offer a broad mix in many media. Items for the home, jewelry and accessories, vintage Hawaiiana, and accouterments at various prices and for various tastes can make great gifts to go, as can locally made food products such as preserves, cookies, flowers, Kona coffee, and macadamia nuts. You'll find that bowls made of rare native woods such as koa are especially abundant on the Big Island. This is an area in which politics and art intersect: Although reforestation efforts are under way to plant new koa trees, the decline of old-growth forests is causing many artists to turn to equally beautiful, and more environmentally sensitive, alternative woods.

1 The Kona Coast

IN & AROUND KAILUA-KONA

Kailua-Kona's shopping prospects pour out into the streets in a festival atmosphere of T-shirts, trinkets, and dime-a-dozen souvenirs, with Alii Drive at the center of this activity. But the **Coconut Grove Market Place,** on Alii Drive, across the street from the seawall, has changed that image and added some great new shops around a sand volleyball court. Next door in the **Alii Sunset Plaza,** next to the Hard Rock Cafe, beaders can make a beeline for **Kona Beads** (© 808/331-2161) to peruse a dizzying collection of beads from all over the world.

Shopping stalwarts in Kona are the **Kona Square,** across from **King Kamehameha's Kona Beach Hotel;** the hotel's shopping mall, with close to two dozen shops; and the **Kona Inn Shopping Village,** on Alii Drive. All include the usual assortment of T-shirt shops. One highlight is **Alii Gardens Marketplace** at the southern end of Kailua-Kona, a pleasant, tented outdoor marketplace with fresh fruit, flowers, imports, local crafts, and a wonderful selection of orchid plants. There's cheesy stuff there, too, but somehow it's less noticeable outdoors.

The newly opened **Kona International Market,** 74-5533 Luhia St (near Kaiwi St), in the Old Industrial Area, is a great idea, a series of small open-air shops in a large pavilion with food vendors, similar to Waikiki's International Market. Unfortunately, with just a few exceptions, I am very disappointed in this "market." I searched all the vendors looking for something made in Hawaii, and with very few exceptions (some jewelry), most of the trinkets sold here were not from the Big Island, and not even from Hawaii, and prices were not that attractive. However, a major exception is **Emma's Flowers** (© 808/329-7746), a great place for leis and just-cut tropical flowers, at reasonable prices.

Honolua Surf Company   This shop targets the surf-and-sun enthusiast with good things for good times: towels, flip-flops, body boards, sunglasses, swimsuits, and everything else you need for ocean and shore action. Quiksilver, Tommy Bahama, Roxy, Billabong, and Kahala are among the top menswear labels here, but I also like the quirky, colorful Toes on the Nose. Also popular is the full line of products with the Honolua Surf Co. label, including T-shirts, hats,

---

Art Appreciation

The finest art on the Kona Coast hangs in, of all places, a bank. Award-winning **First Hawaiian Bank,** 74–5593 Palani Rd. (© **808/329-2461**), has art lovers making special trips to view Hiroki Morinoue's mural, John Buck's prints, Chiu Leong's ceramic sculpture, Franco Salmoiraghi's photographs, Setsuko Morinoue's abstract fiber wall piece, and other works that were incorporated as part of the bank's design. Artists Yvonne Cheng and Sharon Carter Smith, whose works are included, assembled this exhibition, a sterling example of corporate sponsorship of the arts.

bags, dresses, sweatshirts, aloha shirts, and swimwear. At Kona Inn Shopping Village, Alii Dr. ℂ **808/329-1001.**

Kailua Village Artists Gallery   A co-op of four dozen Hawaii island artists, plus a few guest artists, display their works in various media: watercolors, paintings, prints, hand-blown and blasted glass, and photography. Books, pottery, and an attractive assortment of greeting cards are among the lower-priced items. In King Kamehameha's Kona Beach Hotel, 75–5660 Palani Rd. (ℂ **808/329-6653**) and 78–6740 Alii Dr. (ℂ **808/324-7060**).

EDIBLES & EVERYDAY THINGS

The Big Island's **green markets** are notable for the quality of produce and the abundance of island specialties at better-than-usual prices. Look for the cheerful green kiosks of the **Alii Gardens Marketplace,** 75–6129 Alii Dr. (at the south end), where local farmers and artists set up their wares daily from 8am to 5pm. This is not your garden-variety marketplace; some vendors are permanent, some drive over from Hilo, and the owners have planted shade trees and foliage to make the 5-acre plot a Kona landmark. There are 40 to 50 vendors on any given day, selling jewelry, woodcrafts, produce, macadamia nuts, orchids, and—my favorite—the fresh juices of Kay Reeves, owner of Wau, who gets up before dawn to make her sensational fresh *lilikoi* and lime juices. Kona Blue Sky Coffee is also here, as is Lynn Cappell, a fine painter of island landscapes, and Laura de Rosa's sensational A'ala Dreams lotions and oils.

Java junkies jump-start their day at **Island Lava Java** (ℂ **808/ 327-2161**), the hot new magnet for coffee lovers at the Coconut Grove Market Place, on Alii Drive. At the other end of Kailua-Kona, in the new New Industrial Area, between Costco and Home Depot, the handmade candies of the **Kailua Candy Company,** 73-5612 Kauhola St. (ℂ **808/329-2522,** or 800/622-2462 for orders), also beckon, especially the macadamia-nut clusters with ground ginger or the legendary macadamia-nut *honu* (turtle). Other products include truffles, pure Kona coffee, shortbread cookies, toffee, T-shirts, mugs, mustards, and other gift items.

Kona Wine Market, in the King Kamehameha Mall (ℂ **808/ 329-9400**), has a noteworthy selection, including some esoteric vintages, at prices you'll love. This is a wine lover's store, with selections from California, Europe, and points beyond, as well as gift baskets, cheeses, cigars, oils and vinegars, specialty pastas and condiments, Riedel glassware, and friendly, knowledgeable service.

For everyday grocery needs, **KTA Stores** (in the Kona Coast Shopping Center, at Palani Rd. and the Queen Kaahumanu Hwy., and in the Keauhou Shopping Village, on Alii Dr.) are always my first choice. Through its Mountain Apple brand, KTA sells hundreds of top-notch local products—from Kona smoked marlin and Hilo-grown rainbow trout to cookies, breads, jams and jellies, taro chips, and *kulolo,* the decadently dense taro-coconut steamed pudding—by dozens of local vendors. The fresh fish department is always an adventure; if anything esoteric is running, such as the flashy red aweoweo, it's sure to be on KTA's counters, along with a large spread of prepared foods for sunset picnics and barbecues.

My other favorite is **Kona Natural Foods,** in the Crossroads Center (✆ **808/329-2296**). It's been upgraded from a health-food store to a full-on healthful supermarket. And it's the only full-service health-food store for miles, selling bulk grains and cereals, vitamins, snacks, fresh-fruit smoothies, and sandwiches and salads from its takeout deli. Organic greens, grown in the South Kona area, are a small but strong feature of the produce section.

UPCOUNTRY KONA: HOLUALOA

Charming Holualoa, 1,400 feet and 10 minutes above Kailua-Kona at the top of Hualalai Road, is a place for strong espresso, leisurely gallery hopping, and nostalgic explorations across several cultural and time zones. One narrow road takes you across generations and cultures.

Paul's Place is Holualoa's only all-purpose general store, a time warp tucked between frame shops, galleries, and studios.

Prominent Holualoa artists include the jewelry maker/sculptor Sam Rosen, who years ago set the pace for found-object art and today makes beautiful pieces at the rear of Chestnut Gallery; the furniture maker and wood sculptor Gerald Ben; the printmaker Nora Yamanoha; the glass artist Wilfred Yamazawa; the sculptor Cal Hashimoto; and Hiroki and Setsuko Morinoue of Studio 7 gallery. All galleries listed are on the main street, Mamalahoa Highway, and all are within walking distance of each other.

Antiques by Cinderella's *(Finds* Most of the treasures here are tucked away, so don't be shy about asking the owner, Cindi Nespor, where she keeps her prized antique engravings or her out-of-print naturalists' books of hand-painted engravings. There are also rare prints and vases, kimonos, lamps, and home accessories. The rare books will quicken a book lover's heart, while the estate jewelry, vintage linens, rattan furniture, and hats make this a brilliant browse. Gorgeous antique shawls, long-extinct Chanel perfumes, and 1940s Garbo-style hats are among the treasures found here. Call ahead, though; the owner keeps flexible, Island-style hours. Mamalahoa Hwy. $\textcircled{C}$ **808/322-2474.**

Dovetail Gallery and Design   Located behind the old historic post office, Dovetail features contemporary and abstract art, and the works of high-end, fine craftsmen and furniture makers. But the gallery's custom woodworking shop separates it from all the other galleries lining the Mamalahoa Highway. It features top craftsmen and the design work of Gerald Ben, who not only is a skilled ceramicist, but also has been a custom woodworker for 22 years. His expertise is designing furniture and wood accessories for his clients, which include collectors, home owners, interior designers, and architects. 76–5942 Mamalahoa Hwy. $\textcircled{C}$ **808/322-4046.**

Holualoa Gallery   Owners Matthew and Mary Lovein show their own work as well as the work of selected Hawaii artists in this roadside gallery in Holualoa. Sculptures, paintings, koa furniture, fused-glass bowls, raku ceramics, and creations in paper, bronze, metal, and glass are among the gallery's offerings. 76–5921 Mamalahoa Hwy. $\textcircled{C}$ **808/322-8484.**

Kimura Lauhala Shop   Everyone loves Kimura's and the masterpieces of weaving that spill out of the tiny shop. It's lined with lauhala, from rolled-up mats and wide-brimmed hats to tote bags, coasters, and coin purses. The fragrant, resilient fiber, woven from the spiny leaves of the *hala* (pandanus) tree, is smooth to the touch and becomes softer with use. Lauhala also varies in color, according to region and growing conditions. Although Kimura employs a covey of local weavers who use the renowned hala leaves of Kona, some South Pacific imports bolster the supply. At Mamalahoa Hwy. and Hualalai Rd. $\textcircled{C}$ **808/324-0053.**

Studio 7 *Finds*   Some of Hawaii's most respected artists, among them gallery owners Setsuko and Hiroki Morinoue, exhibit their works in this serenely beautiful studio. Smooth pebbles, stark woods, and a garden setting provide the backdrop for Hiroki's paintings and prints, and Setsuko's pottery, paper collages, and wall pieces. The Main Gallery houses multimedia art, the Print Gallery sculptural pieces and two-dimensional works, and the Ceramic Gallery features the works of Clayton Amemiya, Chiu Leong, and Gerald Ben. This is the hub of the Holualoa art community; activities include workshops, classes, and special events by visiting artists. Mamalahoa Hwy. $\textcircled{C}$ **808/324-1335.**

Farmers Market, Fruit Stands & Espresso Bar

South Kona, one of the best growing regions on the Big Island, has a weekly **Farmers Market** every Saturday from 8am to noon at the **Keauhou Shopping Village** parking lot, near Ace Hardware. It's a true farmers market, selling only produce grown on the Big Island. Another great vegetable and fruit stand down south is the **South Kona Fruit Stand,** 84–4770 Mamalahoa Hwy., Captain Cook (*📞* **808/328-8547**), which sells some of the most unusual tropical produce from the Big Island. Way down south, the **Kau Tropical Espresso Bar and Organic Fruitstand** (*📞* **808/929-8785**) has not only organic fruit, but also locally grown, organic coffee to go, or take a moment and "talk story" with Elizabeth or Barney, who can tell you about the fruits, vegetables, and coffee of the Big Island.

SOUTH KONA

In Kealakekua, the **Kamigaki Market,** on Highway 11, also called Mamalahoa Highway, is a reliable source of food items, especially for regional specialties such as macadamia nuts and Kona coffee.

In Honaunau, farther south, keep an eye out for the **Bong Brothers Store,** on Highway 11, and its eye-catching selections of fresh local fruit—from cherimoya (in season) to star fruit and white Sugarloaf pineapples. The Bongs are known for their deli items, produce, and Kona coffee fresh from their own roasting room, but I think their black, very hip Bong Brothers and Bong Sistah T-shirts are the find of the region. The juice bar offers homemade soups and smoothies made with fresh local fruit.

In the town of Captain Cook, look for the big BANANA BREAD sign (you can't miss it) across the street from the fire station on Highway 11, and you'll come across the **Captain Cook Baking Company,** which bakes excellent banana bread with macadamia nuts, under the "Auntie Helen's" label. The bread is made with Big Island bananas and macadamia-nut honey, and baked right there in the kitchen. This bakery-sandwich shop also sells Lilikoi Gold passion butter, cheesecake brownies, and submarine sandwiches on its own house-made breads.

Antiques and Orchids Beverly Napolitan and her husband took over Captain Cook's oldest building (built in 1906) and filled it with an eclectic array of antiques, collectibles, and fresh orchids. There are a few vintage Hawaiian items, lots of teacups, raspberry-colored walls, linens, old kimonos, celadon, etched glass and crystal lamps, a Queen Liliuokalani lanai sofa from the 1800s, and a red wooden veranda where high tea is served on Saturday (11am–4pm), complete with homemade scones, Devonshire cream, and English teacups. You can't miss this green building with white trim, on the mauka side of the highway in Captain Cook. Hwy. 11, Captain Cook. ℂ **808/323-9851.**

The Grass Shack   The Grass Shack has been here for more than 3 decades, with its large selection of local woodcrafts, Niihau shell and wiliwili-seed leis, packaged coffee, pahu drums, nose flutes, and lauhala (woven pandanus leaves) in every form. Bowls, boxes, and accessories of Norfolk pine, the rare kou, and other local woods also take up a sizable portion of the shop. Lauhala baskets, made of fiber from the region and the Hamakua Coast, are among the Shack's finest offerings, as are the custom ukuleles and feather gourds for hula dancing. Hwy. 11, Kealakekua. ℂ **808/323-2877.**

Island Framing Company and Gifts   The owners of this tiny frame shop have great taste, and they've filled their shop with their favorite things: excellent soaps and candles (including Votivo, very chichi), Japanese lanterns, framed prints, koa frames, Indonesian imports, umbrellas, and household accessories and accents that would liven up any home. The shop is in a charming green plantation house with a small veranda, on the ocean side of the street at the border of Kainaliu and Kealakekua. 79–7506 Hwy. 11, Kealakekua. ℂ **808/322-4397.**

Kimura Store *(Finds)*   This old-fashioned general store is one of those places you'll be glad you found—a store with spirit and character, plus everything you need and don't need. You'll see Hawaii's finest selection of yardage, enough cookware for a multicourse dinner, aspirin, Shiseido cosmetics, and an eye-popping assortment of buttons, zippers, and quilting materials. Irene Kimura, the family matriarch, who presided over the store for more than 60 years until she passed away recently, said she quit counting the fabric bolts at 8,000 but estimated there were more than 10,000. Kimura's is the spot for pareu and Hawaiian fabrics, brocades, silks, and offbeat gift items, such as Japanese china and *tabi,* the comfortable cloth footwear. Hwy. 11, Kainaliu. ℂ **808/322-3771.**

2 The Kohala Coast

Shops on the Kohala Coast are concentrated in and around the resorts, listed below.

HILTON WAIKOLOA VILLAGE   Among the hotel's shops, **Sandal Tree** carries footwear with style and kick: Italian sandals at non-Italian prices, designer pumps, and other footwear to carry you from dockside to dance floor.

KINGS' SHOPS   These stores are located at the entrance to Waikoloa Resort. A recent find here is **Walking in Paradise (℗ 808/ 886-2600).** The footwear—much of it made in France (Mephisto, Arche)—can be expensive, but it's worthwhile for anyone seeking comfort while exploring the harsh lava terrain of this island or the pedestrian culture of Kailua's Alii Drive. Toward the mauka (mountainside) end is **Noa Noa,** filled with exotic artifacts from Java and Borneo, and tropical clothing for easygoing life on the Pacific Rim. At **Under the Koa Tree,** some of the island's finest artists display their prints, woodcrafts, and paintings. For snacks, ice, sunscreen, wine, postcards, newspapers, and everyday essentials, there's the **Whalers General Store,** and for dining on the run, a small Food Court with pizza, plate lunches, and the **Wild Boar Juice & Java** bar for fresh-pressed carrot/ginger juice or a steaming cup of brew.

As we went to press, under construction was the $95-million **Queens' MarketPlace (℗ 808/886-8811;** www.waikoloabeach resort.com), located across the street from the Kings' Shops, with a range of shops from Giggles, Island Pearls, Local Motion to Sansei Seafood Restaurant & Sushi Bar, Island Gourmet Markets, and Starbucks.

HUALALAI RESORT   Ka'upulehu Store, in the Four Seasons Resort Hualalai, is a perfect blend of high quality and cultural integrity. Located within the award-winning Ka'upulehu Cultural Center, the store carries items made in Hawaii: handmade paper, hand-painted silks, seed leis, greeting cards, koa bowls, wreaths, John Kelly prints, and a selection of Hawaii-themed books. **Hualalai Sports Club and Spa,** in the same resort, has a winning retail section of beauty, aromatherapy, and treatment products, including Hana Nai'a Aromatherapy Products. The products include mango and jasmine perfumes, Bulgarian rose water, and herbal lotions and potions.

MAUNA LANI RESORT   The recently opened **The Shops at Mauna Lani** is a high-end cluster of well-known name stores and a sprinkle of local, homegrown places such as terrific eateries Kenichi and Dara's Authentic Thai Cuisine. Shops include Lahaina Galleries, Caché, Kohala Goldsmith, Black Perl Gallery, Tori Richards,

A'ama Surf and Sport, and The Market at Mauna Lani. Chain restaurants include Ruth's Chris Steak House, Tommy Bahama, and Starbucks.

3 North Kohala

Ackerman Gallery   Crafts and fine arts are housed in two separate galleries a few blocks apart. Artist Gary Ackerman and his wife, Yesan, display gifts, crafts, and the works of award-winning Big Island artists, including Ackerman's own Impressionistic paintings. There are Kelly Dunn's hand-turned Norfolk pine bowls, Jer Houston's heirloom-quality koa-and-ebony desks, and Wilfred Yamazawa's hand-blown-glass perfume bottles and sculptures. Primitive artifacts, Asian antiques, jewelry, and Cal Hashimoto's bamboo sculptures are also among the discoveries here. The crafts-and-gifts gallery, across from the King Kamehameha statue, has recently doubled in size; it features gift ideas in all media and price ranges. Hwy. 270 (across from the Kamehameha statue; also 3 blocks away, on the opposite side of the street), Kapaau. ✆ 808/889-5971.

As Hawi Turns   You never know what you'll find in this whimsical, delightful shop of women's clothing and accessories. The windows might be filled with painted paper lanterns in the shapes of stars, or retro-painted switch plates, or kicky straw hats paired with bias-cut silk dresses and quirky jewelry. This is the perfect place to pamper yourself with such fripperies as tatami zoris and flamboyant accessories for a colorful, tropical life. Hwy. 270 (Akoni Pule Hwy.), Hawi. ✆ 808/889-5023.

Elements   John Flynn designs jewelry, and his wife, Prakash, assembles fountains and other treasures, and together they've filled their quiet gallery with an assortment of arts and crafts from the Big Island, including local artist Margaret Ann Hoy's wonderful watercolors of island scenes. The lauhala accessories, jewelry, and fountains—simple bowls filled with smooth gemstones such as amethyst and rose quartz—make great gifts and accessories. Hwy. 270 (Akoni Pule Hwy.), Kapaau. ✆ 808/889-0760.

Harbor Gallery ✸✸   Formerly Kohala Kollection, this two-story gallery seems to have made a seamless transition, remaining a big draw next to the Cafe Pesto in this industrial harbor area of Kawaihae. Harry Wishard paintings, Miles Fry's museum-quality model canoes and ships, Kathy Long's pencil drawings, and Frances Dennis' painted island scenes on canvas are among the works by more

than 150 artists, primarily from the Big Island. The range is vast—
from jewelry to basketry, to ceramics, to heirloom-quality koa furniture. In Kawaihae Shopping Center, Hwy. 270, just north of Hwy. 19. © 808/
882-1510.

Kohala Book Shop ✿✿   Jan and Frank Morgan's new- and used-
book store—the largest such store in Hawaii—is a huge success and
a major attraction in the town's historic Hotel Nanbu building. The
yellow building with red-and-green trim is beautifully and faithfully
restored, all the better to house a priceless collection that includes
out-of-print first editions, the $22,500 set of *Captain Cook's Jour-
nals, The Morals of Confucius* (dated 1691 and priced at $350), and
thousands of other treasures. You'll see popular fiction and everyday
books, too, along with titles on Hawaii and Oceania; at last count,
the inventory was 20,000 and climbing. Thoughtful signs, good
prices, and an attractive and welcoming environment are only some
of the winning features. Hwy. 270 (Akoni Pule Hwy.), a block from the Kamehameha statue, Kapaau. © 808/889-6732.

4 Waimea

Waimea is lei country as well as the island's breadbasket, so look for
protea, vegetables, vine-ripened tomatoes, and tuberose stalks here at
reasonable prices. Mainstays include **Honopua Farm** and **Hufford's
Farm,** side by side, selling freshly cut flowers and organic vegetables.

Small and sublime, the **Waimea Farmers Market,** Highway 19,
at mile marker 55 on the Hamakua side of Waimea town (on the
lawn in front of the Department of Hawaiian Home Lands, West
Hawaii office), draws a loyal crowd from 7am to noon on Saturday.

At the other end of Waimea, the **Parker School Farmers Market,** held Saturday from 7:30am to noon, is smaller and more sub-
dued, but with choice items as well. The Kalopa macadamia nuts are
the sweetest and tastiest I've ever had. Hilo's wonderful **Dan De Luz
Woods** (p. 163) has a branch at 64–1013 Mamalahoa Hwy., in
front of the True Value hardware store.

Other shops in Waimea range from the small roadside storefronts
lining Highway 19 and Highway 190, which intersect in the middle of town, to complexes such as **Waimea Center,** where you'll find
the trusty old **KTA Super Store,** the one-stop shop for all your basic
necessities, plus a glorious profusion of interesting local foods.
Across the street, with its upscale galleries and shops, **Parker Square**
will likely be your most rewarding stop.

Bentley's Home & Garden Collection   To its lavish list of glass-ware, linens, chenille throws, home fragrances, stuffed animals, and Wild West gift-wraps, Bentley's has added casual country clothing in linens and cottons. Dresses, sweaters, raffia hats, top-drawer Western shirts, handbags, and woven shoes adorn this fragrant, gardenlike shop. In Parker Sq., Hwy. 19. © **808/885-5565.**

Gallery of Great Things   Here's an eye-popping assemblage of local art and Pacific Rim artifacts. Browse under the watchful gaze of an antique Tongan war club (not for sale) and authentic rhinoceros- and deer-horn blowguns from Borneo, among the plethora of treasures from Polynesia, Micronesia, and Indonesia. You'll find jewelry, glassware, photographs, greeting cards, fiber baskets, and hand-turned bowls of beautifully grained woods. Photos by Victoria McCormick, the sketches of Kathy Long, feather masks by Bety McCormick, and the paintings of Yvonne Cheng are among the treasures by local artists. There are a few pieces of etched glass and vintage clothing, too, along with a small, gorgeous collection of antique kimonos. In Parker Sq., Hwy. 19. © **808/885-7706.**

Mauna Kea Galleries *Finds*   This is the new and expanded version of the gallery I've come to know and love in Hilo, which is now open by appointment only. Mark Blackburn, who wrote *Hawaiiana: The Best of Hawaiian Design,* has made this his showcase for the treasures he loves to collect. He and his wife, Carolyn, amass vintage Hawaiiana in mint condition and then respectfully display it. Their collection includes monarchy and Ming jewelry; mint-condition Santa Anita and Don Blanding dinnerware, including very rare pieces; adz-hewn koa and kou bowls; and vintage photography and menus, all individually stored in plastic sleeves ($10–$300). Rare books and prints, including hand-colored 1870s lithographs; old koa furniture; original Hawaiian fish prints from the early 1900s; and limited-edition, museum-quality reproductions of hula-girl photos from the 1890s are also among the finds. 65–1298 Kawai-hae Rd. (across the street from Edelweiss Restaurant), Waimea. © **808/969-1184.**

Silk Road Gallery   Silk Road offers a rare experience of beauty in a large corner of Parker Square. It's worth a special stop if you love Asian antiques: porcelain teacups, jade cups, kimonos, lacquerware, Buddhas, tansus, bronze bells and chimes, Indonesian woven baskets, Japanese screens, and all manner of delights for elevated living. Fine textiles and baskets, antique dolls, rare woodblock prints, and books, cards, and prints are some of its offerings. You can part with

$15 for a bronze bell, thousands for an antique tansu, or something in between. In Parker Sq., Hwy. 19. (C) **808/885-7474.**

Sweet Wind   Because the owner loves beauty and harmonious things, you'll find chimes, carved dolphins, crystals, geodes, incense (an excellent selection), beads, jewelry, gems, essential oils, and thoughtfully selected books worth more than a casual glance. The books cover self-help, health, metaphysics, Hawaiian spirituality, yoga, meditation, and other topics for wholesome living. In Parker Sq., Hwy. 19. (C) **808/885-0562.**

Waimea General Store   This charming, unpretentious country store offers a superb assortment of Hawaii-themed books, soaps and toiletries, cookbooks and kitchen accessories, candles, linens, greeting cards, dolls, Japanese hapi coats, island teas, rare kiawe honey, preserves, cookies, and countless gift items from the practical to the whimsical. In Parker Sq., Hwy. 19. (C) **808/885-4479.**

5 The Hamakua Coast

Waipio Valley Artworks *Finds*   Housed in an old wooden building at the end of the road before the Waipio Valley, this gallery/boutique offers treasures for the home. The focus here is strictly local, with a strong emphasis on woodwork—one of the largest selections, if not the largest, in the state. A recent expansion has brought more chests and tables and gift items by Big Island artists. All the luminaries of wood-turning have works here: Jack Straka, Robert Butts, Scott Hare, Kevin Parks. Their bowls, rocking chairs, and jewelry boxes exhibit flawless craftsmanship and richly burnished grains. More affordable are the pens and hair accessories. Deli sandwiches and Tropical Dreams ice cream are served in the expanded cafe. In Kukuihaele. (C) **808/775-0958.**

HONOKAA

Honokaa Market Place   I've noticed a proliferation of Balinese imports (not a good sign) mingling with the old and new Hawaiiana. The eclectic selection of Hawaiian, Asian, and Indonesian handicrafts includes wood crafts, Hawaiian prints, and Hawaiian quilts, from wall hangings and pillows to the full-size quilts, plus a few pieces of jewelry. 45–3321 Mamane St. (C) **808/775-8255.**

Honokaa Trading Company   "Rustic, tacky, rare—there's something for everyone," says owner Grace Walker. Every inch of this labyrinthine 2,200-square-foot bazaar is occupied by antiques and collectibles, new and used goods, and countless treasures. You'll find plantation memorabilia, Hawaiiana, bark-cloth fabrics from the 1940s, rhinestone jewelry and rattan furniture from the 1930s, vintage ukuleles, Depression glass, dinnerware from Honolulu's landmark Willows restaurant, koa lamps, Francis Oda airbrush paintings, vintage kimonos, and linens. It's an unbelievable conglomeration, with surprises in every corner. Vigilant collectors make regular forays here to scoop up the 1950s ivory jewelry and John Kelly prints. Mamane St. ⓒ **808/775-0808**.

Kamaaina Woods   The showroom is adjacent to the workshop, so visitors can watch the craftspeople at work on the other side of the glass panel. Local woods are the specialty here, with a strong emphasis on koa and milo bowls. Boxes, carvings, albums, and smaller accessories are also included in the mix, but bowl-turning is clearly the focus. Prices begin at about $10. Lehua St. (down the hill from the post office). ⓒ **808/775-7722**.

Mamane Street Bakery   This bakery on Honokaa's main drag will fill all your coffee-shop needs. Fresh-baked breads, pies, and pastries (including melt-in-your-mouth Danishes) are served with good coffee in a tiny cafe lined with old photographs. 45–3625 Mamane St. ⓒ **808/775-9478**.

Maya's Clothing and Gifts   The Hawaiian-print table runners and locally made soaps and ceramics are only part of the growing selection at this Honokaa newcomer. Napkins, place mats, hula girl lamps, koa accessories, quilted Hawaiian pot holders, aloha shirts, jams and jellies, T-shirts, sportswear, jewelry boxes—it's an eclectic selection for all tastes. Mamane St. ⓒ **808/775-1016**.

Seconds to Go   Elaine Carlsmith spends a lot of time collecting vintage pottery, glassware, kimonos, fabrics, and other treasures to sell to eager seekers of nostalgia. Many beautiful things have passed through her doors, including antique koa furniture, old maps, music sheets, and rare and out-of-print books. The vintage ivory jewelry and Don Blanding dinnerware are grabbed up quickly. The main store is a few doors away from the warehouse, where furniture and larger pieces are displayed. Mamane St. ⓒ **808/775-9212**.

Starseed   Shop here for offbeat holographic bumper stickers, jewelry, beads, incense, and New Age amulets. The selection of crystals is impressive, and there are hundreds of boxes of beads, some of them rare European and Asian imports. The owner also has a special camera that purportedly photographs people's auras, or electromagnetic fields, so you can find out what your colors are. 45–3551 A-2 Mamane St. (*C*) 808/775-9344.

Taro Patch Gifts   Taro Patch carries an eclectic assortment of Hawaiian music tapes and CDs, switch plates printed with Hawaiian labels, Ka'u coffee, local jams and jellies, soaps, pareu, books, ceramics, sushi candles, essential oils, and sportswear, such as Hawaiian-print cowboy shirts. The Hawaiian seed lei selection is the best in town: kamani, blue marble, wiliwili, double sheep eye, betel nut, and several other attractive native species. 45–3599 Mamane St. (*C*) 808/775-7228.

6 Hilo

Shopping in Hilo is centered on the **Kaiko'o Hilo Mall,** 777 Kilauea Ave., near the state and county buildings; the **Prince Kuhio Shopping Plaza,** 111 E. Puainako, just off Highway 11 on the road north to Volcano, where you'll find a supermarket, drugstore, Macy's, and other standards; the **Bayfront area** downtown, where the hippest new businesses have taken up residence in the historic buildings lining Kamehameha Avenue; and the new **Waiakea Plaza,** where the big-box retailers (Ross, Office Max, Borders, Wal-Mart) have moved in. For practical needs, there's a **KTA Super Store** at 323 Keawe St. and another at 50 E. Puainako St.

Basically Books   This bookstore, affectionately called "the map shop," is a sanctuary for lovers of books, maps, and the environment. They have expanded their selection of Hawaii-themed gift items while they maintain the engaging selection of printed materials covering geology, history, topography, botany, mythology, and more. Get your bearings by browsing among the nautical charts, U.S. Geological Survey maps, street maps, raised relief maps, atlases, and compasses, and books on travel, natural history, music, spirituality, and much more. This bountiful source of information, specializing in Hawaii and the Pacific, will enhance any visit. 160 Kamehameha Ave. (*C*) 808/961-0144.

Dan De Luz Woods   The unstoppable Dan De Luz has been turning bowls for more than 30 years. His studio, on the highway on the way to Volcano, is a larger, more stunning showcase than his previous location in Hilo. He turns koa, milo, mango, kamani, kou, sandalwood, hau, and other island woods, some very rare, into bowls, trays, and accessories of all shapes and sizes. You can find

A Special Arts Center & Gallery

Part gallery, part retail store, and part consortium of the arts, the **East Hawaii Cultural Center**, 141 Kalakaua St., across from Kalakaua Park (© **808/961-5711**), is run by volunteers in the visual and performing arts. Keep it in mind for gifts of Hawaii, or if you have any questions regarding the **Hawaii Concert Society, Hilo Community Players, Big Island Dance Council,** or **Big Island Art Guild.** The art gallery and gift shop exhibit locally made cards, jewelry, books, sculptures, and wood objects, including museum-quality works.

---

bookmarks, rice and stir-fry paddles, letter openers, and calabashes, priced from $3 to $1,000. Hwy. 11, Kurtistown. © **808/935-5587.**

Dragon Mama *(Finds*   For a dreamy stop in Hilo, head for this haven of all-natural comforters, cushions, futons, meditation pillows, hemp yarns and shirts, antique kimonos and obi, tatami mats sold by the panel, and all manner of comforts in the elegantly spare Japanese esthetic. The bolts of lavish silks and pure, crisp cottons, sold by the yard, can be used for clothing or interior decorating. Dragon Mama also offers custom sewing, and you know she's good: She sewed the futon and bedding for the Dalai Lama when he visited the island a few years ago. 266 Kamehameha Ave. © **808/934-9081.**

Hana Hou *(Finds*   Michele Zane-Faridi has done a superlative job of assembling, designing, and collecting objects of beauty that evoke old and new Hawaii. If you are looking for Hawaiian lauhala weaving, this is the place for mats, hats, purses, place mats, slippers, and even tissue box covers. But that's not all: Vintage shirts, china, books, women's dresses, jewelry, handbags, accessories, Mundorff prints, 1940s sheet music, and fabrics are displayed in surprising corners. The feathered leis and collectibles—such as vintage silver-and-ivory jewelry by Ming—disappear quickly. 164 Kamehameha Ave. © **808/935-4555.**

Hawaiian Force   Artist Craig Neff and his wife, Luana, hang their shingle at the original location of Sig Zane Designs (good karma), where they sell bold, wonderful T-shirt dresses, mamaki tea they gather themselves, lauhala fans and trivets, surf wear, aloha shirts, and jewelry made of opihi and Niihau shells. Everything here is Hawaiian, most of it made or designed by the Neffs. Their handsome two-toned T-shirt dresses are a Hawaiian Force signature, ideal for island living, and very popular. 140 Kilauea Ave. ✆ 808/934-7171.

Sig Zane Designs *(Finds)*   My favorite stop in Hilo, Sig Zane Designs evokes such loyalty that people make special trips from the outer islands for this inspired line of authentic Hawaiian wear. The spirit of this place complements the high esthetic standards; everyone involved is completely immersed in Hawaiian culture and dance. The partnership of Zane and his wife, the revered hula master Nalani Kanaka'ole, is stunningly creative. The shop is awash in gleaming woods, lauhala mats, and clothing and accessories—handmade house slippers, aloha shirts, pareu, muumuu, T-shirts, and high-quality crafts. They all center on the Sig Zane fabric designs. The Sig Zane bedcovers, cushions, fabrics, clothing, and custom-ordered uphol-stery bring the rainforest into your room. To add to the delight, Sig and his staff take time to talk story and explain the significance of the images, or simply chat about Hilo, hula, and Hawaiian culture. 122 Kamehameha Ave. ✆ 808/935-7077.

EDIBLES
Abundant Life Natural Foods   Stock up here on healthful snacks, fresh organic produce, vitamins and supplements, bulk grains, baked goods, and the latest in health foods. There's a sound selection of natural remedies and herbal body, face, and hair prod-ucts. The takeout deli makes fresh-fruit smoothies and sprout- and nutrient-rich sandwiches and salads. Seniors get a 10% discount. 292 Kamehameha Ave. ✆ 808/935-7411.

Big Island Candies   Abandon all restraint. The chocolate-dipped shortbread and macadamia nuts, not to mention the free samples, will make it very hard to be sensible. Owner Alan Ikawa has turned cookie making into a spectator sport. Large viewing windows allow you to watch the hand-dipping from huge vats of chocolate while the aroma of butter fills the room. Ikawa uses eggs straight from a nearby farm, pure butter, Hawaiian cane sugar, no preservatives, and premium chocolate. Gift boxes are carted interisland—or shipped all over the country—in staggering volumes. The Hawaiian Da Kine line is irrepressibly local: mochi crunch, fortune cookies, animal crackers, and other morsels—all dipped in chocolate. By far the best are the shortbread cookies, dipped in chocolate, peanut butter, and white chocolate. If you get thirsty, there's a juice-and-smoothie bar. Outside are picnic tables on the manicured grounds. 585 Hinano St. ✆ 800/935-5510 or 808/935-8890. www.bigislandcandies.com for mail orders.

Hilo Farmers Market *Finds*   This has grown into the state's best farmers market, embodying what I love most in Hawaii: local color, good soil and weather, the mixing of cultures, and new adventures in taste. More than 120 vendors from around the island bring their flowers, produce, and baked goods to this teeming corner of Hilo every Wednesday and Saturday from sunrise to 4pm. Because many of the vendors sell out early, go as early as you can. Expect to find a stunning assortment: fresh, homegrown oyster mushrooms from Kona; the creamy, sweet, queenly Indonesian fruit called mangosteen; warm breads, from focaccia to walnut; an array of flowers; fresh aquacultured seaweed; corn from Pahoa; Waimea strawberries; taro and taro products; foot-long, miso-flavored, and traditional Hawaiian laulau; made-from-scratch tamales; and fabulous ethnic vegetables. The selection changes by the week, but it's always reasonable, fresh, and appealing, with a good cross-section of the island's specialties. Although it's open daily, Wednesday and Saturday are the days when all the vendors are there. Kamehameha Ave. at Mamo St. ℂ **808/933-1000.**

O'Keefe & Sons   You can enjoy O'Keefe's breads throughout the island, served in the best delis, coffee shops, and restaurants. But come to the source, this friendly Hilo bakery, for the full selection of artisan breads and pastries hot from the oven: Hilo nori bread, black-pepper/cilantro bread, focaccia in many flavors, cracked rye, challah, three types of sourdough, carrot-herb bread, and the classic French country loaf. Located opposite the *Hawaii Tribune Herald* building, O'Keefe's serves sandwiches, soups, and quiche for lunch. 374 Kinoole St. ℂ **808/934-9334.**

7 Hawaii Volcanoes National Park

Kilauea Kreations   This is the quilting center of Volcano, a co-op made up of local Volcano artists and crafters who make quilts, jewelry, feather leis, ceramics, baskets, and fiber arts. Gift items made by Volcano artists are also sold here, but it's the quilts and quilting materials that distinguish the shop. Starter kits are available for beginners. I also like the Hawaiian seed leis and items made of lauhala, as well as the locally made soaps and bath products and the greeting cards, picture frames, and candles. Old Volcano Rd. ℂ **808/967-8090.**

Volcano Art Center   The Volcano Island's frontier spirit and raw, primal energy have spawned a close-knit community of artists, and the Volcano Art Center (VAC) is the hub of the island's arts activity. Housed in the original 1877 Volcano House, VAC is a not-for-profit art-education center that offers exhibits and shows that change monthly, as well as workshops and retail space. Marian Berger's watercolors of endangered birds, Dietrich Varez oils and block prints, Avi Kiriaty oils, Kelly Dunn and Jack Straka woods, Brad Lewis photography, Harry Wishard paintings, Ira Ono goddess masks, and Mike Riley furnishings are among the works you'll see. Of the 300 artists represented, 90% come from the Big Island. The fine crafts include baskets, jewelry, mixed-media pieces, stone and woodcarvings, and the wood diaries of Jesus Sanchez, a third-generation Vatican bookbinder who has turned his skills to the island woods. In Hawaii Volcanoes National Park. ✆ 808/967-8222.

Volcano Store   Walk up the wooden steps into a wonderland of flowers and local specialties. Tangy *lilikoi* butter (transportable, and worth a special trip) and flamboyant sprays of cymbidiums, tuberoses, dendrobiums, anthuriums, hanging plants, mixed bouquets, and calla lilies make a breathtaking assemblage in the enclosed front porch. Volcano residents are lucky to have these blooms at such prices. The flowers can also be shipped (orders are taken by phone); Marie and Ronald Onouye and their staff pack them meticulously. If mainland weather is too humid or frosty for reliable shipping, they'll let you know. Produce, stone cookies (as in hard-as-stone) from Mountain View, Hilo taro chips, bottled water (a necessity in Volcano), local *poha* (gooseberry) jam, and bowls of chile rice (a local favorite) round out the selection. Even if you're just visiting the park for the day, it's worth turning off to stop for gas here; kindly clerks give directions. At Huanani and Old Volcano Hwy. ✆ 808/967-7210.

Volcano Winery   Lift a glass of Volcano Blush or Macadamia Nut Honey and toast Pele at this boutique winery, where the local wines are made from tropical honey (no grapes) and tropical fruit blends (half-grape and half-fruit). It's open daily from 10am to 5:30pm; tastings are free. No tours yet, but plans are in the works to expand the winery to accommodate tours. You can order wines online at www.volcanowinery.com. Pii Mauna Dr., off Hwy. 11 at mile marker 30, all the way to the end. ✆ 808/967-7479.

STUDIO VISITS

The airy Volcano studio/showroom of **Phan Barker** (✆ 808/985-8636), an international artist, is a mountain idyll and splendid backdrop for her art, which includes batik paintings on silk, acrylic painting on wood, oil on paper, dye on paper, and mixed-media sculptures. Her work has been exhibited in galleries and museums ranging from the Smithsonian to Saigon. In addition to studio visits (by appointment only), she also offers beginner classes in silk painting and drawing.

Adding to the vitality of the Volcano arts environment are the studio visits offered by the **Volcano Village Art Studios.** Several respected artists in various media open their studios to the public by appointment. Artists in the hui include **Ira Ono** (© 808/967-7261), who makes masks, water containers, fountains, paste-paper journals, garden vessels, and goddesses out of clay and found objects; **Pam Barton** (© 808/967-7247), who transforms vines, leaves, roots, bark, and tree sheddings into stunning fiber sculptures and vessels, from baskets to handmade paper and books; raku and jewelry artist **Zeke Israel** (© 808/965-8820); and sculptor **Randy Takaki** (© 808/985-8756), who works in wood, metal, and ceramics.

7

The Big Island After Dark

Jokes abound about neighbor-island nightlife being an oxymoron, but there are a few pockets of entertainment here, largely in the Kailua-Kona and Kohala Coast resorts. Your best bet is to check the local newspapers—*Honolulu Advertiser* and *West Hawaii Today*—for special shows, such as fundraisers, that are held at local venues. Other than that, regular entertainment in the local clubs usually consists of mellow Hawaiian music at sunset, small hula groups, or jazz trios.

Some of the island's best events are held at **Kahilu Theatre,** in Waimea (© 808/885-6017; www.kahilutheatre.org), so be on the lookout for any mention of it during your stay. Hula, the top Hawaiian music groups from all over Hawaii, drama, and all aspects of the performing arts use Kahilu as a venue.

1 Big Island Luau

Kona Village Luau ★★★ *Moments* The longest continuously running luau on the island is still the best—a combination of an authentic Polynesian venue with a menu that works, impressive entertainment, and the spirit of old Hawaii. The feast begins with a ceremony in a sandy kiawe grove, where the pig is unearthed after a full day of cooking in a rock-heated underground oven. In the open-air dining room, next to prehistoric lagoons and tropical gardens, you'll sample a Polynesian buffet: *poisson cru,* poi, laulau (butterfish, seasoned pork, and taro leaves cooked in ti leaves), lomi salmon, squid luau (cooked taro leaves with steamed octopus and coconut milk), ahi poke, opihi (fresh limpets), coconut pudding, taro chips, sweet potatoes, chicken long rice, steamed breadfruit, and the shredded *kalua* pig. The Polynesian revue, a fast-moving, mesmerizing tour of South Pacific cultures, manages—miraculously—to avoid being clichéd or corny. The luau takes place Wednesday and Friday at 5pm. In Kona Village Resort. © 808/325-5555. www.konavillage.com. Reservations required. Part of the Full American Plan for Kona Village guests; for nonguests, $95 adults, $56 children 6–12, $30 children 2–5. AE, DC, MC, V.

Moments   An Evening under the Stars

This is one of those "unique Hawaii experiences" that you will remember long after your tan has faded. Perched from the vantage point of 3,200 feet on the slopes of the Kohala Mountains, **"An Evening at Kahua Ranch"** is a night under the stars with wonderful food, great entertainment, fun activities, and storytelling around a traditional campfire.

The evening begins when you are picked up at your hotel. As you relax in the air-conditioned van, enjoying the scenic coastline, your guide spins stories about this historic area. Arriving at the 8,500-acre working cattle ranch, you are personally greeted by the ranch owner, John Richards. When the sun starts to sink into the Pacific, beer, wine, and soft drinks are served as John talks about how cattle ranching came to Hawaii and how they manage the ranch in the 21st century.

A traditional ranch-style barbecue of sirloin steak, chicken, locally grown potatoes, Waimea corn-on-the-cob, baked beans, Big Island green salad, Kona coffee, and dessert is served shortly after sunset.

After dinner the fun and games begin: Local entertainers pull out guitars, line dancing gets going on the dance floor, and several *paniolo* (cowboy) activities take place. You can choose from learning how to rope, playing a game of horse shoes, or trying your hand at branding a cedar shingle.

Fairmont Orchid   "A Gathering of Kings" is the luau/Polynesian show at the Fairmont. The show, a series of traditional Polynesian dance and music, blended with modern choreography, island rhythms, and high-tech lighting and set design, tells the story of the Polynesians' journey across the Pacific to Hawaii, featuring the culture and arts of the islands of Samoa, Tahiti, New Zealand, and Hawaii. Complimenting the show, the luau also highlights the cuisine of these Pacific islands. Fairmont Orchid, One North Kohala Dr., Kohala Coast. © **808/329-8111.** www.islandbreezeluau.com/gotk. $65 adults, $29 children 4–12, 3 and under free. AE, MC, V. Tues and Sat 5pm.

Sheraton Keauhou Bay Resort & Spa   If you are unable to get into the Kona Village Resort luau, this is my second pick. The food is fine, but you really come here for the show: Kamaha'o, The Wondrous Myths of Hawaii. Filled with lavish theatrics woven into

When the stars come out, there's an 8-inch telescope to gaze into the moon or search for distant planets. A campfire gets started, and the ranch's cowboys come over and start telling stories as you toast marshmallows over the campfire.

The entire experience, from transportation to dinner and entertainment, is $89 per person (20% less if you book online). For more information call ⓒ 808/987-2108 (www.EveningAt Kahua.com).

You may have so much fun that you'll want to come back to see the working cattle ranch during the day. The best way to experience ranching in Hawaii is to see the ranch like the cowboys do: on an ATV. Each guest on the **ATV Adventure at Kahua Ranch** (www.kahuaranch.com/profile.html) is given a top-of-the-line 15–350 Polaris ATV; helmet, gloves, and goggles; and a training session. Although it is a guided tour, with a guide for every six guests, it is not a single-file/stay-on-the-road type of ATV experience. You travel across range lands and cattle pastures of the 8,500-acre ranch, from the Kehena rainforest to the Pohakuloa desert and from 2,500 to 4,500 feet. Novices have the assurance of a guide to watch over their safety, while experienced riders have the freedom to ride the rolling hills. Cost is $85 adults and $60 for children under 16.

Hawaiian chants, legends, hula, with acrobatic performing arts. This is definitely not your tired Polynesian revue. Sheraton Keauhou Bay Resort, 78-128 Ehukai St. ⓒ 808/930-4828. www.kaikehawaii.com. $80 adults, $40 children 5–12. AE, MC, V. Mon, Wed, and Fri 6pm. Reservations required.

2 Music, Dancing & Comedy in Kailua-Kona

A host of bars and restaurants feature dancing and live music when the sun goes down, all of them on Alii Drive in Kailua-Kona. Starting from the south end of Alii Drive, **Huggo's on the Rocks** (ⓒ 808/329-1493) has dancing and live music on weekends, and next door at **Huggo's Restaurant** there's jazz and blues and a piano bar. Across the street from Huggo's, **Durty Jake's Café & Bar** (ⓒ 808/329-7366), in the Coconut Marketplace, has live rock 'n' roll on Saturday and karaoke on weeknights. Upstairs, **Lulu's** (ⓒ 808/321-2633) draws a 20-something crowd with music and dancing Friday and Saturday until 1am.

Just down the street, the **Hard Rock Cafe** (© 808329-8866), in the **Alii Sunset Plaza,** has music most nights. Sometimes it's live, sometimes it's DJ, but it's always a happening kind of place.

If you are in the mood for a few laughs, the **Big Island Comedy Club** usually has a live performance once a week of stand-up comedians on tour. Performances are at the Royal Kona Resort; for information, call © **808/329-4368.**

3 The Kohala Coast Resorts

Evening entertainment here usually takes the form of a luau or indistinctive lounge music at scenic terrace bars with scintillating sunset views. But newcomer Waikoloa Beach Marriott's **Clipper Lounge** is a bright new venue for local musicians, with live music nightly from 8:30 to 11:30pm.

The Wednesday and Friday luau at the **Kona Village Resort** (see above) is the best choice on the island. Otherwise, the resort roundup includes the **Hilton Waikoloa Village's Legends of the Pacific** (© **808/885-1234**) Tuesday and Friday dinner show ($78 adults, $39 children 5–12, 4 and under free), and the Tuesday luau at the **Mauna Kea Beach Hotel** (© **808/882-7222;** $86 adults, $43 children 5–12, 4 and under free).

A popular nightspot on the Kohala Coast is the **Honu Bar** (© 808/ 885-6622) at the Mauna Lani Bay Hotel, a sleek, chic place for light supper, live light jazz with dancing, gourmet desserts, fine wines, and after-dinner drinks. You can also order toothsome pastas and light suppers when most other restaurants are closing.

If you get a chance to see the **Lim Family,** don't miss them. Immensely talented in hula and song, members of the family perform in the intimate setting of the Mauna Lani Bay Hotel's **Atrium Bar** (© **808/885-6622**) and at the Hapuna Beach Prince Hotel's open-air **Reef Lounge** (© **808/880-1111**).

The Hilton Waikoloa Beach's newly opened **Malolo Lounge** (© **808/886-1234;** www.hiltonwaikoloavillage.com) has nightly live entertainment of Hawaiian music (5–8pm) and jazz (9pm–midnight).

Just beyond the resorts lies a great music spot—the **Blue Dolphin Restaurant,** 61–3616 Kawaihae Rd., Kawaihae (© **808/882-7771**), where you can enjoy an eclectic mix of music (jazz, rock, swing, Hawaiian, even big-band music) Wednesday through Saturday.

Moments **Old-Style Hawaiian Entertainment**

The plaintive drone of the conch shell pierces the air, calling all to assemble. A sizzling orange sun sinks slowly toward the cobalt waters of the Pacific. In the distance, Mauna Kea mountain reflects the waning sun's light with a fiery red that fades to a hazy purple and finally to an inky black as a voluptuous full moon dramatically rises over her shoulder.

It's **Twilight at Kalahuipua'a,** a monthly Hawaiian cultural celebration that includes storytelling, singing, and dancing on the oceanside, grassy lawn at Mauna Lani Bay Resort (© **808/885-6622**). These events hark back to another time in Hawaii, when family and neighbors would gather to sing, dance, and "talk story."

Each month guests, ranging from the ultra-well-known in the world of Hawaiian entertainment to the virtually unknown local *kupuna* (elder), gather to perpetuate the traditional folk art of storytelling, with plenty of music and dance thrown in.

Twilight at Kalahuipua'a, always set on a Saturday closest to the full moon, really gets under way at least an hour before the 5:30pm start, when people from across the island and guests staying at the hotel begin arriving. They carry picnic baskets, mats, coolers, babies, and cameras. A sort of oceanside, premusic tailgate party takes place as local families chat with visitors in a truly old-fashioned demonstration of aloha.

4 Hilo

Hilo's most notable events are special or annual occasions such as the **Merrie Monarch Hula Festival,** the state's largest, which continues for a week after Easter Sunday. The festivities include hula competitions from all over the world, demonstrations, and crafts fairs. A staggering spirit of pageantry takes over the entire town. Tickets are always hard to come by; call © **808/935-9168** well ahead of time, and see the "Big Island Calendar of Events," in chapter 1, for further information.

A special new venue is the old **Palace Theater,** 38 Haili St. (© **808/934-7010;** www.hilopalace.com), restored and back in action thanks to the diligent Friends of the Palace Theater. The neoclassical wonder first opened in 1925, was last restored in 1940, and has reopened for first-run movies while restoration continues. Film festivals, art movies, hula, community events, concerts (including the Slack Key Guitar Festival), and all manner of special entertainment take place here.

Special concerts are also held at the **Hawaii Naniloa Hotel's Crown Room** (© **808/969-3333**), the Hilo venue for performers from Oahu and the outer islands. You can always count on a great act here, whether it's the Brothers Cazimero or Willie K.

5 Volcano

Tucked into the rainforest of Volcano Village, on a 25-acre parcel of land, close to the Hawaii Volcanoes National Park, lies Jason Scott Lee's latest work of art, the **Ulua Theatre** (© **808/936-1193;** www. ulua.org). Lee is a Hawaii resident who has starred in films (*Map of the Human Heart, Dragon, Jungle Book, Rapa Nui,* and *Lilo & Stitch*) and performed on stage (the lead in *The King and I* in London). He built his dream theater on his land in Volcano.

"While I was traveling in England and Czechoslovakia, I saw small villages, hamlets really, with theaters, just lodges with candlelight and kerosene light," he said. "I wanted to bring back that sort of storytelling."

His list of upcoming productions ranges from music concerts to poetry slams, to plays. He just finished the one-man show from Los Angeles *Shadow Boxing,* with Grant Sullivan, who was nominated for an Ovation Award for Best One-Man Show.

Also new in Volcano is the **Hawaii at the Volcano Art Center's Niaulani Campus** in Volcano Village (© **808/967-8222;** www. volcanoartcenter.org). The name Niaulani, which means "brushed by the heavens" or "billowing heavens," actually describes the way the clouds and fog move through the rainforest. The new 4,400-square-foot administration building houses an intimate Great Room with a fireplace, sofas, and large windows looking out to the fern forest outside. Check local listings for the free events ranging from cultural talks to music and dance performances.

Index

See also Accommodations, and Restaurant indexes below.

ACCOMMODATIONS

FROMMER'S® COMPLETE TRAVEL GUIDES

Alaska
Amalfi Coast
American Southwest
Amsterdam
Argentina & Chile
Arizona
Atlanta
Australia
Austria
Bahamas
Barcelona
Beijing
Belgium, Holland & Luxembourg
Belize
Bermuda
Boston
Brazil
British Columbia & the Canadian Rockies
Brussels & Bruges
Budapest & the Best of Hungary
Buenos Aires
Calgary
California
Canada
Cancún, Cozumel & the Yucatán
Cape Cod, Nantucket & Martha's Vineyard
Caribbean
Caribbean Ports of Call
Carolinas & Georgia
Chicago
China
Colorado
Costa Rica
Croatia
Cuba
Denmark
Denver, Boulder & Colorado Springs
Edinburgh & Glasgow
England
Europe
Europe by Rail
Florence, Tuscany & Umbria

Florida
France
Germany
Greece
Greek Islands
Hawaii
Hong Kong
Honolulu, Waikiki & Oahu
India
Ireland
Israel
Italy
Jamaica
Japan
Kauai
Las Vegas
London
Los Angeles
Los Cabos & Baja
Madrid
Maine Coast
Maryland & Delaware
Maui
Mexico
Montana & Wyoming
Montréal & Québec City
Moscow & St. Petersburg
Munich & the Bavarian Alps
Nashville & Memphis
New England
Newfoundland & Labrador
New Mexico
New Orleans
New York City
New York State
New Zealand
Northern Italy
Norway
Nova Scotia, New Brunswick & Prince Edward Island
Oregon
Paris
Peru
Philadelphia & the Amish Country

Portugal
Prague & the Best of the Czech Republic
Provence & the Riviera
Puerto Rico
Rome
San Antonio & Austin
San Diego
San Francisco
Santa Fe, Taos & Albuquerque
Scandinavia
Scotland
Seattle
Seville, Granada & the Best of Andalusia
Shanghai
Sicily
Singapore & Malaysia
South Africa
South America
South Florida
South Pacific
Southeast Asia
Spain
Sweden
Switzerland
Tahiti & French Polynesia
Texas
Thailand
Tokyo
Toronto
Turkey
USA
Utah
Vancouver & Victoria
Vermont, New Hampshire & Maine
Vienna & the Danube Valley
Vietnam
Virgin Islands
Virginia
Walt Disney World® & Orlando
Washington, D.C.
Washington State

FROMMER'S® DAY BY DAY GUIDES

Amsterdam
Chicago
Florence & Tuscany

London
New York City
Paris

Rome
San Francisco
Venice

PAULINE FROMMER'S GUIDES! SEE MORE. SPEND LESS.

Hawaii

Italy

New York City

FROMMER'S® PORTABLE GUIDES

Acapulco, Ixtapa & Zihuatanejo
Amsterdam
Aruba
Australia's Great Barrier Reef
Bahamas
Big Island of Hawaii
Boston
California Wine Country
Cancún
Cayman Islands
Charleston
Chicago
Dominican Republic

Dublin
Florence
Las Vegas
Las Vegas for Non-Gamblers
London
Maui
Nantucket & Martha's Vineyard
New Orleans
New York City
Paris
Portland
Puerto Rico
Puerto Vallarta, Manzanillo & Guadalajara

Rio de Janeiro
San Diego
San Francisco
Savannah
St. Martin, Sint Maarten, Anguila & St. Bart's
Turks & Caicos
Vancouver
Venice
Virgin Islands
Washington, D.C.
Whistler

FROMMER'S® CRUISE GUIDES

Alaska Cruises & Ports of Call | Cruises & Ports of Call | European Cruises & Ports of Call

FROMMER'S® NATIONAL PARK GUIDES

Algonquin Provincial Park | National Parks of the American West | Yosemite and Sequoia & Kings
Banff & Jasper | Rocky Mountain | Canyon
Grand Canyon | Yellowstone & Grand Teton | Zion & Bryce Canyon

FROMMER'S® MEMORABLE WALKS

London | Paris | San Francisco
New York | Rome

FROMMER'S® WITH KIDS GUIDES

Chicago | National Parks | Toronto
Hawaii | New York City | Walt Disney World® & Orlando
Las Vegas | San Francisco | Washington, D.C.
London

SUZY GERSHMAN'S BORN TO SHOP GUIDES

France | London | Paris
Hong Kong, Shanghai & Beijing | New York | San Francisco
Italy

FROMMER'S® IRREVERENT GUIDES

Amsterdam | London | Rome
Boston | Los Angeles | San Francisco
Chicago | Manhattan | Walt Disney World®
Las Vegas | Paris | Washington, D.C.

FROMMER'S® BEST-LOVED DRIVING TOURS

Austria | Germany | Northern Italy
Britain | Ireland | Scotland
California | Italy | Spain
France | New England | Tuscany & Umbria

THE UNOFFICIAL GUIDES®

Adventure Travel in Alaska | Hawaii | Paris
Beyond Disney | Ireland | San Francisco
California with Kids | Las Vegas | South Florida including Miami &
Central Italy | London | the Keys
Chicago | Maui | Walt Disney World®
Cruises | Mexico's Best Beach Resorts | Walt Disney World® for
Disneyland® | Mini Mickey | Grown-ups
England | New Orleans | Walt Disney World® with Kids
Florida | New York City | Washington, D.C.
Florida with Kids

SPECIAL-INTEREST TITLES

Athens Past & Present | Frommer's Exploring America by RV
Best Places to Raise Your Family | Frommer's NYC Free & Dirt Cheap
Cities Ranked & Rated | Frommer's Road Atlas Europe
500 Places to Take Your Kids Before They Grow Up | Frommer's Road Atlas Ireland
Frommer's Best Day Trips from London | Great Escapes From NYC Without Wheels
Frommer's Best RV & Tent Campgrounds | Retirement Places Rated
in the U.S.A.

FROMMER'S® PHRASEFINDER DICTIONARY GUIDES

French | Italian | Spanish

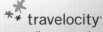